INTRODUCTION

Aims of the book

This book has two objectives:

1 to prepare you for the CAE exam Paper 2 (Writing) and Paper 3 (English in Use).
2 to develop your practical writing skills to an advanced level.

There is no conflict between these two objectives, because CAE writing tasks are as close to real-life situations as possible, and the examiners use real-life criteria in assessing candidates' work. If a piece of writing would 'do the job' effectively in real life, it should also satisfy the examiners.

Why combine Papers 2 and 3?

For those unfamiliar with the CAE exam, it may seem surprising that this book combines Paper 3 (the 'grammar' paper) as well as Paper 2 (the 'writing' paper). In fact, this combination is inevitable, given the many areas the two papers have in common. A characteristic of the CAE exam is that grammar is tested *in context*. Paper 3 tests the ability to *use* grammar in order to *communicate*, and focuses on many of the key areas of written communication – including register, cohesion, and even punctuation.

The Paper 3 exercises:

• provide exam practice for Paper 3.
• are integrated with the Paper 2 work, as controlled practice in writing skills.
• are models (well written, well organized, and usually about 250 words long), which may be referred to when doing the writing tasks that follow them.
• demonstrate different registers and explore different aspects of the theme of the Unit.
• are usually based on authentic texts.

How the book is organized

Part 1: the first part of the book contains an introduction to CAE Papers 2 and 3, followed by preliminary work on three key areas of writing skills at this level: style and register, cohesion, and punctuation. It is intended that this part of the book should be used for preparatory work, remedial work, and reference.

Part 2: Units 1–5 divide writing into types (descriptions, instructions, narrative and argument), to develop the skills specific to each type. At the same time, each Unit looks at a variety of registers, to focus on the importance of the context and the purpose of a piece of writing.

Part 3: Units 6–10 cover all the writing task types in the CAE Paper 2 syllabus.

Task bank: a further selection of writing tasks, indexed to the appropriate units.

Key: answers to all exercises and Paper 3 questions. Model answers to Paper 2 Part 1 tasks.

Working through the book

It is suggested that you work through Units 1–5 before going on to Units 6–10, as each writing task in Units 6–10 practises skills that have been developed in one or more of the first five units. Nevertheless, as there is no progression through the book in terms of difficulty, and as Units 1–5 also contain writing tasks in the style of the exam, the Units may be taken in any order.

Classroom work and self study

This book can be used in class, for self study, or for a combination of the two.

In class
Each Unit is divided into modules which can be taught in class in about 90 minutes (plus homework). Explanations, presentations and activities are followed by Paper 3 exercises and either mini writing tasks or full-scale Paper 2 tasks. Suggestions for pairwork are sometimes included when an exercise would be more enjoyably done with a partner; many other exercises can also be done in pairs and groups.

For self-study
Many features of the book make it especially useful for self study:

• the introductory units, with their thorough treatment of register, style, cohesion and punctuation.
• the use of Paper 3 writing tasks as controlled writing practice, easily corrected with the key when working without a teacher.
• the inclusion of model texts in the form of Paper 3 tasks, and the inclusion of model answers in the key.
• the fact that it is self-contained: it is the student's book, the teacher's book and the key all in one.

Non-exam use

Because of the 'real-life' nature of the CAE writing syllabus and assessment criteria, this book can be used just as successfully as a general writing course at advanced level focusing on practical writing tasks.

CONTENTS

Papers 2 and 3

1.0   Format

The writing paper is a two-hour paper in two parts, Part 1 and Part 2. In each part, you are given a writing task of about 250 words, which can be of the following types.

Articles and reviews for a newspaper or magazine	Unit 9 (also 1, 2, 3, 4, 5)
Leaflets, information sheets, notices, announcements	Unit 10 (also 1, 2, 3, 5)
Formal letters	Unit 6 (also 2, 3, 4, 5)
Informal letters, personal notes, messages	Unit 7 (also 2, 3, 4, 5)
Reports	Unit 8 (also 1, 2, 5)
Instructions and directions	Unit 2 (also 6, 7)

Part 1 (e.g. page 64–65)
1 In Part 1, you have no choice of task. There is just one question that all candidates must answer.
2 In Part 1, you need to read a lot before you can plan your writing. The instructions for the task include information in the form of a number of texts from different sources, such as an advertisement or an extract from a letter. In order to complete the writing task in a satisfactory way, you must 'process' this information by selecting from it, summarizing it, or adapting it to suit the reader(s) you are writing for.
3 In Part 1, you are sometimes asked to produce more than one piece of writing, for example a report (200 words) which you must send to a friend accompanied by a note (50 words); the total number of words is still 250 words in all. This kind of question enables the examiners to see the difference between, for example, your *formal* and your *informal* writing.

Part 2 (e.g. page 53) offers a choice of four different tasks from which you must choose one. As in Part 1, the instructions for the task give a clear idea of *who* you are writing for, and *why*.

Timing
Because of the amount of reading in Part 1, and the time needed to process the information, you will probably need to spend longer on this section than on Part 2, even though the two tasks are worth an equal number of marks.

2.0   Marking criteria – what the examiners are looking for

CAE Paper 2 uses a marking system in which:
every piece of writing is marked by at least two examiners.
a piece of writing does *not* have to be perfect in order to obtain full marks.

The examiners are not only interested in how many mistakes you make. In fact, they give credit for **successful task achievement** and for **accuracy and range**. The seven criteria by which writing is assessed in Paper 2, described in the following exercise, all relate to one or both of these perspectives. A guide to how the examiners allocate marks is given in the mark scheme after the exercise.

Understanding the criteria

The following criteria are used in the assessment of writing in Paper 2.

range   content
accuracy   register
cohesion   organization
target reader

Which of the criteria match each of the explanations below? Write them in the spaces provided. (The examiners reduce this list to six by combining 4 and 5.)

1 _____

- Have you written in the appropriate style – should this task be written in a cold, precise style, or should your writing be entertaining?
- Does your writing have the right degree of formality or informality?
- Are you too personal, or not personal enough?

2 _____

- How many things did the task description ask you to do?
- Have you done all of them, and covered all the points raised?
- Is your writing interesting, informative or convincing, as appropriate? Have you included anything else that is appropriate, e.g. a friendly greeting in a personal letter?

3 _____

- Have you made a lot of mistakes in grammar, spelling or punctuation? Have you used vocabulary in a precise way?
- Do your mistakes make your writing difficult to understand?
- You can make a number of mistakes and still pass the writing paper, provided that your errors do not interfere with communication.

4 _____

- Have you clearly indicated the connections
- between your ideas?
- between your sentences?
- between your paragraphs?
- Do you use linking words and phrases as appropriate?

5 _____

- Are the following all appropriate?
- the beginning of your piece of writing
- the ending
- the layout (e.g. letter, note, leaflet)
- the order and use of paragraphs
- the use of titles, subtitles, headings

6 _____

- Would your writing be successful and effective in a real-life situation?
- Would the company receiving this letter of complaint refund your money?
- Would you be forgiven by the person receiving this letter of apology?
- Would the magazine editor publish this article, and would anyone read it?

7 _____

- Do you have enough mastery of both vocabulary and grammar to accomplish the task? Or is your vocabulary too elementary, and your choice of grammar and sentence structure too simple and limited?

▶▶ Use this list of questions when checking your writing! ◀◀

CAE Paper 2 mark scheme

5	Totally positive effect on target reader. Minimal errors: resourceful, controlled and natural use of language, showing good range of vocabulary and structure. Completion of task: well organized, good use of cohesive devices, appropriate register, no relevant omissions.
4	Sufficiently natural. Errors only when more complex language attempted. Some evidence of range of vocabulary and structure. Good attempt at task, only minor omissions. Attention paid to organization and cohesion; register not always natural but positive effect on target reader achieved.
3	Accuracy of language satisfactory; adequate range of vocabulary and structures. Reasonable task achievement. Or, an ambitious attempt at task, with good range of vocabulary and structures, causing a number of non-impeding errors. There may be minor omissions, but content clearly organized. Would have a positive effect on target reader.
2	Errors sometimes obscure communication and/or language too elementary. Some attempt at task but notable omissions and/or lack of organization and cohesion. Would have negative effect on target reader.
1	Serious lack of control and/or frequent basic errors. Narrow range of language. Totally inadequate attempt at task. Very negative effect on target reader.
0	Not sufficient comprehensible language for assessment.

Omissions

If the task instructions ask you to produce two different pieces of writing, or answer two questions in one piece of writing, you can't get a 'pass mark' unless you do both.

Spelling

1 If you want to use American spelling instead of British spelling, you must spell everything the American way.
2 You can lose a mark for bad spelling if it makes your writing hard to read and understand.

Handwriting

You can lose one or even two marks if your writing is difficult to read.

Length

For a 250-word task, nobody is going to count the words BUT:
– in practice, it is very difficult to write a completely satisfactory answer in fewer words
– if you write much too much, your writing is very likely to 'have a negative effect on the target reader' and to include irrelevant material, for both of which you would be penalized.

Layout

You are expected to lay out your writing (letters, reports, instructions, leaflets, etc.) in the appropriate way. If in doubt, read the instructions.

The English in Use paper tests your ability 'to apply knowledge of the language system, including control of the grammar, register, spelling, punctuation, cohesion, coherence and formulaic language.'

In other words, it is a practical grammar test: it tests not so much what you know about grammar as how well you can *use* it. The paper comprises six questions, and you have one hour and 30 minutes.

Part 1

Vocabulary cloze (e.g. page 98)

Part 1 consists of an authentic text of about 250 words. There are 15 gaps in the text. For each gap you have a choice of four words. Typically, the four words will fit the gap grammatically, but one of the words will be much more appropriate in the context.

Advice on answering Part 1

1 Cover up all the suggested answers.
2 Read through the whole text.
3 Read through the text again, stopping at each gap. Try to think of a suitable word before looking at the four words suggested. If the word you have thought of is one of the four you are offered, then choose it. Do *not* allow yourself to be distracted by the others.
4 If the word you thought of is not there, it may help if you start by eliminating those that are definitely wrong.
5 Make sure the word you choose is possible grammatically:
   • does it fit with the prepositions in the text?
   • if it is a *noun*, is it *singular / plural* to match the verb and the article?
6 If you don't know the answer, guess! Never leave a blank on your answer sheet.
7 When you're doing practice exercises, don't use the key to correct your answers. You won't learn much that way. Use a good English–English dictionary and look at the ways each of the four suggested words are used. The examples given in the dictionary will explain all the most common collocations. Only when you've worked out answers should you check in the key. A more enjoyable way of studying collocations is to read a lot of English for pleasure: magazines, fiction, or whatever interests you most.

Part 2

Grammar cloze (e.g. page 57)

This focuses on *grammar* (e.g. prepositions) and *cohesion* (linking words, articles and pronouns). Like Part 1, it takes the form of an authentic text of about 250 words. Again there are 15 gaps, but this time the choice is open.

Advice on answering Part 2

1 Read through the whole text first.
2 Make sure that the word you choose fits
   • grammatically with the words before it.
   • grammatically with the words after it.
   • the punctuation.
   • the meaning of the text.
3 Remember, most of the answers in this question are 'little' words – pronouns, articles, prepositions, conjunctions, etc. Don't imagine that the answer is going to be difficult: often it's a simple word such as *the* or *a*.

Part 3

Error correction (e.g. page 42)

This question requires you to correct mistakes in a text. You are given a text in which there is one mistake in most of the lines. One mark is awarded per line, whether for successfully correcting a mistake or for recognizing a correct line and marking it with a tick (✓). The mistakes are all of a similar type: the instructions tell you what kind of mistakes to be looking out for.

The possible types are
- one unnecessary word.
- punctuation and spelling.

This is one of the questions in Paper 3 that can contribute most towards developing your writing skills. Apart from the opportunity it affords for work on grammar, punctuation and spelling, it gives practice which will help you in correcting your own writing.

Advice on answering Part 3

1 Read the question carefully. Make sure you know what kind of mistake you're looking for, and how you must write it on your answer sheet.
2 Read the whole text through first.
3 Don't make unnecessary 'corrections' while ignoring obvious and serious mistakes: look for the big mistakes first.
4 About 20% of the lines are correct. Don't forget to mark any lines where you cannot find any mistakes with a tick (✓).

One unnecessary word
1 For a word to be an error in this question it is either grammatically incorrect or it does not fit in with the meaning of the text.
2 The grammar mistakes can include word order and prepositions or articles where there shouldn't be any.
3 The mistakes in meaning can include connecting words or even negatives that seem to work grammatically, but in fact don't make sense.
4 In every case, make sure that the sentence as a whole is correct and reads well once the unnecessary word has been deleted.

Punctuation and spelling
1 Do the punctuation work in this book (pages 29–37). Not only will it help you with this question, but it will also improve your writing.
2 The punctuation errors in this question are basic mistakes. Look out for:
   - missing capital letters.
   - brackets or speech marks that open but do not close.
   - questions that are not marked with a question mark.
3 If a comma is 'optional' (see page 33) you will usually find that there is a real mistake elsewhere in the line, often a spelling mistake.
If you have serious problems with spelling, read more and study the rules for English spelling (see 'Spelling' in Michael Swan: *Practical English Usage*, OUP).

Part 4

Word formation (e.g. page 50)

Part 4 consists of two different texts, each with eight gaps. For each gap you are given a 'prompt word'. You fill the gap by changing the prompt word so that it fits into the text.

Advice on answering Part 4

1 Read through the whole text first, for meaning.
2 Try marking each gap 'noun', 'adjective', 'verb', 'adverb', etc. This will help you focus on the grammar of the word you are looking for.
3 Make sure your answer fits the meaning of the text, as well as the grammar. For example, you might need a negative prefix (<u>un</u>believable) or suffix (hope<u>less</u>). If you write believable or hopeful, your answer will fit the grammar, but it will be completely wrong in terms of the meaning of the text.
4 When doing practice exercises, use an English-English dictionary to correct them.
5 For further practice, make an effort to notice word formation when you are reading English, and note down anything interesting you find. You will also find word formation exercises in published vocabulary materials.

Part 5

Register transfer (e.g. page 17)

This question tests your command of *register* – in other words, your ability to choose the appropriate style and vocabulary for a specific situation. This is a key area of advanced writing skills and is tested throughout Papers 2 and 3, but it is relatively unfamiliar and problematic to many candidates. For this reason a unit on style and register is included in this book (pages 12–18), while every unit explores a variety of registers through contrasting text types.

In Part 5 there are two texts, containing the same information but written in different registers (one of them may be an informal letter, the other a formal notice). The first text appears in full, while the second contains gaps. You have to fill the gaps in the second text with information borrowed from the first, but because of the change of register you **cannot** use the same words. The instructions tell you how many words you can use for each gap.

Part 6

Phrase gap (e.g. page 46)

This question again consists of a gapped text. This time, the gaps correspond to phrases or whole sentences which have been removed and which are printed below the text, together with a few other phrases or sentences which do not fit. This question focuses particularly on discourse – the way ideas are organized into phrases, sentences and paragraphs. It is therefore a very useful exercise in the development of writing skills.

Advice on answering Part 6

1 Read through the whole text to get an idea of the subject matter, the overall meaning and the register. Where does the text come from? Who wrote it? Why?
2 Read through *all* the suggested phrases.
3 Don't make your choices too quickly. Even when a phrase looks good for a gap, it may be wrong.
4 Work through the text slowly, making sure that the phrase you choose for each gap matches for:
   • meaning – does your choice fit with the phrase before it *and* the phrase after it? Does it fit with the meaning of the whole paragraph?
   • grammar – many of the suggested phrases may not fit grammatically.
5 Don't get stuck on a difficult gap. Leave it and come back to it later.
6 Start by crossing out the phrase you are given as an example, then gradually cross out the other phrases as soon as you are *certain* you have found their place. This process of elimination simplifies the task.

Style and Register

In matters of grave importance, style, not sincerity, is the vital thing.
Oscar Wilde

A Introduction

At the Advanced level, you should of course aim to write grammatically correct English. But is that enough? For example, it is grammatically correct to write 'Give me a job!', but that is not the way to write a successful job application. In fact, the employer is more likely to forgive a number of grammar or spelling mistakes than to employ an applicant whose letter was too rude or too informal. In the CAE exam, writing is assessed with this in mind: what effect would the piece of writing have on the person who is going to read it?

The ability to use the right *style*, whether you are writing a business letter or a holiday postcard, is one of the skills assessed in Paper 2; it is also examined throughout Paper 3.

But perhaps *style* is not the best word: you do not necessarily have to write stylishly. We could instead speak of *register*: the style appropriate to a particular kind of writing.

1.0 Story

This murder mystery in ten short texts is an exercise in recognizing register.

1 First, identify the origin of each text by writing the letter **A–J** by the descriptions of the texts. (Some of the descriptions do not correspond to any texts given.) What aspects of each text helped you to decide?

Business letter _____
Tourist brochure _____
Newspaper review of restaurant _____
Spoken: job interview _____
Short newspaper report _____
Spoken: polite conversation _____
Back cover of a novel _____
Informal telephone conversation _____
Advertisement _____
Love letter _____
Police officer's report _____
Recipe _____

A
Main courses at Maximilien's range from duck in raspberry vinegar sauce to a really excellent hare, still shedding its shotgun pellets, and presented as a Gaudiesque tower: slices of marvellously tender saddle on top of the braised leg (a little overdone), itself resting on buttery noodles. Another speciality of the house is the Andalucian rabbit with wild mushrooms

B 4 Return the rabbit to the pan. Cover with the wine. Season. Add the fresh thyme and simmer for 30–40 minutes with the lid on. Add the mushrooms and stir well.

C
'Tell me, Miss Lee, do you have any previous experience as a waitress?'
'Well, I did silver service at the Royal Hotel in Bognor for five years. That was before coming to Leicester. But since I've been here I've been assistant chef in the canteen at International Defence Systems.'
'And why have you given in your notice at I.D.S.?'
'Well, to tell you the truth, it was some pictures I saw on the television. And I realized that if it wasn't for the weapons we were selling them,

D Dear Mr Ball

We were most impressed by your plans, which we received last week.

Our representative in Europe, Colonel Lamont, will be contacting you upon his arrival in London.

E
How much, did you say? This must be a bad line, I thought you said 5,000! . . . Sounds like an awful lot of money for a tummy ache! Foreigners, were they? Wouldn't trust 'em if I were you. Just you make sure you get the money up front, in cash . . . Here, you don't think they're trying to do him in, do you? . . . That'd be worth 50, not five . . . Tell you what, try some on Henry Hungerford first and see what happens.

F
'Wonderful restaurant, Stefan. Do you know, I think this is possibly the best hare I've ever eaten. And as for the St Emilion: I doubt you'd find as good a bottle as this anywhere in Paris. How are you getting on with the rabbit?'

G

Arms boss poisoned

Mr Stefan Ball, managing director of the Leicester company, International Defence Systems, died in hospital at midday yesterday. He had complained of stomach pains after eating in a restaurant on Monday evening, and was rushed to hospital after being found unconscious in the morning. Mr Kevin Truckle, a waiter at the restaurant where Mr Ball had eaten, was also admitted to hospital with suspected food poisoning, but has now been discharged.

H

Words cannot describe how I feel when I think back to Friday night. And I do think of it, all the time, and of the look in your eyes when we said goodnight. Oh Stefan, say we can meet again soon! But we must be very careful, darling. My husband must never find out. Max has such a fiery temper, and so many sharp knives in his kitchen!

I

Having ascertained that the deceased had been seated at table 13, a window seat equidistant between the kitchen door and the ladies' toilets, I proceeded to question the manager about the waiting staff. He replied that Mr Ball's table had been attended by Mr Truckle, and that in the normal course of events neither of the two waitresses, Miss Lee and Miss Fairfax, would have had cause to serve at that table. He suggested that I question the waitresses themselves, but regretted that Mr Truckle was unavailable, having phoned in to say he had to take his dog to the vet.

J

It's a recipe for murder when the sinister Colonel Lamont dines with brilliant young scientist Stefan Ball. But which of his many enemies puts paid to Stefan's career on his own expense account? And who is the mysterious Henry Hungerford? Stefan won't be eating at Maximilien's again, but Holmes finds this menu very much to his taste, and presents the solution on a plate.

2 Identify the murderer by filling in the grid and making your own deductions.

Name and job	Motive	On the other hand	Opportunity
Miss Lee Job:			
Maximilien Job:	His wife was having an affair with Stefan (text H)		
Colonel Lamont Job:			Could easily have poisoned Stefan's food while dining with him (text J)
Kevin Truckle Job:		Was himself poisoned (text G)	
Henry Hungerford Job:			

1.1 Spot the mistake

Making a mistake with register can have unintentionally comic results. With a partner, write a dialogue containing register errors. Some suggested situations:

- a politician speaking to a close personal friend or family as if (s)he was addressing a political meeting or giving a press conference.
- a TV game show host conducting a job interview.
- a primary school teacher or a football coach advising the President of the USA on foreign policy.

When you have finished, swap your dialogue with another pair. Underline the register errors in their dialogue. Can you suggest a more appropriate word or phrase? Or is the whole phrase so out of place and irrelevant that it should be deleted?

B Formal and informal

One of the most important areas to master in terms of register is the difference between formal and informal English. Of course, there are many degrees of formality, and most written English (including newspapers, magazines and novels) is situated somewhere between the two extremes.

Here is a list of some of the most characteristic features that differentiate formal and informal English, followed by some preliminary exercises. Many further exercises to practise the use of different registers, and particularly to distinguish between formal and informal usage, occur throughout the rest of the book.

Formal	Informal
Words of Latin / French origin	Words of Anglo-Saxon origin
Single-word verbs	Phrasal verbs, idioms with *get*
Formal connecting words	Informal connecting words
Impersonal constructions *it is said that* *the price has been increased* *one never knows*	Active constructions *they say that* *they've put the price up* *you never know*
Abstract nouns	Modal verbs, adjectives, clauses, etc.
Is happiness possible during unemployment? *After clarification of the problem areas . . .*	*Can people be happy when they haven't got a job?* *When the bits everyone was getting wrong had been explained . . .*
Not ending with preposition; use of *whom* *To whom were you speaking?*	Ending with preposition *Who were you speaking to?*
Complex sentences	Simple sentences
Use of inversion for conditionals and emphasis *Should you require further information, please contact . . .*	Inversion sometimes used for emphasis *Only then did I realize . . .*
No contractions in writing *I will, we would*	Contractions in writing *I'll, we'd*

1.0 Vocabulary

A Origin

Why are some English words considered to be more polite or refined, whereas others which mean the same thing are thought rude or vulgar?

English vocabulary comprises words taken from many languages, particularly Anglo-Saxon, French and Latin. In 1066 the Anglo-Saxon inhabitants of Britain were conquered by the French-speaking Normans. As French was the language of the ruling classes (and Latin the language of education), words derived from French or Latin have been considered more formal than those derived from the language of the Anglo-Saxons.

The table below compares relatively formal words of Latin / French origin with their less formal alternatives, many of Anglo-Saxon origin. It is an illustration of a general tendency, not a conversion table: the choice of vocabulary always depends on the context. Supply the missing words.

Formal	Informal	Formal	Informal
Verbs		*Nouns*	
to depart	to go	carnivore	meat-eater
to retain	_____	putrefaction	_____
to cease	_____	deficiency	_____
to function	_____	vision	_____
to masticate°	_____	residence	_____
to demonstrate	_____	respiration	_____
to reside	_____	somnambulist	_____
_____	to seem	comprehension	_____
_____	to shorten	perspiration	_____
_____	to end		
_____	to help	*Adjectives*	
_____	to begin	incorrect	wrong
_____	to want	amiable	_____
_____	to get	vacant	_____
_____	to free	insane	_____
_____	to eat	inexpensive	_____
		_____	lively
Adverbials		_____	better
subsequently	next / later	_____	childish
principally	_____	_____	enough
_____	so	_____	whole
_____	at first	_____	older
_____	in the end		

°Bodily functions are an area where the difference of formality is particularly marked.

B Phrasal verbs and single-word verbs

Killing a parrot (a true story)

a Mr Lamprey and Mr Pear are neighbours. Mr Pear and his wife keep parrots. The noise made by the parrots has finally made Mr Lamprey so angry that he has broken down the fence between their two gardens and strangled one of the parrots. You are the lawyer defending Mr Lamprey, who is being sued by Mr Pear for the damage done to his property. The following is how your client describes the events to you.

This has been going on for three years, ever since the Pears *came along* and brought their infernal parrots into the neighbourhood. The noise of the birds *got on my nerves* from the very start **so** I did use to complain a bit. I **finally** *gave up hope* of *getting* used to it when in the middle of the night, I heard someone calling out my name. It was a trick he'd put one of his parrots up to, just to *wind me up*! In the morning I had it out with him, **but** he had the cheek to say that the bird wasn't saying my name at all, **and** it wasn't his fault if the bird's love call sounded a bit like "Herbert".

'I didn't know what to do. I *talked it over* with my mates at work, who suggested I *get in touch with* the City Council **and** maybe *put in* a formal complaint . **So** I rang them up **and** they *put me through* to the Social Services. The woman there said she'd come and *check out* the parrots the next week, **but** she never *turned up*. **So** we *fixed up* another time, **and** she stood me up again. They kept on *putting it off* till one day, out of the blue, a bloke *showed up*. He left after five minutes, saying he'd *pass the matter on* to the Environmental Health Department.'

Now you are speaking in court, before a judge and jury. Note that your account appears more concise and less emotive than your client's. Fill the blanks by replacing the phrasal verbs and phrases with *get* in the original (*in italics*) with a single-word verb selected from the list below. Put the verb into the appropriate tense.

lodge	irritate	despair	arrive
contact	refer	postpone	visit
become	discuss	provoke	investigate
connect	arrange	come	

'Ever since the Pears (**1**)_____ in the neighbourhood three years ago my client, Mr Lamprey, has been (**2**)_____ by the birds. He finally (**3**)_____ of (**4**)_____ accustomed to the noise the night that one of the birds started to call out his name. Mr Pear would appear to have taught the bird to say the name "Herbert" with the sole intention of (**5**)_____ my client.

'Having (**6**)_____ the problem with his colleagues, my client (**7**)_____ the City Council with a view to (**8**)_____ a complaint. The switchboard (**9**)_____ him to the Social Services Department, where a woman promised to (**10**)_____ the matter the following week. The woman never (**11**)_____. Another time was (**12**)_____, but again the woman failed to appear. In fact, this initial visit was continually (**13**)_____ until six months later, when a council officer finally (**14**)_____. After a brief inspection, the officer said he would (**15**)_____ the case to the Environmental Health Department.'

b Now, reverse the process. The rest of the story is in your words. Read it, then complete Mr Lamprey's more informal version by filling each gap with a phrasal verb selected from the list below, or with the verb *get*.

'The prospect of another six months waiting *angered* my client. He told the council officer he was no longer prepared to *tolerate* the situation; **moreover**, he felt it was the Council's job to *restore* peace and quiet to the neighbourhood. **Nevertheless**, in the twelve months that have *elapsed* since the officer came, the Council has *taken no further action*.

'Matters *deteriorated* **recently** when Mr Pear's wife Dolores *entered the quarrel*. My client had previously *enjoyed good relations* with Mrs Pear, **but** *all good will ended* when it *transpired* that Mrs Pear had been phoning the police, *claiming* that the Lampreys had threatened to kill the birds.'

make out	turn out	fall out
go by	bring back	join in
get on with	put up with	get

'Well I don't mind telling you that I (**1**)_____ pretty angry. I told him that if he thought I was going to (**2**)_____ another six months of being messed about by the City Council and taunted by screaming parrots he had another think coming. I told him it was his job to (**3**)_____ peace and quiet to the neighbourhood. Well, 12 months have (**4**)_____ now and the council hasn't (**5**)_____ anything done about it.

'Recently, things (**6**)_____ worse when Mrs Pear (**7**)_____ . We used to (**8**)_____ her OK, but then we (**9**)_____ when it (**10**)_____ she was the one that kept phoning the police about us, (**11**)_____ we had threatened to kill the birds . . .'

c Look back at the connecting words in **bold** in the boxed parts of the story (beginning with '**so** I did use to complain'). What is the difference between the connecting words in the formal speech and those in the informal spoken English?

1.1 Grammar

Impersonal constructions

One of the most common register mistakes made by inexperienced writers involves using too personal a manner in a piece of formal writing. A chatty style, characterized by the use of the words *I* and *you*, could be inappropriate and even offensive in a formal letter or a magazine article.

1 Me, myself, I

Everybody likes to talk about themselves, but when (for example) you're reviewing a film, you should be talking about the film and not about yourself.

Rewrite these three passages so that the writers are no longer talking about themselves.

Example
In my opinion, this is a highly amusing film.
This is a highly amusing film.

a I would say that the best place to spend an autumn afternoon in Paris is probably the Jardins de Luxembourg.
b The actress playing his lover is Juliette Binoche, and although I personally don't like her very much I must admit that her performance is very good.
c From my point of view, this guidebook is very helpful. It tells me about many little-known places and, as I'm not the kind of person who likes to be part of a crowd of tourists, I think this is the right guidebook for me.

2 The informal *you*

The way the word *you* is used in informal speech ('You should have seen it!' 'if you know what I mean') is not appropriate in formal writing. At best it sounds chatty and informal; at worst, disrespectful or even offensive.

The word *you* points a finger at the reader. But the readers are not friends of yours, and you have no right to make assumptions about them. Consider the following sentence from a film review written by a student.

The film is about what happens when you become middle-aged: you comb your hair over the bald patch; . . .

A man reading this will be offended because you accuse him personally. A woman might say you are talking nonsense. What the student meant was:

*The film is about what happens to **a man** when **he** becomes middle aged: **he** combs . . .*

Who exactly are you referring to?
To yourself?

This book convinces you of the advantages of vegetarianism, and after reading it you never want to eat a dead animal again.
*This book convinced **me** of the advantages of vegetarianism, and after reading it **I** never wanted to eat a dead animal again.*

To a specific person or group of people?
If your house is burgled, you can feel violated.
***Victims of a burglary** can often feel violated.*

Or to people in general?
This film makes you meditate on the meaning of life and reconsider your attitude to religion.
*This film makes **one** meditate on the meaning of life and reconsider **one's** attitude to religion.*

(Use *one* only in formal written English, and don't use it to refer just to yourself.)

Rewrite the following sentences without using the word *you*, as if you were writing a fairly formal article or review in a newspaper or magazine.

a If you marry now, in the '90s, you only stand half a chance of staying married for a lifetime.
b You easily forget how different life was 50 years ago.
c It's incredible when you hear about how much they spend on the army, especially when you think of all the poor and homeless people.
d *The Happy Kitten Beginners Picture Dictionary* is a good way of improving your vocabulary.
e As you read this book, you gradually become less ignorant about what it is like to belong to an ethnic minority that suffers from racial discrimination and abuse.
f The open fire and the dogs roaming around the restaurant will remind you of home.
g This book tells you everything you need to know about banking.
h Focusing on the problems faced by working class people in the States today, this is a film that really makes you think.
i In my home town, you're always seeing violence in the streets, but you soon learn to turn a blind eye.
j In my country there are few jobs for school leavers, but when you're desperate you'll do anything to get ahead.

3 The aggressive *you*

When the word *you* would sound unnecessarily direct and even aggressive, it can often be avoided by use of the passive.

You didn't send us the cassettes we ordered, and we've paid you for them.
We have not yet received the cassettes, which were ordered and paid for.

Rewrite the following sentences, replacing the personal construction with a passive.

a What I don't like about your club is that you don't offer enough activities for young people.
b You must do something about these problems.
c If you want to keep your customers happy, you shouldn't break the promises you make in your brochure.

1.2 Register transfer

Read the following piece of informal, spoken English in which someone describes a job advertisement to a friend, then use the information in it to complete the numbered gaps in the job advertisement itself. **Use not more than two words for each gap.** The exercise begins with an example (**0**). The words you need **do not** occur in the informal, spoken English. See page 11 for information and advice about this exam task type.

Informal spoken English

'There's an advert here in the paper for a job that might interest you, Maria. A young airline executive wants a Personal Assistant. The money's not bad – £1,300 a month – but the job's only temporary. The person who normally does the job is off for six months, having a baby.

'Actually, the job sounds right up your street. You've only got to know how to use a word processor and be a bit of a linguist: they're asking for good English and at least one other European language. And you mustn't mind working overtime.

The other thing they say is that they want to give the job to somebody who's got "good interpersonal skills". I'm afraid that means being charming, sociable and articulate. (Never mind, I'm sure they'll accept a rude, sulky delinquent if she's good enough at bluffing her way through interviews!) Oh yes, and you've got to be good on the telephone.

If you're interested in the job, you've got to phone to get an application form. The woman you speak to will also be able to tell you more about it. Then you've got to fill out the form and send it off by the end of February, otherwise you'll be too late. Doesn't give us much time to work on your "interpersonal skills", does it?'

Job advertisement in a newspaper

RICHTHOFEN AIR

Personal assistant   (based in Manchester)
Fixed term contract
Salary £1,300 per month plus paid overtime.

A young airline executive (**0**)___*requires*___ a Personal Assistant for six months while the present postholder is on (**1**)_____.

The successful (**2**)_____ should have word processing (**3**)_____, a good (**4**)_____ of the English language and a keen interest in air travel. Fluency in one or more European languages is highly (**5**)_____, as is a willingness to work overtime.

The person (**6**)_____ would also be expected to (**7**)_____ good interpersonal skills and an excellent telephone (**8**)_____.

Application forms and (**9**)_____ information concerning the post are (**10**)_____ from Sue Murphy (phone 0171 606 9999).

(**11**)_____ application forms must be returned by February 28th. No applications will be (**12**)_____ after that date.

1.3 Writing practice

Nicole Renault works in Public Relations in Lille, where she shares a flat with Jane, an English secretary. Unfortunately, Nicole doesn't seem to understand the difference between a formal letter and a personal note: the result of her confusion may amuse her flatmate, but is likely to offend the important Japanese client.

Rewrite the letter as a note and the note as a letter. When rewriting each, borrow useful phrases from the other.

37 Rue du Vieux Faubourg
59002
Lille
April 4th

Dear Jane,

I write with reference to your phone call of April 1st.

I sincerely regret that I shall be unable to be present at our shared residence at the moment of your return from your vacation: unfortunately, I have previous commitments, namely a luncheon engagement and a dental appointment.

Nevertheless, please allow me to assure you that not only myself but also a number of my colleagues are very much looking forward to obtaining more information concerning your recent travels and, in particular, concerning Adonis. In view of this, might I suggest a meeting at your earliest convenience? We could perhaps meet at 6pm for an apéritif in the Café des Sports, followed by dinner at one of the more inexpensive restaurants in town? I should be very grateful if you would phone to confirm.

I look forward to hearing from you.

Yours sincerely,

Nicole

Mon. 10am

Miss Akiko Kurosawa –

Thanks for the letter. Actually, I've already got something on for Thursday – there's a business lunch, and then I've got to go to the dentist's – so I won't be able to meet you at the airport. But me and the others are dying to get to know you, so perhaps we could get together as soon as possible after you get here? Why don't we come over to your hotel at eight, and take you out for a bite to eat? Give us a ring and say if that's OK.

Nicole Renault

p.p. Jean Émar, Export Manager.

COHESION

What is the difference
   between a pile of stones and a stone wall?
   between lines of words and a good piece of written
   English?

The answer to both these questions is **organization** and **cohesion**: the way things are ordered and joined together. Like a stone wall, a good piece of writing is carefully constructed and all the parts are properly linked, not just put next to each other. Phrases are connected to form sentences; sentences are joined to make paragraphs; paragraphs are linked together to build a text.

A Here are two versions of a fable from Aesop, one well written and the other badly written. In terms of organization and cohesion, what four things does the good writer do that the other doesn't?

A vixen* who had four young cubs was walking down a road one day when she met a lioness with her cub.

The vixen started to boast about her family, saying that she had four cubs, whereas the poor lioness only had one.

'Only one,' replied the lioness, 'but he's a lion!'

vixen – female fox

A vixen was walking down a road one day and had four young cubs and a vixen met a lioness with a cub and a vixen started to boast about a vixen's family and said a vixen had four cubs and a lioness only had one cub and a lioness said a lioness only had one cub but one cub was a lion.

Mastery of cohesion is extensively tested in the CAE so this module, as well as developing writing skills, could also be the key to a greatly improved exam performance.

B A bed with a view

This is the first part of a story – but the narrative lacks cohesion. Each idea is written in a short, isolated sentence which does not connect to the sentence before or after it. Rewrite each one as a **single** sentence; sometimes it will be necessary to add a connecting word. Divide those six sentences into four paragraphs.

- Mick and Keith were two bed-ridden old men. Mick and Keith were sharing a room in an old people's home.

- Mick had the bed next to the window. Mick used to describe in loving detail to his friend the children playing in the sunshine, the dogs running in the park and any really nasty street fights.

- Keith loved the descriptions. Keith soon became sick with jealousy.

- This went on for years. One night Mick was very ill. Mick called out, 'Please, Keith, ring for the nurse. I don't think I'll last the night.'

- His friend reached for the alarm. His friend thought, 'If he dies, I'll get the bed next to the window.'

- He ignored the calls. He pretended to be asleep.

Your narrative will start like this:

Mick and Keith were two bed-ridden old men sharing a room in an old people's home.

C Here is the final paragraph of the story. Some of the words that contribute to the cohesion have been left blank. What are they? Write one word in each blank.

Sadly, (1)_____ the morning, the nurse found Mick dead, (2)_____ she reassured Keith that he would soon have some more company. (3)_____ hearing this, Keith was quick to insist that it was his turn to have the bed by the window. (4)_____ first, the nurses tried to tell him why it would be easier if he stayed where he was, but he became (5)_____ angry that they finally carried him across to the other bed. He lay still for a while, waiting to be alone. Then, as (6)_____ as the nurses had gone, he lifted himself up expectantly (7)_____ peered through the window – to see a solid brick wall.

B Linking words

1.0 Conjunctions and sentence adverbials

A conjunction connects two clauses in the same sentence. (A clause is a phrase with a verb in it.)

I have been watching television **since** *I got home at six o'clock.*

A sentence adverb (or adverbial phrase)

- can connect a sentence with another sentence.
  I got home at six o'clock. **Since then**, *I have been watching television.*

- can connect a sentence with the whole text.
  . . . and then I went to bed. **All in all**, *I had a very boring evening.*

- can signal the writer's attitude to what they are saying.
  Frankly, *I wish I didn't have a television.*

The lists on pages 21 and 23 group these words according to their function (for example, to indicate a relationship of time). Note that a few conjunctions can also be used as sentence adverbials. But note also that the practice of beginning a sentence with *and*, *but* or *or*, though common today – even among good writers – is often thought incorrect.

A These sentences focus on the distinction between conjunctions, in the *a* sentences, and sentence adverbials. Using the lists on page 23, fill the gaps in the *b* sentences with a sentence adverbial, so that the two sentences have the same meaning. The first has been done as an example.

Time

1a (conj) Silvia went for a swim *after* she had done her homework

1b (adv) Silvia did her homework. *Afterwards*, she went for a swim.

2a She was dying for a swim *by the time* she had finished studying.

2b She studied till midday. _____, she was dying for a swim.

3a *While* she was swimming, I continued to study.

3b I continued to study. _____, she was swimming.

Reason and result

4a The Addams live in a strange house, *so* they don't get many visitors.

4b The Addams live in a strange house. _____, they don't get many visitors.

5a *Since* she had promised to visit him, she went there the next day.

5b She had promised to visit him. _____, she went there the next day.

Contrast and concession

6a A lot of men are uncomfortable with Morticia, *even though* she has a sweet nature.

6b Morticia has a sweet nature. _____, a lot of men are uncomfortable with her.

7a The English eat potatoes, *whereas* the Chinese eat rice.

7b The English eat potatoes. The Chinese, _____, eat rice.

Addition

8a *Not only* does Marcel play the trumpet, *but* he can *also* juggle.

8b Marcel plays the trumpet. _____, he can juggle.

B Conjunctions (and prepositions)

Most of the words in this table are conjunctions and join two clauses. The words marked (P), however, are prepositions, and are followed by either a noun or a gerund (-ing form).

Time	Contrast, Concession, Alternatives		if	much as
after+		just in case	on condition that	the way
after which	although	on account of (P)	provided (that)	
and	apart from (P)	seeing as / that	providing (that)	**Addition**
as	but	since	so long as	and+
as long as	despite (P)		unless	as well as (P)
as soon as	even if	**Purpose**	whether . . . or	besides (P)
at which (point)	even though	in case		besides which
before+	except that	in order that	**Manner**	in addition to (P)
by the time	in spite of (P)	in order to	as	not only*
hardly*	or	so	as if	
no sooner*	much as	so as to	as though	**Giving examples**
now (that)	nor	so that	in a way	for instance (P)
once	not that	to	in the way	for example (P)
since	though		just as	in particular (P)
the moment	whereas	**Conditional**	like	
then	while	as long as		
till+	whilst	even if		
until+	yet			
when				
whenever	**Reason**			
whereupon	as			
while	as a result of (P)			
	because			
Result	because of (P)			
and	considering			
and so	due to			
else	for			
or else	in case			
otherwise	in view of the fact			
so	that			
so that				

* Inversion – note the word order after these words when they begin the sentence.

We had hardly left the ground when the storm broke.
Hardly **had we** left the ground when the storm broke.

The plane had no sooner taken off than I regretted not taking the train.
No sooner **had the plane** taken off than I regretted not taking the train.

+ These words can act as either prepositions or conjunctions.
He went to bed **after** midnight. (preposition)
He went to bed **after** he had finished his book. (conjunction)

The sentences below illustrate many of the linking words in the table. Note that many conjunctions can be used either in the middle of a sentence

I wouldn't have told the police **even if** I had known. (sentences 1–9)

or at the beginning.

Even if I had known, I wouldn't have told the police. (sentences 10–12)

Complete the sentences by adding any appropriate word or phrase: note which conjunctions are used with commas in the examples.

1 We are advised to do this exercise very
   a carefully, *otherwise* we will make a lot of _____.
   b carefully(,) *while* our teacher _____.
   c carefully, *even though* it looks _____.

2 My weeks in captivity weren't too
   a unpleasant(,) *considering* the terrible reputation of my _____.
   b unpleasant *once* I got used to _____.
   c unpleasant, *even if* the _____ was terrible.

3 The tigers ran away from the
   a Englishwoman *as if* she _____.
   b Englishwoman *the way* _____ run away from a _____.
   c Englishwoman *the moment* they saw _____.

4 Her Olympic gold medal was
   a remarkable, *though* many people _____.
   b remarkable, *not that* she didn't deserve _____.
   c remarkable *in view of the fact that* she had just _____.

5 His clothes smelled of
  a Chanel Number 5, *just as* _____ had expected.
  b Chanel Number 5, *besides which* he had lipstick on his _____.
  c Chanel Number 5 *now that* he was going out with _____.

6 I'll look after your crocodiles while you're on
  a holiday *provided that* you look after _____.
  b holiday *as though* they were my _____.
  c holiday(,) *as well as* watering the _____.

7 I told him I had decided to break off our
  a engagement, *much as* I regretted losing _____.
  b engagement, *whereupon* he started to _____.
  c engagement, *so* he made me _____.

8 The FBI took the
  a photographs *so that* they could put pressure on _____.
  b photographs *in case* evidence against_____ was needed.
  c photographs *in spite of* _____ asking them not to.

9 I've decided to do two hours of aerobics every
  a day *in order to* lose weight and _____.
  b day *as soon as* I can afford _____.
  c day *as long as* _____ comes with me.

10 a *By the time* we arrived in Barbados, I was sorry I had _____.
   b *No sooner* had we got to Barbados than I discovered _____.
   c *Whenever* I return to Barbados, I am filled with _____.

11 a *Hardly* had Ana entered the room when everyone started to _____.
   b *As a result of* Ana's recent _____, everyone wanted to meet her.
   c *Despite* her reputation, Ana didn't seem to _____.

12 a *Not only* was their relationship happy, but it also produced _____.
   b *Since* she has been with Bruno, she has forgotten _____.
   c *So as to* celebrate their anniversary, they returned to _____.

C Choose nine of the linking words that you want to learn. Use a dictionary to find another example of how each is used, then write a new sentence of your own.

1.1 Sentence adverbials

Sentence adverbials frequently appear at the beginning of a sentence, and are followed by a comma. Many of them can, however, be used in other positions.

The numbers (2, 3, 4) in the table opposite indicate some of the other positions where the adverbial frequently appears. If no number is written, the adverbial normally appears in position (1). These are suggestions for guidance only and by no means a set of rules.

The following sentence will illustrate the 4 positions.

(1)*The snake* (2)(3) *ate the mouse*(4).

1 Capital letter followed by a comma.
   In the meantime, *the snake was eating the mouse.*

2 Mid position (before the verb), no comma.
   The snake **eventually** *ate the mouse.*

3 Mid position, in parenthesis (between two commas).
   The snake, **in the meantime**, *was eating the mouse.*

4 End position.
   The snake has eaten 12 mice **so far**.

Other notes:
   F   = formal
 INF = informal
   * = when these adverbials are used in position 1, they are not followed by a comma.

Sentence adverbials

Time
After a while
After that
Afterwards (1, 2, 4)
As yet (1, 4)
At first (1, 2, 4)
At last (1, 2, 4)
At once
At present (1, 3, 4) (F)
At the moment
At the same time
Before that / then, etc.
Beforehand
By then / that time (1, 3, 4)
Earlier (1, 4)
*Eventually** (1, 2, 4)
Ever since (then) (1, 3, 4)
*Finally** (1, 2)
*First**
From then on (1, 4)
Hitherto (1, 4) (F)
Immediately (1, 2, 4)
Initially (1, 2, 4)
In no time
Instantly (1, 2, 4)
In the end (1, 3, 4)
In the meantime (1, 3, 4)
Lastly
Later on (1, 4)
Meanwhile
*Next**
*Now**
Previously (1, 2, 4)
Simultaneously
Since then (1, 3, 4)
So far (1, 2, 4)
Soon (1, 2, 4)
Subsequently (1, 2, 4)
Suddenly (1, 2)
*Then**
Until then (1, 3, 4)
Within minutes / days

Comparing & contrasting; alternatives; concessions
Admittedly
All the same (1, 3)
Alternatively
*And yet**

At the same time
Be that as it may
Better still
*But**
By comparison (1, 3)
By contrast (1, 3) (F)
By the same token
Conversely (F)
Despite this
Equally (1, 2)
Even so
However (1, 3)
In comparison (1, 3)
In spite of this
In the same way
Instead (1, 4)
Likewise (1, 2)
Mind you (INF)
Nevertheless (F)
Nonetheless (F)
Of course (1, 3)
On the contrary
On the one hand
On the other hand (1, 3)
*Or**
Similarly (1, 2)
Still
Then again
Though (3, 4)
True
*Yet**

Ordering points; adding information
Above all
Additionally
Again
Also
*And** (INF)
*And then** (INF)
As we shall see later
As well (4)
As well as that
Besides
First(ly) / Second(ly) etc.
First of all
Finally
For one / another thing
Furthermore (F)
In addition
In the first place (F)

Last(ly)
More / most importantly
Moreover (F)
Next
On top of that
What is more

Concluding, summarizing; generalizing
All in all
Altogether
As a rule
Basically (1, 2)
Broadly speaking (1, 3)
By and large
Essentially (1, 2)
Generally (1, 2)
In brief (1, 3)
In conclusion (1, 3)
In general (1, 3)
In other words (1, 3)
In short (1, 3)
Mostly (1, 2)
On average (1, 3)
On balance (1, 3)
On the whole (1, 3)
Overall
*So** (INF)
Then (3)
To some extent (1, 3)
To sum up
Ultimately (1, 2)

Giving examples; focusing
Among others (1, 3)
For example (1, 3, 4)
For instance (1, 3, 4)
In particular (1, 2, 3)
Mainly (1, 2)
Particularly (1, 2)
Primarily (1, 2)
Principally (1, 2)
Specifically (1, 2)

Reformulating; clarifying
Actually (1, 4)
At least
I mean (INF)

Indeed
In fact (1, 2, 3)
In other words (1, 4)
Rather / Or rather
That is (to say)
To put it another way

Changing subject; referring to subject
Anyhow (INF)
Anyway (INF)
As far as . . . is concerned
As for . . . / As to . . .
As regards . . .
At any rate (1, 3) (INF)
By the way (1, 3) (INF)
Incidentally (1, 3)
Now for . . .
Regarding . . .
Speaking of . . .
Talking about . . . (INF)
That brings me on to . . . (F)
That reminds me (INF)
To turn to . . .
With reference to . . . (F)

Cause & effect; reason & result; inference
Accordingly (F)
As a result
Because of this
Consequently (F)
For this / that reason
*Hence** (F)
If not
If so
In that case
Otherwise
*So** (INF)
*That's why**
*Then** (1, 3)
*Thus** (F)
*Therefore** (F)

The exercises below will help you to explore the meaning and usage of sentence adverbials.

For each of the eight lists there is an exercise **A** which focuses on the meaning of the items. (With linking words, a good monolingual dictionary can be very useful; on no account, however, should you use a small bilingual dictionary.)

Exercise **B** then puts the words into context. It consists of pairs of sentences: in each case the second sentence requires a sentence adverbial in order to show how it is connected to the first. Think carefully about
    the meaning,
    the word order,
    the degree of formality,
    the punctuation,
then choose an appropriate word from the list indicated (e.g. **Time**) to fit the gap.

1 Time
A Under the heading **Time**, find
    three items similar in meaning to *immediately*.
    three items similar in meaning to *at the same time*.
    three items similar in meaning to *finally*. Which of these implies a feeling of relief?

B 1 I've been waiting an eternity for this moment. _____ I can hold you in my arms, Clementine.

2 A friend of mine got a job on a ranch near Buenos Aires. _____ he found the life very hard, but it didn't take him long to find his feet.

3 The food's in the oven and dinner will be ready in an hour. _____ let's go and do some gardening.

4 We are always looking for bright young men to join our staff. However, there are no vacancies _____.

5 The police received the bomb threat at 6.15 p.m. and arrived at the scene six minutes later. _____, the cinema had already been evacuated and the adjoining streets cordoned off.

6 On my twelfth birthday, I was finally told where babies come from. _____, I had imagined they came from the supermarket like everything else.

2 Ordering points, adding information
A When giving a number of reasons for something, adverbials can be used to mark each reason, and sometimes to indicate which is most important:

There are three reasons why I crossed the Atlantic in a pedal boat. First, it had never been done before. Second, I was generously sponsored by a soft drinks company. And lastly, I wanted to promote 'green' technology.

Find three items that could be used in the place of *First* in this text.
Find three items that could be used in the place of *Second* in this text.
Find three items that could be used in the place of *lastly* in this text.

B There are ten adverbials in the list similar in meaning to *also*. Two are rather informal, and another two are particularly formal. Concentrating on the formality of the context, choose appropriate words for the gaps in each of these three sentences.

1 It's luxurious, it's not too expensive, and the food's out of this world. _____ there's the Italian barman: my friends think he's the real reason I always go there.

2 I don't want to have a drink with you, because it's too early in the day and also I don't like you very much. _____, I'm not thirsty.

3 We are not wholly satisfied with your work to date, particularly in terms of productivity. _____, on more than one occasion your poor timekeeping record has been brought to our attention.

3 Reformulating, clarifying
A Find three items similar in meaning to *in other words*.

B 1 It came as a surprise to hear that Clea was married. _____, it came as a shock.

2 The only thing Chantal wants for her birthday is a new English grammar book. _____, I think that's all she wants.

3 Our hotel was what the travel agents describe as 'lively and colourful'. _____, it was in the red light district.

4 I don't know how you can listen to that music. _____, it sounds like Rambo's foreign policy: no harmony but lots of explosions.

4 Comparing and contrasting

A 1 Find four items similar in meaning to *similarly*.
2 Find five items similar in meaning to *by contrast*.
3 Find 12 items similar in meaning to *but*. (Note the degrees of formality.)

B 1 All three films give an extremely fine grained result. Delta, _____, cannot quite match T-Max 100 for the fineness of its grain structure.
2 The Delco freezer is cheap and efficient. Sometimes, _____, it can be difficult to open.
3 *Batman Returns* is surely Hollywood at its most original. _____, the film has its faults.
4 He's not much to look at, and he's certainly no hero. _____ I love him.
5 Managers are advised to avoid confrontation. _____ they should encourage staff to discuss their problems.
6 Professional cyclists do not get stomach pains, even though they eat and drink while competing. _____, swimmers rarely suffer.
7 You say I was driving fast and dangerously. _____, I was observing the speed limit and driving with great care.

5 Concluding, summarizing, generalizing

A Find three items similar in meaning to *in brief*.
Find four items similar in meaning to *in general*.

B 1 The earnings gap between men and women in Europe is at its highest in Britain. _____, women in British industry receive 69 per cent of men's earnings.
2 The Personnel Manager interviews all job applicants here. _____, she looks for potential rather than experience or qualifications.
3 And what was worse, it was raining all the time. _____, it was a disastrous weekend.
4 (430 students voted in favour of the motion to ban smoking on the college premises, while 462 voted against.) _____, students at the college are against a smoking ban.
5 At the back of the bookshelf, I found the cassettes of the telephone calls. It was Barbara, _____, who had been tapping the Palace phone lines.

6 Giving examples, focusing

A Find two items that can mean *for example*.
Find two more items that can mean *mainly*.

B 1 My cat seems to think she's a dog. Yesterday, _____, she bit the postman, and this morning she jumped up and started licking my face.

2 Yes, I am studying English at the moment. It's _____ for my job, but it also means that I'll find it a lot easier to travel.
3 His parents said I was a bad influence on him. _____ they accused me of taking him drinking last Sunday morning; they didn't mention any other ways in which I was supposed to have corrupted him.

7 Changing subject, referring to subject

A Find two items similar in meaning to *anyway*.
Find the item closest in meaning to *by the way*.

B 1 I spent the rest of the day watching the cycling on television. _____ bikes, have you got yours mended yet?
2 Darlene is as miserable as ever, and Jackie never comes to visit us. _____, I'm sure you don't want to hear about my problems, so let's get back to those holiday plans.
3 I had a letter from Patrick Eggli the other day. _____, I don't suppose you remember Carine Imhof?
4 Education is still way behind the rest of Europe, and the Health Service is in crisis. _____ the economy, there's no immediate sign of an end to the recession.

8 Cause and effect, reason and result, inference

A Find one informal and four formal items that can mean *as a result*.
Find two words that can mean *in that case*.

B 1 It is not advisable to drink beer after vigorous exercise because alcohol is a diuretic – it makes you urinate. _____ rather than replacing what you have lost in sweat, it promotes dehydration.
2 Finally, I found the pricing to be as attractive as the other features detailed above. _____ I recommend purchase of the A/EU/W4CAE Mark 1.
3 With *The Last of the Mohicans*, Day-Lewis has found that vital element – star quality. _____, he is a strong candidate for an Oscar.
4 Sorry I didn't come out last night, but I was feeling a bit under the weather. _____ I stayed at home and watched telly.
5 Don't forget to pack insect repellent. _____, you may find yourself eaten alive by the local mosquitoes.
6 'She's only inviting you because you've got a car.' '_____ I won't go.'

1.2 Attitude

A Some sentence adverbials describe your attitude to what you are saying. For example, in **Luckily**, *it was raining*, the word *luckily* describes not the rain but the way the writer feels about it. If you are expressing your own opinion, you could say **frankly** or **personally**. If you are expressing an idea that goes against your argument, you can signal this by saying **Admittedly** *it's raining, but I do think we ought to go to the beach*.

Use the following attitude words to complete the table below: for each word in the first column there are two words that can mean almost exactly the same.

predictably	happily	to my mind
granted	of course	incredibly
curiously	frankly	surprisingly
funnily	true	it seems
luckily	supposedly	

A admittedly		
B astonishingly		
C fortunately		
D strangely enough	enough	enough
E naturally		
F apparently		
G in my opinion		

Note that it is very common to say *strangely enough* rather than just *strangely*.

The use of words to refer back to things already mentioned or to refer forwards is a key area of cohesion. Mastery of reference is essential as a writing skill for Paper 2; it is also tested in Paper 3.

1.0 Various devices

Here are some of the devices that contribute towards reference.

Determiners
a, an, the   (articles)
* *my, your, his, her, their, one's, its, our*
(possessive adjectives)
this, that, these, those   (demonstrative adjectives)

Pronouns
* *I, you, one*, etc.; *me, her, it*, etc.   (personal)
mine, yours, his, hers, its, theirs, ours   (possessive)
* *this, that, these, those*   (demonstrative)
* *who, which, where, when, that*   (relative)

This* and *that
Both *this* and *that* can be used to refer to something that has been mentioned before. *This* is preferred when talking about something you are close to (in time as well as space), while *that* refers to something more distant.
Helen says she's fed up with her job. **This** *doesn't surprise me.*
Helen said she was fed up with her job. **That** *was the last time I saw her.*

This but not *that* can be used to refer to something that has not yet been mentioned.
You're never going to believe **this** *– Helen's got a new job!*

Words that can be used as pronouns
My brothers are very successful, but **both** *have a girlfriend problem. Kev hasn't got* **one**, *and Julian has* **too many**.

Words that can replace adverbs
I thought the atlas was on the bookshelf, but I can't find it **there**.
I used it on Saturday, but I haven't seen it **since then**.

***So**
I'm not very tidy; I'll have to be more **so** *in future.*
I don't believe my brother is especially clever, but he certainly thinks **so**.

Ellipsis
They want me to join the army, but I'm not going **to**. (i.e. to join the army.)
I don't think I'll be sent to prison, but I **might**. (i.e. be sent to prison)

Repetition
*Use Halo washing powder. **Halo** washes whitest.*

Synonyms and near-synonyms
*I started reading a novel last night; at dawn, **the book** was still in my hands.*

*General words
*I first visited San Sebastian in '89, and I've loved **the city** ever since.*
*The boys were being unnaturally helpful and polite. I wondered whether they were planning to trick me, but I kept **my suspicions** to myself.*
*A man bumped into me in the market this morning. I thought nothing of **the incident** till lunchtime, when I found that my wallet had been stolen.*

The former and the latter
The former refers to the first of two things or people mentioned while *the latter* refers to the second.
*Neither Reagan nor Bush could deny knowing about this plan: **the former** had thought it up, while **the latter** had actively supported it.*

He / she / they
Compare the following sentences:
a *If you find a good teacher, could you give me **his** address?*
b *If you find a good teacher, could you give me **his/her** address?*
c *If you find a good teacher, could you give me **their** address?*

All the above sentences are grammatically correct, but: sentence *a* assumes that the teacher will be a man. As the systematic use of male pronouns to refer to either a man or a woman has negative consequences for women, this practice is now widely avoided.

Sentence *b* is a non-sexist alternative, but this style – and the usage *s/he* or *(s)he* – can be rather clumsy.

Sentence *c* is another non-sexist alternative, less clumsy than *b*, and now in common usage.

They can be used to refer to one person.
*Someone knocked at the door, but when I opened it **they** had gone.*
*The next time I see a doctor, I'll ask **them** about your problem.*
*If any student wishes not to have **their** exam results sent to **their** home, could **they** please have a word with the school secretary?*

Alternatively, the problem can be avoided by using a plural noun.
*If any **students** wish not to have **their** exam results sent to **their** homes, could **they** please have a word with the school secretary?*

1.1 *It*

These sentences, written by CAE candidates, all include reference mistakes: they all use the word *it* inappropriately. In each sentence, replace *it* with an appropriate word or words. They may not be pronouns: it might be appropriate to use repetition, a synonym or a general word.

a Male employees in Japanese companies are usually willing to be sent to another branch, but Japanese women often refuse *it*.
b When democracy fails, the people's last weapon is civil disobedience. *It* means actions that disobey the authority of the state, for instance illegal demonstrations and refusing to pay taxes.
c There are one or two details I'm not entirely happy about. *It* concerns the office furniture and the heating.
d She spent years researching the causes of cancer. I think *it* is very necessary.
e I'm very satisfied with the atmosphere in the office, my workload and the salary, but I feel, however, that there are some ways in which *it* could be improved.
f Every beach in my country has lifeguards in case you need *it*.
g Increasingly, a university degree is essential. For those who have *it*, there is plenty of work.

'Please send me information about Family Income Supplement. I have a six-month-old baby and I didn't know about it until yesterday.'

1.2 Practice

A This text illustrates many features of reference. It is also one that would be very suitable for the Paper 3 'grammar cloze' question (see page 9). Read through the text and find at least one example of each of the devices marked with an asterisk (*) in 'Various devices' on pages 26–27.

PRINCE PETER
KROPOTKIN

Some years ago I came across a copy of the 1906 edition of Prince Peter Kropotkin's *Memoirs of a Revolutionist* in a second-hand bookshop. I bought it for £3. As soon as I
5 started to read it I recognized a hero.

Being myself a coward and a pessimist, and having been so as long as I can remember (and I can remember falling out of my pram, which confirmed me in my views), the people I most
10 admire are the bold and the optimistic – unless, of course, they are very stupid as well. Kropotkin, however, was as clever as he was kind, and he had a sincere faith in the absolute importance of reading books. In this he was
15 encouraged by his beloved elder brother, who wrote to him when they were separated by the exigencies of their harsh education, 'Read poetry; poetry makes men better.'

Kropotkin was an explorer who mapped some
20 of the wildest and most majestic rivers in the world. He was an anarchist who, when he was imprisoned in the dreaded fortress of St Peter and St Paul in Moscow, escaped by dashing out of the gate into a waiting carriage and galloping
25 through the streets waving to his friends who were waiting at every corner to see that the way was clear; then he shaved off his beard and spent the evening at a smart restaurant, where no one thought of looking for him. He was a pioneer of
30 the ecological movement, and in his book *Mutual Aid* he uses his own observations of nature to support his view that altruism has an important role in evolution; he was also fond of quoting Darwin's description of the blind
35 pelican which was fed by its fellows.

Memoirs of a Revolutionist is a wonderful adventure story, redolent of the generous spirit and vigorous mind of its author; if it has not already been reprinted, it should be.

B Write your own test

1 Imagine that you are a CAE examiner, looking for words to leave as gaps to test the CAE candidates. In the first two paragraphs of the Kropotkin passage, underline all the words that you feel you could reasonably expect a CAE candidate to be able to supply.
Look especially at:
the prepositions (*across*, *in*, *for*, *out of*, etc.).
the conjunctions (including *and*, especially in lines 6, 13 and 30).
the sentence adverbials.
the determiners and pronouns.

2 Choose six of your gaps – a good gap is one where only one or two answers are possible – and test a partner.

3 Now find another English text of between 100 and 200 words. Study the way reference is used in your text, and look closely at the prepositions and linking words. Then turn the text into a CAE grammar cloze for your friends (and enemies), by copying it out with 15 one-word gaps.

PUNCTUATION

What is this thing called love?
What is this thing called, love?
What? Is this thing called love?
What is this thing called? 'Love'?
'What is this thing called?' 'Love.'

A Full stops, sentences, paragraphs

A sentence begins with a capital letter and ends with a full stop (US 'period'), question mark or exclamation mark. Sentences are joined together to form paragraphs. The sentences in a paragraph are related to each other and have the same theme or subject. When the theme changes, a new paragraph is used.

Sentences can be as short as two words, but one or two lines is an average length. If you frequently write more than three or four lines without a full stop, ask yourself:

> could anyone find my sentences difficult to read?
> have I joined together two sentences that should be separate? (1.0 below)
> did I write *and* when I should have used a full stop?

If your sentences are very short (one line or less on average), ask yourself:

> could I combine two sentences to make a complex, but equally clear, sentence? (1.1 opposite)

1.0 Practice

A It is possible to combine two sentences in many ways, but a comma alone cannot join two sentences. Which of these sentences are correct? Which of them need full stops to divide them into two or more sentences? Insert full stops in the place of commas where necessary.

Example
I watched the soldiers march past, when they had gone I went back to my writing.
Incorrect. The correct punctuation is:
I watched the soldiers march past. When they had gone . . .

1 One day he married a cabaret dancer, this woman already had two daughters.
2 She was surprised to see her father, who had come home earlier than usual.
3 I think that a teacher's method is very important, would I have learned as much with another teacher?

4 I seem to have lost Naomi's address, I wonder if you could have a look to see if you've got it.
5 Cinderella was in her room, she couldn't help thinking about the boy who had bought her the Coke, her father came in and asked her how the disco had been, she told him about the boy, and how she didn't even know his name, finally she told her father the worst of it, that she had forgotten her bicycle when she left the disco some time around midnight, suddenly there was a ring at the doorbell, it was the boy who had bought her the Coke, and he had her bicycle with him, 'this bike's much too small for you', he said, 'shall I adjust the saddle? Or better still, if you'll be my girlfriend, I'll buy you a new mountain bike.'

B In the following text, some commas are used correctly, while other commas are used incorrectly in the place of full stops. Use full stops and capital letters, then divide the text into three paragraphs. The first paragraph is an introduction to the theme, the second tells the story, and the third is the writer's (rather curious) concluding comment.

> The Fakirs of India are distinguished by their attempts to demonstrate their resistance to pain and privation, some have been frauds, and some have shown remarkable powers of mind over matter, demonstrating that all pleasure and pain is Maya, or illusion, at the end of the 19th century Fakir Agastiya of Bengal proved the mental control he possessed over his body by raising his left arm above his head and leaving it in that position until he died in 1912, gradually, the blood circulation diminished to almost nothing and rendered the arm completely numb and rigid, even the joint locked, and Agastiya was laid to rest with his arm in the same position, the only poetic touch to an otherwise pointless exercise was the decision by a bird to nest in the palm of his hand, whether the accumulating bird-lime set solid over the years and helped to support his arm is unknown and open to after-dinner speculation,

1.1 Joining sentences

Writing very short sentences – like writing very long sentences – can give a bad impression. Long sentences are difficult to read, and only the best writers can structure them well. Short sentences can look like a child's writing, or can suggest that the writer is not capable of using more complex grammatical structures.

A Rewrite the following pairs of sentences as single sentences in three different ways:
a using a present participle (-ing)
b using a conjunction
c using a relative clause

1 Lucy saw an advertisement in Time Out. She was immediately interested.
   a *Seeing an advertisement in* Time Out, *Lucy was immediately interested.*
   b *As soon as Lucy saw the advertisement in* Time Out, *she was interested.*
   c *Lucy was immediately interested in the advertisement that she saw in* Time Out.

2 Lucy was looking for an adventure. She answered the advertisement.
   a *Looking . . .*
   b *Since . . .*
   c *Lucy, who . . .*

3 She approached the desert island. She was impressed by its beauty.

4 They found a good place to camp. They pitched the tent there.

5 Lucy needed to find food in order to survive. She learned to fish.

B Another way of linking two short sentences is with a past participle. Rewrite the following pairs of sentences as single sentences using a past participle.

1 I was excited about the job interview. I woke up many times in the night.
   Excited about the job interview, I woke up many times in the night.

2 He was frightened by the anonymous phone calls. He went to the police.

3 The stamps were collected by my father. They are worth a fortune.

4 Children must be accompanied by an adult. If they are not, they will be refused admission.

In order to link two sentences in this way, the past participle must have a *passive meaning*. In the sentences below, it might be necessary to transform a clause into the passive in order to achieve the link.

Greece fascinates me. I go there every summer.
I am fascinated by Greece. I go there every summer.
Fascinated by Greece, I go there every summer.

5 I found the film boring. I left the cinema and went to a café.

6 A dog attacked a woman. She received no compensation for her injuries.

7 Diana is wearing an expensive coat. Lauren Bacall wore the same coat in *The Big Sleep*.

8 I won the game of chess by using a clever gambit. I had learnt the gambit from Nigel Short.

B Commas

1.0 Parenthesis and relative clauses

A Parenthesis in the middle of a sentence

When part of a sentence appears in brackets, you can read the sentence without the words in brackets and it will still make sense.

Senna (more than any other sportsman) was loved by the Brazilian people.

The main idea of this sentence is:

Senna was loved by the Brazilian people.

Commas can be used for parenthesis in the same way as brackets.

Senna, more than any other sportsman, was loved by the Brazilian people.

In the following sentences, the material between the commas is not the main idea of the sentence. Although the words in parenthesis give extra information, the sentence would still make sense without it.

Catherine, having set out before dawn, was the first to reach the peak.

Main idea –
Catherine was the first to reach the peak.

More than one parenthesis can occur in a sentence.
Fabiana decided, on hearing about the deer, that she would, after all, climb the mountain.

Main idea –
Fabiana decided that she would climb the mountain.

1 Write the main idea in these sentences.
   a We all agreed that, in view of the condition of our feet, we would spend the next day touring the villages.
   b The deer, which stood, silently gazing at us, about 30 metres away, were not disturbed by our presence.
   c After many years of study, years which I believe I have the right to describe as both long and painful, my brother Matthew, about whom you will hear more later, finally became a good enough trumpet player to join the army.

2 Remember to use *a pair* of commas for parenthesis. If you forget one of the two commas, the sentence can become difficult to read. In each of the following pairs of sentences, one is badly punctuated. Supply the missing commas.

1a She was, however tired after her expedition.
1b She was, however tired after her expedition, still smiling.

2a Politicians have to be fair, lied the Prime Minister.
2b Politicians have to be fair, lied less this year.

3a He told me when his company was going to be taken over by a multinational, so I quickly bought shares.
3b He told me when his company was going to be taken over by a multinational, that he was drinking too much.

4a Jenny told the story of her husband's accident, was angry with him.
4b Jenny told the story of her husband's accident, laughing till the tears ran down her face.

B Parenthesis at the beginning or end of a sentence
You only need one comma if the parenthesis comes at the beginning or end of a sentence: the full stop, colon, semicolon, question mark or exclamation mark takes the place of the other comma.

Catherine was the first to reach the peak, having set out before dawn.

The concept of parenthesis and the punctuation appropriate to it can be applied to many different grammatical structures.

participle phrase
My brothers being very jealous, I never invite boys home.

sentence adverb
Nevertheless, he was a pleasure to live with.

prepositional phrase beginning a sentence
In the Middle Ages, Amanda would have been burnt as a witch.

Supply the necessary commas in each of the following sentences.

1 However I decided to spend the day in the mountain refuge.
2 We found deer near the top of the mountain the highest in Catalonia.
3 On hearing about the deer Fabiana decided that she would climb the mountain.
4 High in the sky an eagle soared effortlessly enjoying the sunshine.

C Defining and non-defining relative clauses
Bearing in mind that a phrase in parenthesis can be omitted without changing the main idea of a sentence, note the difference in meaning between the following sentences.

1 The girls, who went to aerobics classes, found the climb easy.
2 The girls who went to aerobics classes found the climb easy.

The main idea of 1 is *The girls found the climb easy.*
The main idea of 2 is *The girls who went to aerobics classes found the climb easy.*

In other words, in 1 all the girls found the climb easy, whereas in 2 it is only the girls who went to aerobics classes who found it easy and the other girls didn't.

In sentence 1, the phrase 'who went to aerobics classes' is written between commas because it is a *non-defining* relative clause: like any phrase in parenthesis, it adds information but it can be taken away without changing the main idea of the sentence.

In sentence 2, the phrase 'who went to aerobics classes' is written without commas because it is a *defining* relative clause. It tells us *which* of the girls found the climb easy.

D Summary
This exercise revises the use of commas for parenthesis. Insert any necessary commas in the following sentences. At least one of the sentences does not need a comma.

1 My birthday which had begun with sunshine ended with rain.
2 Cleopatra Henry's dog or rather bitch was a nuisance the whole day.
3 Norway being a bit cold in January I've decided to go to Morocco.
4 Marion who was frightened of spiders begged us crying to turn back.
5 What's happened to the car you used to drive when you were in California?
6 Henry's brother the doctor was unable to accompany us but his brother the guitarist did come.
7 However old as she is she has entered the London Marathon again.
8 He told me and I know you're not going to like this after all the drinks you've bought him and all the energy you've put into your attempt to sell him a Jaguar that he's bought a Fiat.

1.1 Commas: verb and object

Don't put a comma between the verb and its object, even when the object is a noun clause.

Verb + object	*I have forgotten my childhood.*
Verb + noun clause	*I have forgotten what . . .*
	I wonder if . . .
	I cannot accept that . . .
	I wish someone would . . .
Verb + two objects	*I told the captain what I thought.*
	I told the captain that . . .

A Taking care not to separate the verb from its object, add any commas that may be necessary in the following sentences.

1 I asked her what time her mother expected her home.
2 I couldn't persuade him to tell me when he had started to indulge in this habit.
3 I told her to simplify matters that I was the boss.
4 There was no way we could have guessed who was going to be at the party.

B The role of punctuation is to make written English easy to read, and to make the meaning absolutely clear. In the following exercise we see how poor punctuation can lead to ambiguity and misunderstandings.

In each of the following pairs of sentences, one of the sentences is well punctuated, while the other needs one or two commas: add those commas.

1a She promised to leave the ball before midnight.
1b She promised to keep her mother happy to leave the ball before midnight.

2a If only you'd told Helen she would be welcome!
2b If only you'd told Helen she wouldn't have been shocked when she saw it.

3a She asked me to cut a long story short to mend her car.
3b She asked me to devote my whole weekend to working on the engine of her Seat 127.

4a I can't remember whether we drank five bottles or six.
4b I can remember whether you can or not.

5a It was she who chose which was unusual for her.
5b It was she who chose which film we went to see.

1.2 Commas: verb and subject

Don't put a comma between the subject and the verb, whether the subject is a single word or a long noun phrase. In the following examples, the subject is in bold.

Dancing *excites me.*
The only thing I have forgotten *is how it ends.*
The way some of her best students spoiled their writing and confused their readers by failing to punctuate properly *was a terrible worry to Miss Brodie.*

A In each of the following pairs of sentences, one of the sentences is correctly punctuated, for the reason given above. The other sentence is incorrectly punctuated, and requires one comma. Decide which sentence is incorrectly punctuated, and add the missing comma.

1a When he started to play polo was when Kate stopped loving him.
1b When he started to play polo Kate stopped loving him.

2a Whether or not you're going doesn't interest me at all.
2b Whether or not you're going I certainly am.

3a Where there used to be a factory now there were fields of wild flowers.
3b Where large sums of money change hands is where lawyers are to be found.

B Revision
Add any commas that may be necessary.

1 Wasn't it Churchill who said that power corrupts and absolute power corrupts absolutely?
2 Many of the students and their friends and supporters were shot at by the police who later claimed that they were only obeying orders.
3 My youngest sister who was a baby during the time I spent in the 'House of the Rising Sun' was strongly advised not to do what I had done.
4 A large number of fairly successful trials had already been completed with laboratory animals before any change in the behaviour of the professor who was responsible for the project was noted.

1.3 Optional commas

As a rule, you should use a comma only if it will make the sentence easier to read, or make the meaning more clear by preventing an ambiguity. For example, why is the comma useful in the following sentence?

Here's a box to carry the cat, and the dog can sit on my lap.

A With conjunctions

Commas are often unnecessary with co-ordinating conjunctions. As a general rule, when sentences are joined together with *and, or* or *but*, commas are not needed provided that both verbs have the same subject.

She saw the bank robbery and phoned for the police.
The mother of the bride loses a daughter but gains a son.

When the verbs have a different subject, a comma is more usual.

She saw the bank robbery, but the robbers did not see her.

In the following sentences, add any commas that may be useful.

1   Australian footballers can kick the ball or throw it.
2   The burglars ate all our food and the baby never woke up.
3   She thought Miss Verner was going to be furious and she waited all morning to be summoned to the 5th floor but the call never came.
4   She squashed a grapefruit in Cagney's face and walked out of his life.

B Subordinate clauses

Commas are generally used when a subordinate clause begins the sentence. For example, *Although I had never seen one before* is a subordinate clause. The sentence is not finished, but must continue with a main clause.

Although I had never seen one before, I knew he was a zombie.

When the subordinate clause follows the main clause, commas are optional. As a rule, only use a comma when you need one to make the meaning of the sentence clear.

I knew he was a zombie(,) although I had never seen one before.
I get a headache whenever I think of you.

Insert commas as appropriate in the following sentences.

1   Before he took off Lindberg made himself some sandwiches.
2   Much as I admire his paintings I wouldn't trust him with my daughters.
3   I bought this bicycle so I could go to the beach every morning.
4   Footballers dream of scoring goals and philosophy students dream of finding the meaning of life.

1.4 Lists and sequences

Commas are used to separate items in a list.

At the school there are facilities for football, tennis, volleyball and croquet.
Charles never drinks beer: he prefers gin and tonic, whisky and soda, brandy and ginger, and wine.

The usual practice is *not* to put a comma between the last two items of a list: they are joined instead by *and*. But sometimes, when each item on the list is more than one or two words long, a comma can make the sentence easier to read and avoid ambiguity.

In the first sentence above, there is no need for a comma after *volleyball*; in the second sentence the comma after *ginger* is strongly recommended, in order to avoid an unpleasant cocktail.

Commas are used to separate a list of nouns (as above) but also adjectives, adverbs, etc.

The month of March was cold, wet, windy and thoroughly English.
She got to her feet slowly, reluctantly and painfully.
I've looked here, there and everywhere.

They are also used to separate items in a sequence or 'list' of clauses (but note the conjunction between the final two items in the following examples).

*Frank packed his bags, put them in his car, closed his front door, threw a petrol bomb through the window **then** drove to the airport.*
*They come home late, they never clean the stairs, I'm often woken up in the night by their noisy parties, **and** worst of all they don't go to church.*

See also page 34 for the use of semicolons in lists.

1.5 Revision of commas

The commas have been removed from the following text, a true story told and illustrated by Ralph Steadman. Put the commas back in the text.

Charles Charlesworth Who Died of Old Age at the Age of Seven.

The ageing process affects us all at different rates. Some people of 53 like the esteemed author look a mere 35 with sparkling brown eyes and a handsome gait. Others like the author's friend Colin look like little middle-aged men at 21 with middle-aged outlooks set ways and planned futures. In women the former condition is common but women rarely suffer from the latter being fired with the insatiable drive of ambition for either an independent and distinguished career in a still male-dominated world or a home and seven children by the time they are 30.

No such luck for Charles Charlesworth who was born on the 14th of March 1829 in Stafford. At the age of four Charles had a beard and was sexually mature.

In the final three years of his life his skin wrinkled and he developed varicose veins shortness of breath grey hair senile dementia and incontinence. Some time in his seventh year he fainted and never regained consciousness.

The coroner returned a verdict of natural causes due to old age.

C Semicolons

To lose one parent, Mr Worthing, may be regarded as a misfortune; to lose both looks like carelessness.
Oscar Wilde

Do not be afraid of the semicolon; it can be most useful.
Sir Ernest Gowers

1.0 Joining sentences

When two sentences are very closely connected in meaning, a semicolon can be used in the place of a full stop.

In which three of the examples below might a semicolon be preferred to the full stop?

1 Neurotic men, from Lord Byron to Cary Grant, have been admired for dominating their condition. Neurotic women, notably Marilyn Monroe, have been admired for surrendering to it.

2 Sir John was found guilty of driving with double the legal limit of alcohol in his bloodstream. 'You are a very foolish man', said the judge, 'but on this occasion I shall turn a blind eye to your folly.'

3 At about two in the morning, the last customers left the bar. The next day, I was awakened early by the sound of laughter outside my window.

4 In winter, I bring the geraniums into the house. All the other plants I leave outside.

5 The strong kept on walking until they reached the safety of the woods. The weak stopped to rest by the side of the road.

6 It was good to be in Italy at last. My grandmother had travelled a lot in Europe, but the rest of the family had little or no curiosity about the Old World.

1.1 Lists

Semicolons are also used to separate items in a list on occasions where commas would make the list ambiguous or difficult to read.

*The **Christine Nielsen** is the most successful boat fishing from North Shields. The wheelhouse is like a video arcade: there is screen after screen of coloured lights; sonar equipment bleeps and pings; radar fingers circle endlessly; the print-out information machine chatters away to itself.*
Peter Mortimer, *The Last of the Hunters*

Could you get me a kilo of potatoes, two salmonsteaks, 500g of pasta (spaghetti or farfalle) and something fresh to make a big salad?

Note the use of the **colon** in the first example to introduce a list, also used in 1 and 3 below.

The following sentences all contain lists. Supply the commas or semicolons, as appropriate. Make sure that the meaning is absolutely clear and unambiguous.

1 Almost half the club will be playing in the doubles tournament: six women including myself Peter Bates and John Wade the twins and of course the team captain with his partner.
2 While working at the hospital she was overworked exploited and constantly criticized at the same time as being underpaid undervalued and taken for granted.
3 When you come to one of our theatre workshops you can expect a whole rainbow of activities: music and singing circus skills including juggling vegetarian cooking mime and acrobatics improvisation and above all a warm group experience.

D Colons

1.0 Joining sentences

A colon can be used between two ideas that are very closely connected. It does not separate two *sentences* like a semicolon does; in fact, it acts like a linking word in the way it connects them, so is not followed by a capital letter. A colon can have the same *meaning* as a number of linking words, as illustrated in the following exercise.

Write a phrase after the colon to complete the unfinished sentences (numbered 1–8). In your finished sentence, the colon should have the meaning of the linking word given so you do not need to use the linking word.

Because
The river is polluted: there is a paper factory upstream.
He must have been very angry: he didn't even say goodnight.
1 I think Mary is in love:
2 I'm sure I will pass my exams:

Indeed / in fact
He comes from an athletic family: both his parents are Olympic gymnasts.
The river is more than polluted: it is an open sewer.
3 Silvia is interested in animals:
4 The dress was elegant, sensual and provocative:

So / as a result
But I was in disguise when I met them: of course they didn't recognize me.
The river is polluted: why are they swimming in it?
The river is polluted: there are no fish, and the ducks no longer swim there.
5 He was bitten by a cobra:
6 I had a terrible hangover this morning:

Namely / and that is / in other words / for example
Empress Wu's eldest son came to a fast Wu-type end: she had him murdered.
The river is polluted: don't drink the water.
7 Suddenly I remembered my grandmother's advice:
8 She thinks she's a model:

1.1 Proverbs

Write your own proverbs.

Punctuation is like a referee's whistle: too much and it interrupts the flow; too little and the result is chaos.
Full stops are like release from prison: they come at the end of a sentence.

1 Studying English is like_____ : _____
2 Life is like _____ : _____
3 Truth is like _____ : _____
4 Fashion is like_____ : _____
5 Money is like_____ : _____
6 Food is like_____ : _____
7 _____ : _____
8 _____ : _____

1.2 Other uses

A It is possible to follow a colon with something less than a sentence; in this case, the colon means *and that is . . .* or *namely.*

There's one thing that nobody understands: death.

Often, the colon is used in this way to introduce a list.

Some astronomers are particularly interested in the bodies that make up our solar system: the Sun, Moon, planets, comets and other smaller objects.

Sebastian contributes three things to the class: energy, hard work and a sense of humour.

What goes before the colon should be able to stand alone, like a complete sentence. A colon must not separate a verb or a preposition from its object.

✗ *Unfortunately, Sebastian understands nothing about: grammar, punctuation or pronunciation.* ✗
✓ *Unfortunately, Sebastian understands nothing about grammar, punctuation or pronunciation.* ✓

B A colon can also introduce direct speech (1) or a quotation (2). In both cases, a comma is normally used rather than a colon when the speech or quotation is only one line long, or shorter (3, 4).

1 *The painter who re-did the sign outside the Dog and Duck pub was berated by the landlord who told him: 'There should be equal spaces between "Dog" and "and" and "and" and "Duck".'*

2 *Another good point made by John McDermott is the following: 'American usage requires a colon in the salutation of a letter (Dear John:) where British English prefers a comma or nothing.'*

3 *Greta Garbo was famous for the line, 'I want to be alone.'*

4 *When asked why she was wearing grass seeds in her hair, Garbo replied, 'I want to be a lawn.'*

1.3 Practice

Add colons and commas where appropriate to these sentences. (Look back at *1.1 Lists* on page 34 first.)

1 Rosewall no longer had the strength and energy of his youth and so his game became more economical nothing was wasted.

2 The string quartet I play with comprises two violins a viola and a cello but my jazz quartet has rather an unusual line-up double bass violin piano and tenor saxophone.

3 But now after a bath a change of clothes and a drink the thought returned to me how was Foxton going to react when he found that I had escaped?

4 I've just decided to emigrate to Canada it sounds like the perfect solution.

5 There are four things we would need to know more about before we could offer you a job we would need to question you further about your education your family background your experience and your plans for the future.

E Dashes

Dashes may be used in three different ways, all of them characteristic of **informal** writing. They should be avoided in formal writing.

1 A single dash can be used in the place of a colon.

The river is polluted – there's a paper factory upstream.

2 A single dash can also be used to add an afterthought (something you had forgotten to say).

He used to be very good at tennis – and golf too, of course.

It can also mark a deliberate pause in order to emphasize a final phrase which is very important to the meaning of what went before.

He used to be very good at tennis – or so he says.

3 A pair of dashes – like this – can be used in informal writing to do the same job as a pair of brackets.

When I'm ready my driver – usually a member of the band – picks me up.

Practice

Punctuate the following sentences, using dashes wherever appropriate and any other punctuation mark necessary.

1 Now at last here in my hands was a book whose entire subject was railway trains in India in the 1940s

2 The people here are always happy and smiling which is more than can be said for Edward

3 Binoculars must be held steadily which means resting them or your elbows on a solid support

4 The writer of this novel is trying to tell us how important it is for us to keep in touch with our own violence and aggression at least I think that's what she's trying to say

5 On the brink of a total breakdown he met Laurie his fourth and greatest love who was to inspire some of his most moving compositions

F Hyphens

1 Hyphens can join two or more words together.

green-eyed	*twenty-one*
big-headed	*nineteen eighty-four*
half-eaten	*three-quarters*
broad-shouldered	*seven-eighths*
out-of-date information	*a Rolls-Royce*
state-of-the-art technology	*the Mason-Dixon line*
	the north-south divide

Hyphens can also be used to add a prefix to a word, especially

when the word starts with a capital letter

un-American.

when the word begins with the letter the prefix ends with

re-edit.

with the prefixes *ex-*, *anti-*, and *pro-*

ex-husband.

2 When an adjective is made up of two or more words (as in the examples above) a hyphen is used, but not when the same combination of words is **not** an adjective.

She is a three-year-old girl.
but
My daughter is three years old.

He's got a part-time job.
but
He's working part time.

A twentieth-century problem.
but
I live in the twentieth century.

3 Some words often written with a hyphen can also be written as two words: *dining-room* or *dining room*. Others can be written either with a hyphen or as one word: *hard-hearted* or *hardhearted*.

4 Hyphens become important when they make your meaning clear: perhaps a *violent butterfly collector* collects violent butterflies, whereas when *violent butterfly-collector* is written we know it is the collector who is violent.

'Look, £1 to see the man-eating tiger!'
'Give me 50p, Dad, and I'll show you a boy eating ice cream.'

5 In handwritten English, don't use a hyphen at the end of a line to split a word that is too long to fit onto that line: write it on the next.

Practice

Add hyphens where appropriate in this newspaper report.

Porsche driving army chief in anti nuclear protest

LOCAL ANGER was revealed yesterday when a cross section of the population was questioned about plans for a new gas cooled nuclear reactor just twenty three miles north west of the city centre. The opinion poll revealed strong anti nuclear feelings among three fifths of the population. Indeed, the coexistence of two pressure groups in the valley came to light: one a small time affair led by a dog loving cat food factory owner cohabiting with a used car saleswoman in a twenty storey high rise block, the other a more threatening operation with left wing Marxist Leninist sympathies. This latter group, coordinated by Lieutenant Colonel James Fox Talbot, the red haired Porsche driving managing director of an ultra modern high explosive factory, is already suspected of having committed a number of acts of low level sabotage. Lady Fox Talbot, the Lieutenant Colonel's university educated wife and cocoordinator of the group, has described these accusations as far fetched.

'We are simply reminding the democratically elected government of its democratic responsibilities,' the Fox Talbots said in a joint statement issued yesterday. 'As parents with a three year old son, we are deeply worried about the government's happy go lucky attitude to radiation. We urge all our fellow valley dwellers to join us and take advantage of this once in a lifetime opportunity to prevent the mistakes of twentieth century technology being carried over into the twenty first century.'

1 DESCRIPTION

Warm up: register exercise

The way you describe and write about an object depends on who you are writing for and why.

1 Where were these descriptions taken from, and why were they written?
2 What helped you to decide?

A

Rucksack: a bag in which you carry things on your back, for example when you are walking or climbing. It has straps that go over your shoulders. Also knapsack, haversack, backpack.

B

all three having a capacity of over 75 litres and describing themselves as 'ergonomic'. Both the Tramonte and the Cougar have adjustable back systems, whereas the Rockman comes in a choice of three back lengths. The Rockman is also the only one to be made of cotton (with synthetic shoulder straps), the other two using proprietary nylon fabrics. Although possibly more agreeable against the back on a hot day, the cotton adds to the weight of the bag; our tests also found this fabric to have 30% less resistance to abrasion than the nylon fabrics

C

I'm having problems with one of your rucksacks, a Rockman, which I bought at the Wild Rover camping shop, Bradford, in March 1994. I am writing to you directly, confident that you will be able to repair the damage under the terms of your 'Lifetime Guarantee'. There are two problems: firstly, one of the aluminium tubes has broken through the fabric at the base of the bag, and the other is threatening to do the same. Secondly, the stitching of the zip of the lid pocket has failed, rendering the pocket useless

D

The Sisyphus Rockman is the classic hardwearing ergonomic rucksack. Crafted out of 100% colour-fast waterproof cotton in a choice of attractive colours around a superlightweight aluminium frame, it is as ideal for walking and climbing as it is practical for tourism. With its capacity of 80 litres, the Rockman will always be able to cope, whether you're in Harrods or the Himalayas. And among the many original design features, the locking lid pocket and the adjustable, detachable waist belt are unique to the Rockman.
The Sisyphus Rockman: *a head and shoulders above the rest.*

E

It is a 12-year-old faded-blue 80-litre 'Sisyphus' rucksack made of thick cotton. The only external pocket, on top of the bag, is ripped, and one of the two aluminium tubes that make up the internal frame has broken through the canvas at the bottom. The arm straps and the two small straps with buckles on either side are gold-coloured; there is no waist strap. There is an embroidered badge on the top pocket, a souvenir of the Lake District.

F

An experienced travelling companion for only £15. Sisyphus Rockman rucksack, tried, tested and well-travelled. Good working order. Blue cotton, lightweight, huge capacity. Phone Eric, 773524.

G

The walker's rucksack, a bold, angular mass of vivid reds and greens painted in short, fine strokes, dominates the lower left-hand quarter of the canvas, while the walker's pale, naked right arm, a strikingly human element, stretches diagonally upwards to the right.

1A Making descriptions interesting

1.0 Descriptive detail

If you're describing a piece of lost property, you don't need to worry about whether the reader will find your writing interesting. But if you're describing something when writing a magazine article or a story, the most important thing is to catch and hold the reader's interest. Here is a checklist of ways to do this.

BORING	INTERESTING
Generalizing a large vegetable an old ship opinions	*Being specific* a three-quarter-pound sweet potato the *Marie Celeste* / the *Titanic* facts, observations, quotations
No 'picture' a glass of wine	*Descriptive details* a long-stemmed glass of aromatic, golden Muscatel
Dull, unobservant vocabulary look ask	*Precise words* gaze, glance, stare, glare, peep beg, implore, request, demand, invite
Repetition car . . . car . . . car . . . car . . . as well . . . as well . . . as well . . .	*Variation* car . . . Ford . . . vehicle . . . car . . . as well . . . also . . . What is more, . . .
Being predictable 'There are five reasons why I like . . .' stating the obvious; 'received' opinions 'The fifth reason I like it is . . .'	*Surprising the reader* starting with something striking* original thinking and observation saving something for the end*
Always talking about yourself	*Always thinking about your* *readers, and how to interest them*

* the openings and closings of magazine articles are practised on pages 124–127.

1.1 The five senses

In order to include specific, concrete details in your description, you must first *observe* in detail. Don't forget there are five senses; you don't have to limit yourself to visual description. If, for example, you wanted to describe sculptures in an African village, would you have thought of observing them in the dark, by touch and smell?

Standing in the darkness, breathing in the smell of woodsmoke and mealie porridge and earth and unfamiliar vegetation, my hands roved over bulges and incized cuts, jutting-out shapes like trunks or horns or beaks and rounded ones that might be eyes; smooth, pointed heads and bulbous lips and noses, fat fingers and protruding belly-buttons and other shapes I couldn't interpret. Some were sticky with oil which impeded the flow of my fingers; the polished ones were sensuous and let me feel them freely.

Write just four or five lines describing one of your favourite possessions using at least three of the senses.

1.2 Adjectives and adverbs: too much of a good thing?

As in the example of the glass of wine in 1.0, you can 'paint a picture' by adding one or more adjectives to a noun. Similarly, you can describe a verb by adding an adverb or adverbial phrase.

He drank the wine delicately / greedily / with abandon / in a careless manner.

However, writing becomes tiresome and predictable unless there is a variety of structures, and often a more concrete image can be achieved with a precise noun or verb.

1a *a tallish man of powerful, athletic build, with short dark hair and green eyes*

1b *a Mel Gibson look-alike*

2a *She entered my room intrusively and aggressively.*

2b *She invaded my room.*

Both of the examples are comparisons. In 1b, the man is compared to Mel Gibson; in 2b, her entry is compared to a military operation. Comparisons are frequently introduced by the word *like* or *as*.

He sipped the wine like a debutante.
She gulped the wine as if she was trying to drown herself.
He drinks as studiously as a camel.

1.3 Writing practice

This short description was written for a magazine series in which readers recommend a local café or restaurant. It was not published, because it is not at all interesting. Nor is it informative: it raises a lot of questions (what colour are the uniforms? what night does the pianist play?) but doesn't answer any. Rewrite it, keeping the same structure, but informing the reader and making the restaurant, and your description, sound interesting.

The Bazaar Restaurant

When you go in, you are taken to the bar area, where one of the waiters or waitresses will look after you. They are very nice and wear interesting uniforms of an unusual colour. They take your order from the long menu which has exciting dishes from different countries. There is also a blackboard on the wall with some other things that are not on the menu. They do a very good dish with fish, which I would recommend, and some of the salads are excellent.

Before long, you are taken to your table in the well-decorated dining room. This room is quite big; the tables are round, and the chairs are made of wood. You can hear soft music, which adds to the atmosphere, and once a week they have someone playing piano.

At the end of the meal, many people like to drink coffee, etc., in the lounge bar, where there are lots of plants and other exotic decorations.

When the bill comes you'll find it isn't very expensive for such good food, and I'm sure you'll want to go again.

1B Describing pictures and objects

<u>1.0</u>   ## The order of adjectives

When a number of adjectives (and other qualifiers) go before a noun, they are generally written in the following order.

1 **Number / determiner**	*a / one / a dozen / 365 / her / my teacher's / too many / Cleopatra's / Genghis Khan's / innumerable*
2 **Opinion**	*favourite / adorable / stylish / priceless / charming / romantic / useful / comfortable / sophisticated decadent / scandalous / dangerous / old-fashioned / cheap / nasty / ugly / useless / disgusting / boring*
3 **Size**	*short / little / microscopic / gigantic / dwarf*
4 **Age**	*antique / brand-new / ten-year-old / second-hand*
5 **Shape**	*oval / square / round / spiral / streamlined / baggy / pointed / tapered / heart-shaped / pear-shaped*
6 **Colour**	*jet black / tartan / canary yellow / shocking pink*
7 **Origin**	*Cherokee / Chinese / Alpine / Renaissance / Roman / Aboriginal*
8 **Material**	*gold / leather / copper / diamond / wooden / marble / glass*
9 **Compound**	*ear / key / wedding / electric / summer / dinner / disco smoking / dining / religious / motor / toy / bird / tree / jazz*
10 **Noun**	*ring / trumpet / jacket / shoes / shirt / skirt / table / painting / car / boat / bath / house / teddy bear / record / hat / room*

A The 'compound' describes the noun's use, type or purpose. This word is often itself a noun; it joins with the noun to form a compound noun (*earring, key-ring, wedding ring*). The compound noun may be hyphenated or written as one or two words: check in a dictionary.

How many other compound nouns can you make from the *compound* and *noun* lists (9 and 10) above?

B It is possible to use more than three or four adjectives to describe something, but it sounds a bit unnatural if you have as many as nine adjectives in front of a noun.

My teacher's charming little antique tapered black Chinese wooden ear trumpet.

Choose five of the nouns above, and describe them using five adjectives (or other qualifiers) for each. You may use the adjectives in the lists, or any others.

Examples
a stylish short Italian leather skirt
a cheap second-hand shocking pink disco shirt
some ugly antique diamond wedding rings

C The three strange items illustrated to the left were invented from words in the table. Describe them. Be creative!

D Writing practice
You have just arrived by plane in an English-speaking country and the airline seems to have lost your luggage. Write a brief but detailed description of the luggage (either one or two items). Do not mention or describe the contents. Write about 100 words.

Task bank: Task 1

1.1   *Au Bon Coin*

In most lines of this description of a famous French photograph, there is one unnecessary word – it is either grammatically incorrect or does not fit in with the sense of the text. Write the unnecessary word in the margin. Some lines are correct. Indicate these lines with a tick (✓). The exercise begins with two examples (**0**). See page 10 for information and advice about this exam task type.

0 One of Doisneau's street scenes is taken after the War shows a ___*is*___
0 thin house at the angle of an intersection like the point of a ___✓___
1 wedge or the prow of a ship. The house is been surrounded by _____
2 the *pavé*, which is glinting in the rain, there is a canal to the _____
3 one side, and a man in a beret he is walking on the _____
4 narrow pavement carrying slowly a small bucket. It is a _____
5 bleak, grimy, misshapen scene but, to anyone who can it _____
6 remember, it says immediately 'France – after the War'. The _____
7 street is poor and foreign and pungent and too full of _____
8 adventurous possibilities. There is one also cheerful point in _____
9 the picture. In the front room of the narrow house at the _____
10 corner of the two streets has a faded sign, 'Au Bon Coin', _____
11 and the both net half-curtains of the café are gleaming _____
12 white. You know that such as you open those rickety doors _____
13 you will after be assailed by the noise of laughter, and by _____
14 blue cigarette smoke and the smell of fresh coffee and _____
15 fresh and bread and cheese and wine and the *plat du jour*. _____

pavé – road made of cobble stones
plat du jour – the cooked meal on the menu that day

How many of the five senses does the writer refer to in his description of Doisneau's photo?

1.2   Describing a photograph

Work with a partner and choose one of these photos each. Don't describe what you can see, but tell your partner something about what the photo shows, or how it makes you feel.

Now read these two descriptions of the photos. The first is someone talking about the family photo, and is written in an informal style. The photograph is being exhibited in an art gallery, and the description is taken from the exhibition catalogue. The phrases printed in *italics* are some that you might find useful in your own writing.

Note also the tenses of the verbs.

- The present continuous is used to describe what is happening in a picture (*I'm having a donkey ride; she's wearing*).
- The present perfect can be used to describe what has just happened (*the coat she has just been given*).

Fill the gaps in the two descriptions. All the missing words are adjectives. Use your imagination! This is a 'creative writing' exercise, not a grammar test. Take risks with vocabulary!

Skegness Donkey Ride

My favourite family photo is this one, taken when I was a little girl back in the '30s. *I'm having a donkey ride* on the beach at Skegness. That's my cousin Sylvia on the left of the photo, holding the reins. We have always got on very well together, even though she is five years older than me. And she has never lost that (**1**)_____ gap-toothed grin.

In the photo, *she's wearing* a (**2**)_____ woollen coat *she has just been given*. I remember how proud she was of it, with its (**3**)_____ collar and cuffs. Here, the coat is almost brand new; two years later she was still wearing it, though the sleeves stopped just below her elbows and the black had faded to something like the colour of that donkey. She was very fond of the hat, too, a dark (**4**)_____ red with a broad satin ribbon. It was meant to be a summer hat, but she seemed to wear it almost all year round – she said it was good at keeping the rain off.

Over my right shoulder, also on a donkey, you can see my cousin David, just one year older than me, and Auntie Jessie, Sylvia's mother. Auntie Jessie seems to be pulling at a donkey's ears, in the same (**5**)_____ way she would always be pulling at my clothes or straightening my hair. And if you look very closely, you can just make out the edge of a hat directly behind my head. That's Uncle Harry. I don't know what he's doing there – probably just waiting for the pubs to open!

If you asked me why I like this photo so much, I couldn't really say. More than anything else, I think the picture sums up what a (**6**)_____, adventurous and (**7**)_____ summer I had that year. That week with Auntie Jessie was the first I had spent away from my parents, but I was never (**8**)_____, and never homesick. Look at my style and cowboy confidence on that donkey! John Wayne, eat your heart out!

São Paolo, 1960

At first we are struck by an atmosphere of stress and oppression. The photographer gives us a glimpse of the tension between the individual and the faceless city, represented as much by the uniform business suits as by the impersonal buildings. For a moment we believe that these four men are the only people to be seen. But (**9**)_____ figures can be discerned in the street below. And we know that every car has a driver, and that behind every window in those (**10**)_____ buildings someone is sitting. The camera itself must have been placed high in one of the very buildings that appear to be so empty of life and humanity.

The contrast between the (**11**)_____ sunshine and the surrounding greyness makes the picture work. The four businessmen, perhaps taking a short break from their work, are walking out of the picture with the afternoon sun on their backs, and we ourselves are led into the (**12**)_____ distance along a line of dazzling light.

<u>**1.3**</u>   ## Writing practice

Whichever of these tasks you choose to do, share your writing with other students. Perhaps you could put your writing, with the picture, on the classroom wall or in a class magazine.

A Find, in a magazine, on a postcard or in a book, a photograph you like very much. Describe it, and say why you like it (100–200 words).

B Describe your favourite family photo, and say why you like it (100–200 words).

C A Game

Everyone brings a family photo to class; you swap photographs with a partner and write about the photograph as if it was your own. Invent names for the people in the photo, pretend you know them well, and tell stories about them. (In fact, the author of 'Skegness Donkey Ride' was playing this game!)

If your partner writes about the same photograph, the rest of the class can try to guess who is telling the truth, you or your partner.

Task bank: Task 2

1C   Describing products

<u>**1.0**</u>   ## The language of advertising

Getaway Car

Are you torn between another executive saloon and something with more freedom of spirit?

2   With the new Toyota 4Runner, you can now have the civilisation of the former with the liberation of the latter.

3   When you slip inside, you'll see that the cabin's as slick as anything in the city. A button's press opens the sunroof, adjusts the mirrors and operates the windows. Including the window on the tailgate.

4   The sound system is something you've got to hear with your own ears. With six speakers surrounding you, be prepared to be transported even before you fire the engine.

5   The 4Runner's three-litre turbo-diesel delivers more power and torque than anything else in its class. (Talking power there's also the option of a 3-litre, petrol V6.)

6   For life in the fast lane, you've got a 5-speed gearbox. Yet, with the flick of a lever, you can be over the hills and far away. Even on the move, that's all it takes to switch from two-wheel drive to four, with both high and low ratios.

7   Steal a day's sailboarding and the 4Runner will go like the wind to the surf. And if the quick way means scaling the rocks, it will relish the climb.

8   On the road, the tilt-adjustable power steering gains firmness as the car gathers speed.

9   Better still, it grows lighter as those alloy wheels confront the furrows in the landscape. (That should keep the furrows off your brow.)

10   In the city or in the wild, the 4Runner is a very tough act to follow. And it's no different when you're towing.

11   You can hitch up over one and a half tons and this car will never make heavy weather of it.

12   Otherwise, it's as free of hitches as every car we build. Which is why it comes with our comprehensive 3-year / 60,000 mile manufacturer's warranty.

13   Dial A Trial: to arrange a test drive or for further information on the 4Runner, call 0800 777555.

14   It's the car in front for getting away to the back of beyond.

<u>The new 4Runner</u>

The car in front is a Toyota

The Toyota advert illustrates many of the stylistic devices used when something is described in an advertisement. The advanced student needs to be familiar with these devices in order to be able to use them when appropriate, (e.g. when trying to sell, persuade, convince or impress) and to be able to avoid them when they are inappropriate.

A Organization around a theme, an image or a key idea

This advertisement is typical in that it has a central theme, suggested in the title, which is used to structure the writing. What is that theme, and what words in paragraphs 1, 2, 6, 10 and 14 contribute to it?

B Playing with words: alliteration and rhyme

As in a poem, every word is carefully chosen, often for its sound as well as its meaning.

Dial A Trial (paragraph 13) – rhyme
as slick as anything in the city (paragraph 3) – alliteration. *Slick* and *city* sound good together as both begin with an *s* sound and have the same vowel.

Find the other instance in the text where a word is chosen solely because of the letter it begins with (this time also, the letter *s*).

C Playing with words: words with double meanings

Just as words can be chosen for their sound, they can also be used because of their second meanings or their associations.

4Runner (paragraph 2) The word *forerunner* suggests that the car is innovative and ahead of its time, and perhaps likely to be imitated and followed; this meaning also corresponds to the slogan *The car in front is a Toyota.*

1 Why is the word spelled differently here, and what is the second meaning?
2 What are the double meanings for the following words?

getaway car (title)   *life in the fast lane* (paragraph 6)
transported (paragraph 4)   *hitches* (paragraph 12)

D Interesting or poetic vocabulary

Words that paint pictures and bring the description to life are used instead of dull, everyday words. Supply the everyday words for these:

slip inside (paragraph 3)
fire (paragraph 4)
scaling (paragraph 7)

E Idioms, quotations, references to songs, proverbs, etc.

Over the hills and far away (paragraph 6) is an idiom that originated in a traditional song. Here it is chosen because it fits well with the 'getaway' theme at the same time as describing the advantages of four-wheel drive.

go like the wind (paragraph 7), *a tough act to follow* (paragraph 10), *make heavy weather of it* (paragraph 11), and *the back of beyond* (paragraph 14) are also idiomatic phrases, chosen to give the writing a friendly, informal tone and to suggest images which fit the theme.

F Comparatives, superlatives and 'limit' adjectives (*unique*, *incredible*)

Find the one sentence where the car is described as better than other cars.

G Appealing to the emotions

Many advertisements use children, animals or sexuality to appeal to the reader's emotions. Another common device is to write about the thing you are selling as if it were a person, attributing to it feelings, emotions, intentions and character.

Find the two examples of this device.

H Freedom with layout

The text is arranged in a visual layout; titles, subtitles and slogans may be printed extra large and in typefaces that will catch the reader's eye; paragraphs may be very short.

Why are long sentences and long paragraphs unusual in advertisements?

I Freedom with grammar

Sentences are usually short, and may not contain a main verb.

Find the two examples here of a sentence with no main verb.

Note also the number of sentences beginning with *And* or *But*, a practice that is sometimes considered incorrect in formal writing.

Other common features of the language of advertising, not illustrated in this advert, are:

J Use of statistics, scientific words or foreign languages

K References to how 'natural' or 'pure' the product is

References to traditions and the past, or to progress and the future, are also very frequent.

L Repetition (either of key words or of the name of the product)

1.1 Practice

Read through the following advertisement and then choose from the list **A–K** the best sentence to fill each of the blanks. Some of the suggested answers do not fit at all. The exercise begins with an example (**0**). See page 11 for information and advice about this exercise type.

IT LOVES THE CITY

No wonder the Cinquecento gets on so well with the city. (**0**)__*F*__

It's attractive. Who could resist its good looks?

Reliable, too. (**1**)_____ (Or into one, come to think of it.)

(**2**)_____ Side impact beams protect your body, whilst 100% galvanization of all external steel panels keeps its own body looking good for years.

Like them sporty? (**3**)_____ And stops when you want it to. (Thanks to servo-assisted brakes.)

(**4**)_____ At 42.8 mpg in the urban cycle, you won't have to spend a fortune every time you take it into town.

A non-smoker. Fiat fit a catalytic converter as standard.

It won't even embarrass you in company. Despite being so compact, it seats four adults comfortably.

(**5**)_____ Now.

To make a date with the new Fiat Cinquecento call 0800 717000 or visit your local Fiat dealer.

(**6**)_____

A You never know, it could be love at first sight.
B To sum up, you should buy one.
C You can always rely on a Cinquecento to get you out of a tight spot.
D It's good with money.
E The car in front is a Toyota.
F It has everything anyone could wish for in a partner.
G It will get you where you want to go.
H And, best of all, it's available.
I The Cinquecento may be small, but it performs brilliantly.
J Like any good mate, it's protective.
K It is a small Italian car.

<u>1.2</u>   Summarizing

This exercise practises two skills:
- recognizing the language of advertising and avoiding it when inappropriate.
- summarizing a text (also known as *précis*).

A Here is a summary of the Toyota advertisement. It expresses, in a third of the length, all the factual information given there. Compare the summary with the advertisement, and find the one place where the summary has omitted important factual information.

The Toyota 4Runner has the advantages of an executive saloon car, but it is also good off the road. Like an executive car, its sunroof, mirrors and windows (including the back window) are electronically operated. The sound system has six speakers. The three-litre engine (a choice of either turbo-diesel or petrol V6) is very powerful. There's a five-speed gearbox, and you can change easily to four-wheel drive even when moving. Off the road, it's good for going uphill. It has power steering and alloy wheels. It's fully guaranteed for three years or 60,000 miles. For a test drive or more information, call 0800 777555.

B In a simple, factual manner, summarize the following advertisement in about 75 words.

Britain does make Europe's finest ovens.
The proof is in the pudding.

Merseyside. Once it gave rise to the best music and football. Now it's giving rise to the best lemon soufflé.

How come? Because it's the home of Stoves, who have been producing ovens there since the 1920s.

And at Stoves we invest millions to make sure they are always the right ones. You see, we believe in delving deeply to find out precisely what people want from a cooker.

We then combine this research with the latest technology cooked up by our boffins. Add the process of continuous improvement which is a way of life at Stoves – and quality is built in.

In the Stoves range, you'll find single and double cavity ovens, gas and electric ovens, fanned and non-fanned ovens. All have Powercool, which keeps doors safe to touch, even during roasting.

While gas models have the unique Maxigrill, which gives a totally even heat.

And naturally, we've taken care of the worst part of cooking any meal: the cleaning-up. All our ovens are stay-clean. In addition, they're designed so that there are no nooks and crannies where grime can gather.

But, of course, all of this really adds up to one thing. While France may be able to claim they have Europe's finest cooks, Britain can definitely claim to have Europe's finest cookers.

STOVES
FINE OVENS

ACTION

Warm up: register exercise

What is the origin of each text? Who is it addressed to and what is it trying to achieve?

A

accelerates rapidly until it is travelling as fast as the wave. The surfer then pushes himself up, first kneeling and then standing on his board.

B

Mix one teaspoon of cocoa with one teaspoon of sugar, add a little cold milk and mix to a smooth paste. Pour on boiling milk, stirring all the time.

C

4 Be direct. Americans, Germans, Dutch and Scandinavians think we're vague in business because they're used to straight talking.
5 Be specific. Germans are likely to want specific figures, whereas the British think in approximations. Fax the hard figures ahead and use the telephone to

D

• Help young children with language by spending time talking to them, reading to them and encouraging them to use language. And remember, parents should still be parents and not behave like teachers.
• Expect children to do their best, offer rewards of extra attention such as

E

Coffee is delivered to the manufacturer ready roasted, blended and ground. It is then percolated in batches of up to 900 kilos at a time. Some of the water is evaporated from the coffee to leave

F

Parachute Jumping for Beginners

1 Put a book on the floor.
2 Climb on a chair and raise your arms.
3 Aiming at the target, jump shouting 'Banzai!' Your friends will be impressed.

H

Put the cooked chick peas, oil, lemon juice, garlic and tahini (sesame paste) into the blender with enough water to allow the mixture to purée satisfactorily. Add salt to taste and more lemon juice or tahini as necessary.

I

'Sit down, shut up and get on with your work. And do try to act your age: this isn't a kindergarten.'

G

g. Finally, the muscles will relax, although the casualty will remain unconscious for a few minutes or more.
h. After the fit is over, the casualty will regain consciousness but may feel dazed and confused. This feeling can

J

First make a fist with your right hand. Steady the foot with your left hand, and with the knuckles of your right hand massage the sole. Move your knuckles in small circles; press hard. Be sure to

K

Wet the hair and apply a small amount of the shampoo. Gently work to a lather. Rinse. Repeat as necessary.

2A Instructions and directions

1.0 Neither too many words nor too few

A These two sets of instructions refer to the same keep-fit exercise. Neither is perfect, but which features make the first set better?

1 You start this exercise by standing upright. Now make sure that your bottom is tucked in and that your knees are slightly bent. Also, your hips should be slightly forward.
2 Bend sideways at the waist, to your left. Let your left arm slide slowly down your leg. At the same time, bring your right arm up above your head. All this time, you should be breathing out.
3 Hold that position for a moment, then start going upright again as you breathe in.
4 Repeat this process a total of five times on the left. Afterwards, do the same exercise another five times on the other side.

1 Stand up straight.
2 Bend left five times, breathing out, with one arm going down your leg and the other in the air.
3 Bend right five times, etc.

B A good set of instructions avoids any misunderstanding, without being too long. The first set could have been written using fewer words without losing any of the details. Rewrite each step in a single sentence, using fewer words.

1.1 Writing practice

When giving instructions, you should explain anything that the other person might not understand, and adapt your instructions to suit your reader. It is better to give too much information than not enough.

Write a set of instructions, numbering them step by step (four or five steps), for **one** of these activities. Imagine you are talking to a friend from a country (or planet) where they don't do these things.

Buying bread   Turning on a television   Shaking hands

1.2 Imperatives

Instructions on shampoo bottles, in recipes and so on, are often given like commands, in the imperative: *Rinse and repeat*; *Add 200g of chocolate*.

Useful language

+

Do it.
Remember to …
Don't forget to …
Do remember to … (for emphasis)
Be sure to … / Be sure you …
Make sure that … / Make sure you …
See that … / See that you …
Try to …

–

Don't do it.
Take care not to …
Be sure not to …
Be careful not to …
Never, ever do it.
Try not to …
Avoid doing it.

Examples
Punctuate your writing.
Do punctuate your writing.
Remember to use paragraphs.
Never, ever use obscene language in an exam paper.
Make sure your writing is legible.

Related structures used for giving advice can be found on page 51.

1.3   Word formation

Use the words in the box to the right of the text to form **one** word that fits in the same numbered space in the text. Write the new word in the correct box below the text. The exercise begins with an example (**0**).

OPERATING INSTRUCTIONS

Warning

To reduce the risk of fire or (**0**) ... shock, do not expose this (**1**) ... to rain or (**2**) ... .

To maintain good (3) ...

– Do not keep the unit in places which are (**4**) ... hot, cold, dusty or humid. In particular, do not keep the unit in an area of high (**5**) ... such as a bathroom.

Note on listening with the headphones

– Listen at a (**6**) ... volume to avoid damage to (**7**) ... .
– To ensure (**8**) ..., do not wear the headphones while (**9**) ... .

Usable power sources

This unit can be (**10**) ... by two R6 (size AA) batteries or AC house current using an (**11**) ... AC (**12**) ... .

Maintenance

Clean the playback/recording head (**13**) ... (every 10 hours of use) for optimum sound quality. Use a cotton swab (**14**) ... moisturized with (**15**) ... fluid.

0 ELECTRICITY			
1 APPLY			
2 MOIST			
3 PERFORM			
4 EXTREME			
5 HUMID			
6 MODERATION			
7 HEAR			
8 SAFE			
9 DRIVE			
10 POWER			
11 OPTION			
12 ADAPT			
13 REGULAR			
14 LIGHT			
15 CLEAN			

0	*electric*	8	
1		9	
2		10	
3		11	
4		12	
5		13	
6		14	
7		15	

1.4   Writing practice

A For a magazine, write your favourite recipe (about 100 words).

B A Scottish friend is staying with you. She promised to phone her family in Scotland tonight, but your phone's not working. You won't see her until very late, so you leave a note telling her where to find the nearest public call-box and how to use it to phone Scotland. Write the note (about 100 words).

C Translate the fire notice on the wall of your classroom into English. If you are in an English-speaking country, translate it into your first language.

Task bank: Tasks 5, 29 and 47

2B   Advice

1.0   Advice for travellers

In most lines of the following text, there is **one** unnecessary word. It is either grammatically incorrect or does not fit in with the sense of the text. Find the unnecessary words and write them in the margin. Some lines are correct. Indicate these with a tick (✓). The exercise begins with three examples (**0**).

What to do if you get a stomach upset

0	It's possible that at some stage in your holidays you will have be struck	_have_
0	down with diarrhoea, maybe just as a result of a change of food or water,	✓
0	but more often also because of a bug of some sort.	_also_
1	Don't go and pumping yourself full of antibiotics at the first sign of trouble.	
2	This is not a good way to treat your stomach and you can often do more of	
3	harm than good by destroying all the useful intestinal flora in your gut as	
4	well as the nasties that are giving all you the problems.	
5	The best course of action is to try starve the little devils out. Rest, eat	
6	nothing and drink only unsweetened tea, citrus juice and clean water. Make	
7	sure you drink plenty of fluids, as though diarrhoea can dehydrate you very	
8	quickly. It is also important to take after salt to help your body retain water.	
9	If you must eat, stick to simple foods such as boiled vegetables, plain bread	
10	or toast, and yoghurt. Keep them away from dairy products (other than	
11	yoghurt), anything to sweet and non–citrus fruits.	
12	If it's not practical to stick to this diet, you may have to take something or	
13	to block you up for a while yourself. Lomotil is effective; codeine phosphate	
14	tablets are another alternative. If at the end of all this happens you	
15	are still suffering, you may have dysentery and should see a doctor.	

1.1   Avoiding the imperative

Imperatives may be used when giving advice, but in many circumstances they can be impolite. Often it is more appropriate to use one of these 'softer' structures. Try to find examples of them in the 'stomach upset' text.

You put _you_ in front of the verb.
You go to the end of the street and turn left.

You could use a modal verb.
You must try to write legibly.
You don't have to write perfectly.
You may want to work on your handwriting.
You could try changing pens.
You might like to look again at the unit on punctuation.

An impersonal construction can be used.
The best / worst thing to do is to . . .
It would be easier / advisable / preferable / useful / a good idea to . . .
It helps to . . . / It pays to . . .
It's worth buying a good . . .
It's no good / no use using a cheap substitute.
(Doing) this will be appreciated / useful / a good start.
Good writing is / should be / must be punctuated with care.

Working with a partner, write seven sentences using these structures to give advice on one of the following subjects.

How to avoid catching a cold.   How to overcome shyness.
How to learn to swim.   How to succeed in class without doing any work.

<u>1.2</u>   *If, to, by*

A Punctuate the following text and divide it into two or three paragraphs.

HOW TO pick up a BABY RABBIT

There are somewhat different methods of picking up a baby or half grown rabbit as opposed to an adult a young rabbit can be easily picked up by sliding a hand under the belly and lifting bodily before it has a chance of jumping away the trick is to have the animals body nicely balanced in the palm of the hand a very young rabbit being picked up for the first time may struggle a little so transfer it to your chest and soothe it by gentle stroking alternatively bring up the other hand and cuddle it gently hold the animal firmly but not tightly otherwise it may struggle all the more vigorously most young rabbits quickly adapt to being picked up in this manner and correctly held rarely struggle however they must have the opportunity to become accustomed to the human hand and it is advisable to handle youngsters of about five to six weeks onwards on a regular basis spare a few moments at feeding time to fondle the youngsters while they are eager for food.

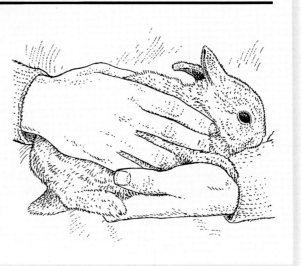

B This exercise practises three structures that are common in giving instructions.

If   *If* you want to pick up a rabbit, slide a hand under its belly.

To   *To* pick up a rabbit, slide a hand under its belly.

By   You can pick up a rabbit *by* sliding a hand under its belly.

If   *If* the rabbit struggles, hold it against your chest. This will soothe it.

To   *To* soothe a rabbit that struggles, hold it against your chest.

By   Soothe a rabbit that struggles *by* holding it against your chest.

Rewrite these sentences using structures with *to* and *by*.

1 If you want to turn right, move the steering wheel clockwise.
2 If you want it to work, kick it.
3 If this is a problem, use cold milk. (use *avoid*)
4 If you want to interrupt the speaker, raise your hand.
5 If you blow harder, you will get a higher note.
6 If you let go as soon as it gets hot, you won't be burnt. (use *avoid*)
7 You may find that your handwriting improves if you write more slowly.

C Practice

Write six sentences giving instructions on how to behave with a new employer or teacher using *if*, *to* and *by* (two sentences using each structure).

<u>2.0</u>   An 'advice' article

The text below is a model answer to this CAE writing task:

*Write, for publication in an English-language magazine, a set of tips (pieces of advice) for students who are preparing to take the CAE exam. Your **article** should be about 250 words.*

1 Write subtitles (A–E) for those paragraphs that don't have them.
2 Write a suitable introduction (between 20 and 40 words recommended).
3 The article is a bit too long. Cut anything that you feel is irrelevant or unimportant.

HOW TO PREPARE FOR THE CAE

(Introduction missing)

Know the exam

As soon as you start working for the exam, make sure you have a clear idea what is tested in each of the five papers. When you know what you are aiming for, you can plan your preparation more effectively and work on your weaknesses.

Take responsibility for your work

You're probably not in a class full of highly-motivated students whose English is exactly the same level as yours, with a teacher you like and whose methods suit you perfectly. But three-quarters of the work you need to do can be done outside the classroom, so the progress you make is your responsibility (and lack of it is not the fault of others). If you have time for more homework than you are given, your teacher will probably be delighted to recommend books for self study and to correct any extra writing you do.

(A)_____

Babies spend a year listening to spoken language before they start to speak; yet some CAE students expect to be able to write English when they never read any! A lot of what you need to know for Papers 1, 2 and 3 can be learned simply by reading widely and extensively, from literature and magazines to song lyrics and food labels.

(B)_____

It's possible to get plenty of reading practice in English without having to buy books, but everyone needs to have a good dictionary. A small bilingual dictionary has its uses, but a medium-sized English–English dictionary is essential at CAE level because it tells you how and when the word is used. A good grammar book, a vocabulary book and a self-study writing skills book can also be very helpful.

(C)_____

If you're lucky enough to have the chance of spending some time in an English-speaking country, this is a good way of making quick progress, particularly in listening and speaking. If you've got a lot of time and come from an EU country, it's not hard to get a low-paid job in Britain (e.g. hotel work). Alternatively, if you can afford it, come to Britain and follow a CAE exam course.

(D)_____

Listen to as much English as possible (BBC World Service and other radio and TV broadcasts, films in English, songs, novels on cassette, etc.) and speak English whenever you can. Talking to your partner or friends in English is just as good speaking practice as talking to a native speaker.

(E)_____

In some exams, the questions are so predictable that you can learn to pass simply by spending a lot of time doing practice tests instead of studying properly. Happily, this is not the case with CAE. Nevertheless, some exam practice is recommended (using practice tests) in order to familiarize yourself with the format of the questions and, above all, to get the timing right.

2.1 Writing

Part 2 writing task

An English language magazine for young adults (aged 16–18) in your country runs a series of articles entitled *How to get the best out of . . .* The articles are sometimes serious, and sometimes light-hearted. Write an **article** of about 250 words for the magazine on the subject of your choice. (*Some ideas: how to get the best out of being a student / your family / your creativity / your television.*)

Task bank: Tasks, 6, 7, 41a and 41b

2C Processes and systems

1.0 The passive voice

A Here are two explanations of the workings of a fire extinguisher. The first is from a talk given by a fireman. The second is from a school text book. The main stylistic difference is that the second is impersonal – the words 'I' and 'you' are not used – and the verbs are often in the passive.

Put the verbs in the second text into the appropriate form. More than one word may be required. Some of the verbs may be participles (*stopping* or *stopped*) rather than full tenses (*were stopping*, *had been stopped*). The first one has been done for you as an example.

HOW A FIRE EXTINGUISHER WORKS

'This one, painted red, is a water-filled fire extinguisher. As you can see, it's a steel cylinder with a hose coming out of the top. This lever here, where the hose joins the cylinder, is what you use to make it work. The cylinder's almost full of water, and inside the water there's a cartridge of carbon dioxide gas at high pressure.

To make it work, you just pull out this safety pin here and squeeze the lever. When you pull down the lever, it pushes a pin down which makes a hole in the carbon dioxide cartridge. And that lets out the gas into the space above the water in the cylinder. The gas, which is still of course under high pressure, pushes down on the water and makes it go up the tube in the middle, through the hose and out through the nozzle at the end. The nozzle is smaller than the tube, to make the water come out faster. This means it's going to send the water far enough so you can stand back from the fire.'

The CO$_2$-propelled water-filled fire extinguisher

A water-filled fire extinguisher comprises a red-painted steel cylinder (connect) ___*connected*___ to a hose and (control) _____ by an operating lever. The cylinder (fill) _____ almost to the top with water. Inside the cylinder is a cartridge (contain) _____ CO$_2$ gas at high pressure.

When the safety pin (remove) _____, the operating lever can (squeeze) _____, pushing a pin down to (pierce) _____ the CO$_2$ cartridge. The high-pressure gas (release) _____ into the space above the water in the cylinder. The gas (push) _____ down on the water, which (force) _____ up the discharge tube to a hose (connect) _____ to a nozzle.

The nozzle is narrower than the discharge tube, so the speed at which the water (leave) _____ is increased. The water (throw) _____ far enough so that the operator can (stand) _____ back from the fire.

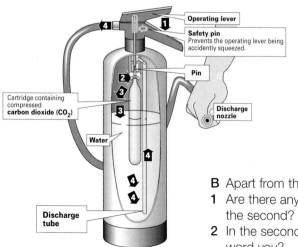

Operating lever

Safety pin
Prevents the operating lever being accidently squeezed.

Pin

Cartridge containing compressed carbon dioxide (CO$_2$)

Discharge nozzle

Water

Discharge tube

B Apart from the verbs, there are other differences between the two texts.
1 Are there any words or phrases in the first text which would be out of place in the second?
2 In the second text, what words and structures replace the phrases with the word *you*?

1.1   The organization of a process description

This model is taken from a travel book describing a journey down the Mississippi. The author has visited a button factory. The organization of the passage is exemplary; what is more, although the process is described in the past (the factory visit is seen as an event in the writer's journey), the writer uses the passive voice in the characteristic manner.

A Read through the text and choose the best phrase (A–K) to fill each of the gaps. Write one letter in each gap. Four of the suggested answers do not fit at all. The exercise begins with an example (**0**).

⊙ *Making buttons* ⊙

The whole process of button making was nicely contained and comprehensible. It started (**0**)___*G*___ of the factory and rose, machine by machine, to the top. On (**1**)_____ , the liquid plastic was poured into an oil drum, mixed with dye and hardener, and slopped into a centrifuge like a big spin-drier, where (**2**)_____formed an even, translucent sheet of soft rubbery stuff. The sheet was passed into the machine that punched it into a thousand or so round button blanks; (**3**)_____ were fed on a conveyor belt into an oven where they were baked hard; then they were cooled and sent on up (**4**)_____ . Here more machines drilled needle holes in them and carved patterns on (**5**)_____ . They were polished in a tumbling vat of wooden shoe pegs, and (**6**)_____ they were sorted into cardboard boxes.

A   to the next floor
B   upstairs again
C   the first floor
D   the top floor
E   up the path
F   their fronts and backs
G   at the bottom
H   the blanks
I   it was whirled around until it
J   the sheet
K   pieces of soft stuff

B Can you find three words in the text that the writer would not have used if he had been writing this for a scientific study of manufacturing industries?

1.2   Writing practice

Write a short description of one of these processes. Write in a fairly formal style, using the previous two texts as models.
- The production of milk, from grass to table
- How the human body works
- The greenhouse effect
- *A Star is Born* – the process of stardom from birth to death, in one field of your choice (rock music, sport, film, etc.)

2.0 Organization and cohesion

How are soft centres put into chocolates? Can you or your partner answer that question before reading the text below?

Putting the soft centre in a chocolate

The secret of putting creamy centres into chocolates is that the centres are made into solid shapes **first**, covered with liquid
5 chocolate, **then** made creamy inside the chocolate coating.

Soft-centred chocolates contain fondant, <u>which</u> is made by mixing sugar with a quarter of <u>its</u> own
10 weight of water. The <u>solution</u> is heated slowly **until** the sugar dissolves, and **then** <u>the syrup</u> is boiled **until** it reaches 115°C. The hot, sticky, clear solution is **then**
15 poured out **and** left to cool to 38°C, **when** <u>it</u> becomes a mass of tiny sugar crystals.

The fondant is re-heated to 43°C, **when** <u>it</u> is soft enough for
20 natural or artificial colours or flavours to be kneaded* in. **At the same time**, another ingredient is added – an enzyme called invertase.

The next step is to mould <u>the</u>
25 <u>kneaded fondant</u> into fancy shapes, by re-heating it until it is just liquid and pouring it into cornflour moulds. A shallow flat bed of cornflour passes under a machine
30 which stamps indentations for the shapes, <u>which</u> are then filled with

the liquid fondant. As <u>it</u> cools and hardens, the fondant centres pull away from the cornflour slightly,
35 and are then turned out onto another conveyor.

<u>This</u> carries the fondants through a bath of melted chocolate, <u>which</u> covers the base, **while** a curtain of
40 melted chocolate covers the rest of the shape. **When** the chocolate has hardened, <u>the covered sweets</u> are heated to 30°C, <u>which</u> is not hot enough to melt the chocolate but
45 activates the invertase. Invertase breaks down the sugar in the fondant into its two main components — glucose and fructose. <u>These</u> are both more
50 soluble than sugar, and they combine with the water in the fondant to liquefy the centres and make them creamy. The process takes several days.

*to knead = to mix

A The words in **bold** in the text help to signal the chronological order of the process (note that the word *after* is not needed). Apart from these words, what else contributes to the chronological ordering of the description?

B The <u>underlined</u> words all refer back to a word or idea that has been mentioned before. In each case, say exactly what the underlined word is referring to.
EXAMPLES
which (line 8) refers to *fondant* (line 8).
the kneaded fondant (line 25) refers to the fondant which now contains colours, flavours and invertase (lines 20–23).

C What is the function of the first paragraph in relation to the rest of the text?

D How are the following ideas expressed in the text?
• The hot, sticky, clear solution is then poured out. When it has been poured out, it is then left to cool until it reaches 38°C. When it reaches that temperature, it becomes a mass of tiny sugar crystals.
• The next step is to mould the kneaded fondant into fancy shapes. In order to achieve this, the kneaded fondant is re-heated until it is just liquid, then immediately poured into cornflour moulds.
Which are better, the sentences here or those in the text? Why?

2.1 More on cohesion

This text was written for school science students. The exercise focuses on cohesion, including the features studied in 2.0. Complete the text by writing the missing word in each gap. The exercise begins with an example (**0**). See page 9 for information and advice about this exercise type.

How a **metal detector works**

Electronic metal detectors use the principle of electromagnetic induction. (**0**)___***This***___ means that, if an object is placed in a changing magnetic field, an electrical voltage is created in (**1**)_____ object. In a metal detector, an electrical current is passed through a coil of wire, called the search coil, (**2**)_____ create a magnetic field. (**3**)_____ alternating current (AC) generator converts the direct current (DC) from the battery into the AC needed to drive the coil. (**4**)_____ AC regularly reverses direction, it produces the necessary ever-changing magnetic field.

Currents are generated in a metal object (**5**)_____ comes within the magnetic field by a process known as induction. When a current is induced in a metal object (for example, a buried coin), (**6**)_____ in turn produces its own magnetic fields. (**7**)_____ magnetic fields are capable of inducing a small amount of electricity in the detector's search coil itself.

The simplest kind of metal detector is the pulse induction type. A powerful current is passed from the battery through the search coil and (**8**)_____ switched off. The pulse of magnetism causes currents to flow in any target objects below the ground. (**9**)_____ , unlike the current in the search coil, the current in the object cannot be switched off; it (**10**)_____ to die away naturally. As it fades, the current in the object reactivates the search coil. This voltage is (**11**)_____ amplified to indicate with a sound or a flashing light that an object has been found.

2.2 Writing practice

The following advertisement appeared in the newsletter of The Green Cross, an organization dedicated to promoting more efficient use of the world's natural resources and to reducing pollution.

A thousand and one ways to save the planet

Is everything in your town 100% efficient? Think of rubbish collection, transport, office hours, recycling, etc. Whatever system you choose, get together with some friends and find ways in which it could be made more efficient, either saving energy or reducing pollution. Remember, "small is beautiful" – even if your idea only saves a few calories, it's still part of a giant step for mankind! Then write to us, describing the present system in detail, and outlining your plans for improvement. The best ideas we receive will be included in our new publication, *1,001 Ways To Save The Planet*, and should be about 250 words long.

Work in a group to choose an appropriate system and make it more efficient, then write your ideas so they can be included in the book.

Task bank: Tasks 8, 9, 35 and 40

NARRATIVE

A Narratives and connecting words   page 59

B Biographical narratives   page 62

C Newspaper stories   page 66

Warm up: register exercise

Read the following descriptions (**A–H**) then match them with the contexts from which they were taken (**1–8**).

1 Obituary
2 Accident report
3 Letter of complaint
4 Job application

5 Film review
6 Joke (spoken)
7 Local history section of a guide book
8 Newspaper story (from 'popular' press)

A

After graduating from Newcastle University in 1987, I spent two years travelling around the world (Europe, India, Malaysia, Australia, South America). In the course of the second year, I became fluent in Portuguese and worked as an aerobics instructor and tennis coach for six months in São Paulo. As you will see from my CV (enclosed) I returned to Newcastle in June '89 and worked as Community Liaison Officer on the Byker Community Arts Programme

B

The oncoming car had taken the corner too fast and was on the wrong side of the road. The car in front of me, a Ford Escort, tried to pull in to the side of the road to avoid being hit. The Ford managed to avoid a head-on collision, but nevertheless the driver's door was ripped off by the glancing impact. The speeding car was also damaged, and lost a wheel; it rebounded towards me, sideways on. I swerved to the left in an attempt to avoid it

C

There's this new man working at Cape Canaveral. It's his first day at work. He sits down at the microphone. 'Fifty-four thousand, three hundred and twenty-one . . . Sorry, I'll read that again . . . Five, four, three, two, one.'

D

Born Frederic Bulsara in Zanzibar, he moved to London with his family in 1959, and took his first exploratory step into music with a group called Wreckage. He joined Queen in 1970, while studying Art and Design and running a stall at Kensington Market. He also met Mary Austin, manageress of Biba's boutique. They lived together for seven years, and she remained a close friend.

E 'I cannot understand why a lioness should step over some of my mates to have a go at me,' he said. Snoring was one of the reasons put forward by his colleagues. But London Zoo expert Doug Richardson said: 'Lions are not terribly brave and would more likely have gone for someone quiet.'

F

In addition to this, on one gloomy morning the landlady asked me to switch off the light in the room where I was having breakfast, claiming that electricity in England was too expensive. On two other occasions, she came into my room in the morning and turned the light off before even saying 'Good morning'.

G

Charlie, a young New York tax consultant on the verge of promotion, walks out of a diner without paying for his lunch. He is challenged on the street by a strange girl in a black wig, reminiscent of the silent movie star Louise Brooks. She offers him a lift back to his office, but once he is in her car she throws his portable telephone out of the window, puts her foot down and heads into the Holland Tunnel and the distant reaches of New Jersey. He is so startled he does not even notice that she robs a liquor store on their journey.

H

During the English Civil War, Lyme Regis remained a staunch supporter of Cromwell, and was besieged by royalist forces. Heavily outnumbered, the men of Lyme held back the 5,000-strong force of Prince Rupert until, after two months of skirmishes, the royalist forces gave up and

3A Narratives and connecting words

1.0 Telling the story of a town

In most lines of this text, there is one unnecessary word. It is either grammatically incorrect or does not fit in with the sense of the text. Find the unnecessary words and write them in the margin. Some lines are correct. Indicate them with a tick(✓). The exercise begins with three examples (**0**).

Cambridge

0	Cambridge was important long before the University has existed. In the	*has*
0	first century BC an Iron Age tribe built a settlement on what is now known	*known*
0	Castle Hill. This site was taken over by the Romans around 40 AD;	✓
1	the Saxons had followed, then the Normans under William the Conqueror,	_____
2	who he raised a castle on a steep mound as a base for fighting the Saxon	_____
3	rebels at Ely. The earthworks of William's castle are still stand, and	_____
4	Ely Cathedral is visible from the top on a clear day.	_____
5	The first scholars didn't there arrive until 1209, and another 75 years	_____
6	passed before Hugh de Balsham founded Peterhouse, the first college. Five	_____
7	more colleges were being established in the first half of the 14th century,	_____
8	then another ten during the 15th and 16th centuries were.	_____
9	Henry VI took off nearly a quarter of the medieval city for King's	_____
10	College; after Henry VIII united two existing colleges to make Trinity	_____
11	grand enough to rival Christ Church in Oxford. But these women didn't have	_____
12	a proper college building until Girton was first founded in 1869.	_____

<u>1.1</u>   ## Connecting words

This exercise looks at words that are useful for connecting sentences in a narrative, and aims to develop your range of linking words and practise the tenses that accompany them.

Box A		
Earlier[1]	*Meanwhile*	*Next*
Before that / then	*At the same time*	*After a while*
Beforehand	*In the meantime*	*After that*
Previously	*Simultaneously*	*Afterwards*[2]
		At once
By that time / by then		*Before long*
		Later on
Until that time / until then		*Soon*
		Immediately
		At that moment
		Instantly
		Suddenly
		Then
		Within seconds / days / etc.

[1] The six words and phrases in this column are often followed by the past perfect tense.
She started work in Geneva yesterday. Previously she had worked in Rome.
I first met him in '91. By then, he had already mastered the flute and piano.

[2] After should **not** be used to mean *next*, *then* or *afterwards*.
After can be used in the following structures:
After + gerund (*After meeting them, . . .*)
After + clause (*After he had introduced himself, . . .*)
After + noun (*After her birthday, . . .*)

A Practice

Starting with **one** of the sentences given below, work with a partner to continue the narrative for as long as possible. Take it in turns to add one or more sentences to the story. Each time, use one of the linking words given in Box A before adding your sentences.

Example
Soon after midnight, the sound of gunfire echoed across the desert.
A **Then** *we heard screams coming from the prisoner's tent. It sounded as if he was in terrible pain,.*
B **Until that moment,** *he had been so quiet we had been afraid he was dying. He hadn't even told us his name or what he had done with the steering wheel of our jeep.*
A **At once** *we ran over to investigate.*
B **Within seconds,** *we realized it was a trap.*

• Everything went well for the first 20 minutes, and even the tiger seemed friendly.
• Amy managed to escape, leaving her mechanic a prisoner on the island.
• After 13 days their rations were exhausted and they were dying of hunger.
• Ablaze with fiery emotions, Jane walked self-consciously away.
• The spacecraft was immediately surrounded by small green creatures.
• Marvelling at her beauty, the prince kissed her sleeping face.
• I was in the Tupinamba, having a *bizcocho* and coffee, when this girl came in.

Box B		
To start with	**Now²**	**In the end**
At first¹ / First	*At present*	*At last³*
	At the moment	*Eventually*
Initially	*For the time being*	*In time*
In the beginning	*Nowadays*	*In the end*
	Right now	
	These days	

¹ *Firstly / First* emphasizes the sequence of events.
  First . . . then . . . finally . . .
  At first implies a contrast with what happens later.
  At first I was incompetent, but in the end I became reasonably proficient.

² *Actually* means *in fact*; it **never** means *now*.

³ *At last* implies a feeling of relief, so it is **not** the usual partner to *at first* (use *in the end* or *eventually*).

B Practice

Now, using **one** of the new opening sentences below, start your continuation with a word or phrase from Box B column 1 (e.g. *at first*). Continue, using any words from either box, especially Box B column 2 (taking your narrative into the present) or Box B column 3 (which brings your narrative to a conclusion). This time, be especially careful with the tenses of your verbs.

- I dreamed I was flying in a hot air balloon.
- Did I ever tell you about the time I was kidnapped by aliens?
- It has been a fantastic holiday.
- Harrison was beginning to wish he had never entered the jungle.
- When I lost my job, I decided to become a criminal.
- I haven't enjoyed this party at all.

1.2 Writing practice

Write a brief history of your town or region (150–200 words) for the English-language edition of a tourist guide. Use the text about Cambridge on page 59 as a model.

1.0 The story of a life

Six phrases have been removed from this text. Match the gaps (**1–6**) with the phrases (**A–H**) given below. Two of the suggested phrases do not fit at all.

OBITUARY:
Francis James

1 Had there been Olympics to select a champion eccentric, the gold would have been won for Australia by the journalist and former fighter pilot Francis James,
5 who has died in Sydney at the age of 74.

We were at the same New South Wales country school in the late twenties. His brilliance shone (**1**)_____. Then, without the knowledge of the staff,
10 he founded a school newspaper with help from local advertisers, but that admirable initiative was marred by the fact that his editorials accused the staff of practically every criminal act. He knew it was
15 untrue but felt that society needed an external stimulus. His expulsion was dramatic. His father, (**2**)_____, came to the school to thrash Francis in public.

The family moved to Canberra to a
20 new life and a new school. There he exploded another laboratory in a failed experiment and dared Gough Whitlam,

(**3**)_____, to climb a high tree with the help of a ladder. Francis removed the
25 ladder and left Gough in the stratosphere for the best part of a day before a search party found him.

Francis became (**4**)_____. He thought officers should fraternize with the lower
30 ranks and emphasized the point by flying our most powerful fighter aircraft along the main streets of Melbourne almost below roof level. Expelled again, he took ship to England and joined the RAF as an
35 aircraftsman in 1939.

By 1942 he had become a Spitfire pilot and I was at the BBC in London. I asked him how he had managed to get into the firing line. 'Easy, dear boy. Forged my
40 log books to prove I had been flying fighters in China.' Weeks later he was shot down over France and badly burned. Taken prisoner, he was asked his name and rank and replied 'Group Captain
45 Turtledove'. He tried to escape from a Stalag five times, once in a hot air balloon he had made. It crashed back into the compound, setting it alight.

In 1944 I had, (**5**)_____, a telephone
50 call from Francis. 'Dear boy, I am in London. I shall be with you in half an hour.' He was. In the biggest staff car I had ever seen. How, I asked. 'Easy, dear boy. I was at RAF HQ, just repatriated
55 from Germany as wounded, and I said to the desk "A car please for Air Vice Marshal James of Australia", and as you see it came.'

He was given a scholarship to Balliol,
60 Oxford. I used to visit but once found him absent. The porter explained, 'Mr James has left. A fellow student had not paid his gambling debts and Mr James took him to the river to explain that he
65 must do so, but unfortunately took a loaded pistol to explain.'

Many years later he became the owner / editor of Sydney's *Anglican Times*, had a profound effect on Church leaders with
70 blistering editorials, and joined Australia's *Sydney Morning Herald* as Religious Editor, writing many of his pieces on a typewriter (**6**)_____ parked in Sydney's main streets.

A to my astonishment
B a fellow student and future prime minister
C in the back of a 1936 Rolls Royce
D but he was a very good rugby player
E the youngest cadet in the Australian Air Force
F although he once wrecked a laboratory in an explosion
G a six-foot-two amateur boxer and Anglican priest
H while riding a police horse

1.1 Narrative technique

The obituary of Francis James manages to tell his life story clearly yet retain a sense of drama. The writer is able to give so much information without his writing becoming heavy and slow by using short sentences and participle clauses.

A Short sentences
Look back to see how these two ideas were actually written in the text.

1 And indeed he did arrive just half an hour later. What is more, he came in the biggest staff car I had ever seen. I asked him how he had obtained such a car. (line 52-3)

2 From time to time I used to visit him there, but on one occasion when I went to see him I found that he wasn't there. (line 60–1)

B Participle clauses

Can you remember how these ideas were expressed – in single sentences and fewer words – in the text? Do your best to express the ideas more economically, then compare your ideas with the original.

1 As a result of this exploit he was expelled, as he had been from his school. Then he took ship to England. (line 33-4)
2 He was taken prisoner. When he was asked his name and rank, he replied 'Group Captain Turtledove'. (line 43-5)
3 It crashed back into the compound. The crash set the compound alight. (line 47-8)
4 'I was at RAF HQ. I had just been repatriated from Germany as I had been wounded. I said to the desk . . . ' (line 54-6)

1 An alternative to linking words.

Participle clauses are often used to imply reason or result, so they can have the same function as linking words such as *consequently*, *because*, *which is why*, and *so*.

Never having learned to swim, I rarely go to the seaside.
implies   *I have never learned to swim, **which is why** I rarely go to the seaside.*
Defeated in the debate, the Prime Minister resigned.
implies   *She was defeated in the debate, and **as a result** she resigned.*

2 Structure

Three different structures may be used, depending on the tense.

Present participle – relates to present tenses, past continuous, and past simple when two events are more or less simultaneous.

In the first scene Travis is crossing the Mojave desert. He looks like a tramp.
In the first scene Travis is crossing the Mojave desert, looking like a tramp.

I was dying of thirst. I drank water from the river.
Dying of thirst, I drank water from the river.

He turned his back on his problems and took a long holiday in the sun.
Turning his back on his problems, he took a long holiday in the sun.
OR *He turned his back on his problems, taking a long holiday in the sun.*

Past participle – relates to past simple passive.

He was shot down over France. He was interned in a camp.
Shot down over France, he was interned in a camp.

Having + past participle – relates to present perfect, past simple, and past perfect.

I've worked very hard for this exam. I'm confident that I'll do well.
Having worked very hard for this exam, I'm confident that I'll do well.

I had never eaten raw fish. I had mixed feelings about the invitation.
Never having eaten raw fish, I had mixed feelings about the invitation.

As a child, he had been attacked by a dog. He was terrified of them all his life.
Having been attacked by a dog as a child, he was terrified of them all his life.

3 Practice

Rewrite the following in single sentences using a participle clause.

Example

Many people hope the government will do something. They are writing to their MPs.

Many people, hoping the government will do something, are writing to their MPs.

1 He heard what his daughter had done. He was proud.
2 The soldiers were singing 'Flower of Scotland'. They marched through the blizzard.
3 I visited the Sudan last year. I was shocked by what I saw.
4 She was born in 1975 and educated at Hirst. Susan Gallon became a star in 1996.
5 I pulled a muscle yesterday. As a result, I can't do any training today.
6 I haven't been to the States. Consequently, I don't know what you're talking about.
7 He insisted that we should all be punctual. Then he himself was half an hour late.
8 I hadn't opened the letter. As a result, I hadn't realized I had won first prize.
9 When they look around old houses, some people get a sense of history.
10 I wasn't fluent in their language. I had to use a lot of mime.
11 Her son was inspired by the concert. He started to learn the piano.
12 I only brought T-shirts and beach clothes. I had assumed that August would be hot.
13 I wasn't frightened of the cobra. I had been bitten by snakes many times before.
14 If you told me that Francis James spent three years in prison in China, I wouldn't be surprised. I have just read an article about his life.
15 I was delighted about winning the prize, so I took all my friends out to celebrate.

1.2   A letter to the editor

Part 1 writing task

The texts below are taken from a review, in a British newspaper, of a collection of short stories. Cindy Vitale once stayed with you during her travels and since you have a very good memory of her and her friendship, you are shocked by the inaccuracy of the information printed in the newspaper. With the help of a rock music encyclopedia, you decide to write to the newspaper and set the record straight.

Study the extracts from the book review together with the biographical information from the encyclopedia, then write your **letter** to the newspaper (about 250 words).

Surprisingly, the remarkable last short story in the book was written by punk rocker Cindy Vitale, who died in 1994 in a plane crash. Given the quality of the writing, it seems a real pity that she wasted so much of her life on the music scene, where her unsuccessful career with the punk band DGeneration culminated in her disappointment at failing to secure the leading role in the film *Broken English*.

If only Miss Vitale had devoted more of her energy to writing, where she seems to have had enormous talent, instead of music, where she obviously had none

CINDY VITALE

1952 Born São Paulo, Brazil. Irish mother, Brazilian father. Mother singer in nightclub, father jazz guitarist.

1957 Starts classical piano.

1968 Appears on Brazilian TV (piano: Chopin, Liszt).

1969–70 Leaves home, travels (USA, Caribbean, Africa). Studies drums and percussion.

1971–74 LAMDA Drama School, London. Continues drums and percussion with leading African, Brazilian and jazz musicians.

1974–75 Theatre: 18 months with Royal Shakespeare Company.

1976 Travels in Africa and Asia, studying percussion, folklore, Buddhism.

1977 London. Beginning of punk rock. Forms band, DGeneration. In TV interview, describes classical music and theatre as 'the dead culture of the middle classes' while punk is 'the living folk music of the people'.

1979 Dissolves DGeneration after two and a half years touring Britain, Europe and USA, five Top 40 singles and two albums.

1980 Refuses leading role in punk rock film Broken English because film 'doesn't understand punk – our ideals, our lifestyle or our art; we're not cinema, we're for real.'

Major role as punk rocker in Derek Agios's independent film Street Party. Critical success.

1981–82 Travels around world, studying music and theatre.

1981 Marriage to Diego Aguirre, Cuban writer. Moves to Cuba.

1981–94 Successful career as performer and music teacher in Cuba.

Music (dance orchestras, jazz quartet), theatre and TV work.

Starts to write in '86: many short stories published, one novel.

1994 Death (car accident).

Useful words and phrases

I was shocked / horrified / deeply offended / angered / surprised to read . . .
defamatory / ill-informed / unprofessional
contrary to Mr Bacon's allegations / despite Mr Bacon's assessment
not, as your reviewer suggests, . . . / far from being 'unsuccessful' . . .
a scandalous misrepresentation of the remarkable career of . . .

Guidance

1 First, read the question very carefully and think:
   Who am I going to write this letter for? (*target reader*)
   Why am I going to write it? (*task achievement*)

   When you write to a newspaper you write to the editor, but your letter is in fact intended for publication in the newspaper. Your 'target reader' is therefore the reader of the newspaper. Don't expect a reply or an apology from the editor. Your main task is calmly to correct the false information and thus clear Cindy's name.

2 Study the information in detail, underlining all the inaccuracies in the review. Some of these errors may be harmless mistakes and perhaps not worth mentioning, while others may be extremely offensive.

3 Plan your letter. It should include:

First paragraph • clear reference to newspaper article (title of article and date); in tasks when these are not given, you may invent them.
   • explanation of your connection to this story (brief details of your personal acquaintance with Cindy)
   • expression of your reaction to the article.

Middle section • paragraphs dealing with the most important errors. Give a clear account of the facts, perhaps in the form of a biographical narrative. Point out where the reviewer gives false information, and correct the false overall impression of Cindy's career and qualities.

Last paragraph • a conclusion which summarizes your whole letter.

4 Don't accuse the writer of the article of 'lying'. If somebody doesn't have a good grasp of the facts, they are 'mistaken' or 'misinformed'.

5 This kind of writing task is in fact a role-play. You can use your imagination but you mustn't change any of the facts you are given.

Task bank: Tasks 26 and 28

3C Newspaper stories

1.0 Model

Newspaper stories are good examples of economical narrative writing. The writer tells the story clearly in as few words as possible.

Divide the following report from the *Guardian* into five short paragraphs and punctuate it, taking particular care to mark any direct speech.

a doctor who came across a mock rail disaster exercise thought it was the real thing and joined in the rescue effort robert lambourn realized his mistake when he gave one of the injured a painkilling injection and the surprised actor looked up to ask do we really have to go that far the volunteer patient explained to the doctor that the 40 casualties lying around the crash scene were all acting then he was stretchered away to sleep off the effects of the injection in hospital doctor lambourn had inadvertently joined in an exercise with police fire and ambulance services at choppington northumberland he was thought to be part of the medical team and was allowed through the police cordon doctor lambourn was not available for comment yesterday but his colleague in ashington northumberland dr john campbell said my colleague acted with the very best intentions

1.1 Organizing a story

News reports are usually written in short paragraphs: the first generally summarizes the whole story, while the last often includes a quotation. Narrative tenses and linking words for time are key features.

A Putting events in order

1 Rearrange the following sentences to make a newspaper story.

2 Comment on the tenses of the two verbs in *italics*.

3 Write a title, or headline, for the story by summarizing it in 12 words or fewer.

a He pulled onto the hard shoulder and hobbled off for help with the aid of his two walking sticks.

b 'I was very surprised when the police phoned.'

c But he never returned.

d Absent-minded husband Tom Brown sparked off a police search after he left his wife in their broken-down Skoda on the M5, and forgot to collect her.

e Soon afterwards, Mrs Brown was picked up by a police patrol and a manhunt was launched, with a helicopter and sniffer dogs.

f 'I suppose I must have got confused,' Mr Brown said.

g He was discovered five hours later having tea at home.

h Police found that Mr Brown, a retired British Rail worker, *had taken* a bus to Bristol and a train home to Tewkesbury, Gloucester.

i Mr Brown, aged 73, and his wife Catherine, aged 84, *were heading* for Totnes, Devon, on Saturday when the car stuttered to a halt at Clevedon, near Bristol.

B Write a suitable first paragraph for this newspaper report by summarizing the whole story in one sentence.

(First paragraph missing)

Iain and Sue Baughan, who have 4 children, said 19-year-old Johan Egelstedt was perfect for the post.

He was detained at Heathrow airport when he arrived on Monday, and immigration officials were to fly him back to Sweden until the Baughans intervened. Mr Egelstedt was then allowed to stay for seven days with the couple at their home in Leicester.

'We are all outraged that the authorities have to deport him,' said Mrs Baughan, aged 38. 'The only reason he cannot stay is because he is a man.'

Mr Egelstedt said: 'I've a friend who went to France as a male au pair without any trouble. I don't see why I cannot do the same here.'

The immigration service states that an au pair must be 'an unmarried girl aged 17–27 inclusive without dependants.'

C Here you have the first and last paragraphs of a newspaper story, but the middle section is missing. Taking the three preceding stories as your models, use your imagination to complete the story by writing a few paragraphs giving all the details.

The Golden Hoard That Lost Its Glitter

The retired Suffolk gardener who will become a millionaire after finding a hoard of Roman gold and silver now wishes it had never happened.

(Middle paragraphs missing)

'We expect the next thing will be begging letters, and what are we supposed to do about them? There are times we wish this had never happened.'

GIVING YOUR OPINION

Warm up: register exercise

Read the following extracts (**A–G**), then match them with the contexts from which they were taken (**1–7**).

A

I wasn't at all surprised to hear that Mum and Dad are against the marriage. The thing is, Jutta, both of you are really much too young to get married. What's the harm in waiting, at least until Mike has finished college? And how do you two plan to set up home together, when neither of you has a job?

B There are three different ways of buying a second-hand car: privately, from a dealer, and at an auction. Each has its advantages and disadvantages.

Buying Privately
This is usually cheaper than buying from a dealer, but your legal protection is weaker. It's a good idea to take someone along with you when you go to look at a car, as a witness to what the seller tells you about it.

C What a shame all this technology couldn't make the music even slightly interesting. Although recent pieces like 'No Son Of Mine' at least have a tune, a trip down Genesis's interminable memory lane is like being locked in a musical-aversion chamber, where synthesizers plonk aimlessly, and guitars huff and bluster until they're blue in the face, but bear no relation to anything going on around them. And they called this 'progressive rock'?

D I was both surprised and saddened to read your recent publication of a letter from V. Meldrew regarding what was described as the 'appalling conditions that exist at Jericho Hospital'. Direct reference was made to Ward C9. I feel very strongly that I should reply to the criticisms. I was recently a patient on Ward C9, where I received a liver transplant. I have the utmost admiration and appreciation for the professionalism, dedication and patient care I received.

E don't blame your father if, knowing your mother is there for him, he uses her. Remember that she too must take responsibility for the position in which she finds herself. In other words, be very careful not to take sides.

I think the best thing you can do is to urge them both to help themselves and possibly find help outside

F No matter where in the world you go, you'll find some deranged Brit setting up a donkey sanctuary. Isn't it time we tuned the dial to a better reception, started caring a bit more about humanity, a bit less about donkeys?

We ought, as a nation, to grow up and stop trying to pretend that Peter Rabbit is still our best friend. In the greater scheme of things, the worst of humanity is worth considerably more than the best of bunnies.

G Louis Sarno's account of his strange journey away from modern civilization is disarmingly frank and completely lacking in self-importance. Longing to be accepted by these people, but ashamed at his lack of basic skills, he appears to be the ultimate innocent in paradise.

1 A concert review
2 A magazine article
3 Consumer advice in a consumer magazine
4 A book review
5 An informal letter
6 The advice page of a magazine
7 A letter to a newspaper

4A Argument

1.0 Arguments for and against

Here we look at the type of writing where the writer argues a case, or expresses an opinion, by looking at a problem from two sides. In this type of writing, the way ideas are connected is very important; this is achieved by the use of connecting words, by the way the ideas are grouped together into paragraphs, and by the way the paragraphs themselves are ordered. The following mini-composition is an example of the basic structure.

Telling the truth may be a virtue, but is it not more important to know how to tell lies? Obviously, modern civilized society couldn't exist if everybody lied all the time. But at the same time, would it not be equally disastrous if everybody always told the truth? So it seems to me that lying is an essential skill, and that schools are quite right to teach children how to do it.

This expresses the whole argument in four sentences. A longer piece of writing would develop the ideas in each of these sentences into four (or more) paragraphs, but the same basic structure would be retained.

Use your imagination and creativity to complete the sentences in the mini-compositions below. Note that **A–E** look at both sides of the argument, whereas **F** and **G** are one-sided and simply list reasons.

A Students often wonder whether it's worth going to Britain to study English.

I would say it depends on _____

_____

Some students _____

Others, however, _____

_____

All in all, _____

_____

B This is only the third time I've _____ and I still don't know if I really enjoy it.

In some ways, _____

_____

Also, _____

_____

But at the same time, _____

By and large, I think _____

_____

C I'm often told I'm lucky to be a man / woman, but in fact it's a mixed blessing.

_____

While it is true to say that _____

_____, I nevertheless _____

_____

On balance, I suppose _____

_____

D Many young actors and actresses dream of becoming stars, but in reality stardom
has its drawbacks as well as its attractions.

On the one hand, _____

_____

Also, _____

_____

On the other hand, _____

_____

Not only that, but _____ also _____

_____

Ultimately,_____

_____

E As an Olympic Gold Medallist, I am often asked what is the best way to spend
the night before a big race.

On the one hand, _____

_____

On the other hand, _____

_____

Personally, though, _____

_____

F There are many reasons why I love _____

One reason is _____

_____

Another_____

_____

What is more, _____

_____

Above all, _____

_____

G Of all the soap powders in the world, I would recommend that you use_____

In the first place, _____

_____

More importantly, _____

_____

On top of that, _____

_____

In short, _____

_____

1.1   Expanding your argument

Below is the mini-composition on page 69 developed into a magazine article.

A The connecting words that signal the structure of the argument have been removed. For each of the numbers (**1**, **2**, **3**) which **four** of the following adverbials would be appropriate?

a Admittedly	b By and large	c Then again
d Of course	e All in all	f But in the same way
g Granted	h Conversely	i Naturally
j To sum up	k On the other hand	l Ultimately

1 _____, _____, _____, _____

2 _____, _____, _____, _____

3 _____, _____, _____, _____

B What is the function of each paragraph?

*T*he importance of *not* being earnest

*T*elling the truth may be a virtue, but is it not more important to know how to tell lies? Any idiot can tell the truth, but lying is a skill, a science, an art. Fortunately schools, with the unrealistic expectations that they have of young people, provide early training in the art of lying. For example, is it realistic to expect a 15-year-old to write a 250-word composition and spend six hours watching television in the same evening? So we watch television but tell the teacher we did our homework, but that the dog / cat / baby got hold of it . . . Then, later in life, when the really uncomfortable questions come, like 'I know you're 18 years old now, but wouldn't it be nice if we all went on a family holiday together, with grandma and grandpa?', we know better than to say that frankly it would be our idea of hell. Instead, we're really sorry we can't come but we've got that project to finish for school, plus fitness training, piano practice, or even English grammar exercises.

(**1**) ___ modern civilized society couldn't exist if everybody lied all the time. Before a business deal could be concluded, lawyers would have to be brought in to make sure there was no trickery; but the lawyers themselves would be lying, and leave both companies bankrupt. And how could democracy operate unless politicians occasionally kept at least some of their electoral promises?

(**2**) ___ would it not be equally disastrous if everybody always told the truth? How many families depend for their stability on the little white lie? How much unhappiness, how many wars are avoided simply because people have the good taste to hide the hatred and contempt they feel for other people? And as for love and desire, could these emotions not be ultimately more destructive to society than any negative feelings?

(**3**) ___ it seems to me that lying is an essential skill, and that schools are quite right to teach children how to do it. And if the editor of this magazine wonders why this article reached her so late this week, please note that I did in fact write it on time, but unfortunately the dog, the cat and the baby ganged up together, mugged me and buried the article in the garden.

Note that in this article the key sentences ('topic sentences') are the first sentences in each paragraph; this is often, but not always, the case. Similarly, many adverbial connecting words are not necessarily written at the beginning of a sentence.

1.2 Writing

Opinions are like belly buttons: everybody has got one, but do other people want to hear you talk about yours?

This writing of opinions only becomes interesting when the writer has something to say. Your opinion will not be interesting or worth expressing until you have thought about the subject. So the first stage in writing your opinion happens in your head, while you get your ideas straight. Many of the best writers find it useful to make notes of all their ideas before they start writing.

Part 2 writing task

Choose one of the mini-compositions **A–E** on pages 69–70, and develop it into a full-length magazine article (about 250 words) using *The Importance of Not Being Earnest* as a model.

Task bank: Tasks 13, 14 and 15

4B Reviews

Consumer reviews

A When reviewing a consumer product, whether for publication in a magazine or in a letter to a friend, it is necessary to look at the product's bad points as well as its good points. What does this product *do*, and what does it *not* do? What are the advantages of one particular dictionary? Are there any ways in which other dictionaries are preferable?

1.0

In this review of a new car:

 what is the function of the first sentence?
 what does the rest of the first paragraph do?
 what does the second paragraph do?

There are two schools of thought about multi-purpose vehicles (MPVs) such as the Mitsubishi Space Wagon. Critics dismiss them as marketing ploys with no sound technical merit. Why waste energy pushing a tall, van-like body through the air when a lighter, lower, more penetrating one is so much more efficient and stable? Why create space above your head where it is not wanted?

Advocates point to the lofty MPV's down-to-earth advantages. You get a better (and safer) view – over hedges and blind brows, for instance. Sitting upright, the need for leg-stretching space is reduced. Versatility comes into the reckoning, too, especially when you can squeeze a third row of seats into a vehicle that is no longer than a family car.

B Modelling your writing very closely on the Space Wagon review, use these notes to write two paragraphs looking at the advantages and disadvantages of a new mountain bike called the Lamia Anboto. Start your review, 'There are two schools of thought about mountain bikes such as . . .'

Against the Lamia Anboto
- expensive (£400)
- 21 gears: unnecessary in cities of mountain bikes used only in cities)
- attractive to thieves, so seldom used

For the Lamia Anboto
- useful in city
- shock absorbers, thick tyres: good (95% for rough surfaces and potholes of city roads
- can climb onto pavement
- ecology: car owners tempted into cycling by fashionable machine

1.1   Film review

A Complete the review by writing the missing word in each gap. Use only one word for each space. The exercise begins with an example (**0**).

B This film review is mainly the writer's opinion, but he never says 'I' or 'in my opinion'. How does he convey such a strong opinion without using the first person?

FILM REVIEW
High Heels

Pedro Almodovar, almost a national institution in Spain and certainly the only Spanish director everybody knows, comes up with a nasty surprise in *High Heels*. (**0**)_____**This**_____ is that he's no longer capable of surprising us.

There are, (**1**)_____, moments in his new film, (**2**)_____ has made a mountain of pesetas in Spain, when things happen (**3**)_____ are, to say the least, odd. (**4**)_____ as when Victoria Abril, as a television newscaster, announces the murder of her husband on the box, calmly adding that it is she who is the culprit.

Almodovar's film is stylish, garishly decorated, and dressed with great and fashion-conscious aplomb. It is (**5**)_____ equipped with a real capacity to allow its two splendid stars to display (**6**)_____ acting and other assets.

But it doesn't exactly roll along in the (**7**)_____ fluent way as *Women On The Verge Of A Nervous Breakdown*, (**8**)_____ does it contain the frissons of *Tie Me Up, Tie Me Down*. (**9**)_____ fact, it is not above a certain flatness in places and is distinctly (**10**)_____ long.

(**11**)_____ some funny jibes at the media and some suitably eccentric minor characters, this is a melodrama that not only lacks real emotion but, dare one say it, (**12**)_____ hasn't a lot of real flair. It is (**13**)_____ worth seeing; Almodovar would have to grow a different skin actually to be dull. (**14**)_____ the inspiration isn't (**15**)_____ any means consistently there, and it shows in the film's slightly disorganized and spray-gun approach.

<u>1.2</u> **Concert review**

A Six sentences have been removed from this extract from a review of a concert. Match the gaps (**1–6**) with the sentences (**A–H**) given below. Note that two of the suggested sentences do not fit at all.

B How many words can you find which show how the writer feels without him needing to say 'In my opinion'?

In a fickle world, one certainty remains. Every year at this time Eric Clapton returns to the Albert Hall for a dozen shows sold out months in advance. (**1**)_____ It could easily become a cosy ritual, an annual report from that ever-reliable trading company, Clapton PLC. (**2**)_____ It began as expected, then developed into an extraordinary, emotional blend of the tragic and triumphant.

He and his band strolled on in immaculate grey suits and buttoned-up shirts, with only the dark granny glasses of percussionist Ray Cooper providing a clue that this wasn't a meeting of smart city executives. (**3**)_____ Not great songs, any of them, but the playing was tight and the guitar solos as effortless and perfectly crafted as ever.

(**4**)_____ Clapton has had more publicity for his painful private life than his music since he last played here, as he acknowledged with three songs about the death of his four-year-old son.

'My Father's Eyes' had speed, attack and melody that was almost welcome as defence against the anguished, thoughtful lyrics. (**5**)_____ His finger-picking was rolling and slick, now with a Spanish edge, but the lyrics of 'The Circus Left Town' were at times almost unbearably painful. This wasn't a blues but a lament with the personal heartfelt intensity of a great blues, and it quite literally reduced some of the audience to tears. (**6**)_____
(The review continues)

    A But then he sat down and switched to acoustic guitar.
    B They kicked off with a trio of bluesy pieces from the '89 album, *Journeyman*.
    C 'Tears In Heaven' had much the same effect.
    D Ticket touts line the entrances, and 'Crossroads' is the encore.
    E What a change from those wild days of the sixties.
    F But the first night this year was unforgettable.
    G In fact, it's one of my favourite songs.
    H Suddenly, the noisily soporific, easy-going mood changed.

<u>1.3</u> **Writing a book review**

A This review of the novel *Heat and Dust* is spoiled by a number of weaknesses. Underline examples of where the writer fails to follow each of the numbered pieces of advice given below.

1 *Write for the reader.*
Always bear in mind who you are writing for. If you're writing for a magazine, think of the kind of people who read that particular magazine. A book review is intended for people who have not read the book, so don't assume that your readers already know the story.

2 *Don't talk about yourself.*
When giving your opinion, whether in a review or elsewhere, be careful not to fall into the trap of talking about yourself. Try to be objective. One way of testing for objectivity is to check your writing for the words *I, me, my, myself*. Similarly, phrases such as *in my opinion, to my mind, I think* should be used as little as possible; any more than once in the first paragraph and once in the last, and your review seems to focus on yourself, not your subject.

3 *Write in an impersonal style.*
Many students spoil their articles and reviews by writing in a chatty, informal style as if they were talking to a friend. On the contrary, essays, articles and

reviews should be relatively impersonal. Your readers are not particularly interested in you: they need information, description and narrative more than they need your opinion. Finally, you don't know your reader, so be careful about using the word *you*.

4 *Use precise, descriptive vocabulary.*
Generalizations such as *This book is boring* communicate very little to the reader. Specific observations and concrete facts, on the other hand, help the reader to share your experience. If you have strong feelings about your subject, this should make your writing more interesting – but be careful! Strong feelings must be given form and coldly translated into precise words.

Heat and Dust,
by Ruth Prawer Jhabvala

'A writer of genius . . . a writer of world class – a master storyteller . . .' it says on the dustjacket. Can they really be talking about the same writer, the same book? Personally, I can't see what distinguishes Heat And Dust from any of those cheap romantic novels that you get at railway stations.

What on earth is so remarkable about the story of a bored expatriate who leaves a dull husband for someone richer, more intelligent and totally exotic? In my opinion, if Jhabvala was really a good writer she would have written instead about a much more interesting phenomenon, the typical colonial who clings absurdly to the behaviour, traditions and even dress of his mother country. Alternatively, Olivia could have really 'gone native', instead of just being seduced by a Nawab with a Rolls-Royce, an Alfa Romeo and an intimate knowledge of the best hotels of Paris and London.

The plot too is corny: the idea of someone retracing someone else's life, and then (surprise, surprise!) finding parallel events happening in their own lives. Thousands of writers have used this device, and to much better effect. So what makes Jhabvala such a great writer? It can't be her prose, surely, which is quite boring. The words 'heat' and 'dust' appear frequently, but I for one certainly never get any impression of heat or dust. I don't know about you, but the impression I get is of a very literary, upper-class woman sitting at her typewriter drinking tea.

Finally, what really annoys me personally about this book is the writer's morality. You can see she's a romantic and a moralist: she looks down on her narrator with a patronizing attitude, and paints a degrading picture of modern love by giving her narrator a kind of abject promiscuity in the place of a love life. And incredibly, the message of the book seems to be that the best thing that can happen to a woman – even an unmarried woman, without a boyfriend, travelling abroad – is to get pregnant. I'm sorry, but if you think that, you're living in another world.

B Rewrite the last 26 lines from 'It can't be her prose . . .', bearing in mind the four paragraphs of advice.

 Writing

Part 2 writing tasks

A A friend of yours is thinking of buying a consumer item (e.g. a personal stereo, a bicycle, a tennis racket, a pair of shoes, a musical instrument, an English dictionary). Your friend knows that you have one, and writes to you asking if the one you have is a good model to buy, or whether you would advise them to choose a different model. Write your reply in about 125 words.

B A British friend of yours is studying your language. Using a satellite dish, they are capable of receiving TV programmes from your country. Write a letter of about 250 words recommending two programmes your friend should watch to help improve their language, bearing in mind that your friend's level in your language is about the same as your level in English.

Task bank: Tasks 16, 42, 43 and 44

4C Personal advice

Writing advice – to friends, or in a magazine – is another opportunity to express an opinion. But what distinguishes this from most of the other writing in this unit is that you are often writing on a person-to-person basis. Unlike in the argument and the review, the writer addresses the reader as *you* – and the reader is often just *one* individual.

1.0 Problem page

The following advice was printed on the 'Problem page' of a women's magazine, in response to a reader's letter. Study the advice, and decide what the reader's problem is.

In a partnership where both of you expect to do well, success almost never comes for two people at the same time. You are at the crucial breakthrough stage of your career, so it's only natural to feel unsure. Your boyfriend must also be feeling vulnerable as he is building his career, too. No matter how much men may accept intellectually that women are entitled to succeed, it can still be hard for them when we push ahead.

Talk this over honestly and establish precisely what is bothering him. Reassure him of your confidence in him and remind him, too, that it's much better to be with a successful woman than with a dissatisfied one. Make sure he reaps the benefit of your new prosperity in the form of fun and treats, so that he sees a tangible reward for his loyal support. Then give him time to adjust. But don't let his problem of confidence undermine you. If he can't cope with a woman who makes money, you may have to look for someone who can.

1.1 Advice structures

When giving advice, a range of structures may be used. Some of them are stronger than others – *Do this!* – whereas others are more tentative suggestions – *I wonder if you've ever considered doing this*. Your choice of structure should suit the *situation* rather than just your strength of character. Two of the following are particularly strong and should only be addressed, in moments of anger and frustration, to a close friend or relative.

Grade the advice structures on a scale of 1–5: 1 for very weak or tentative; 5 for aggressive or authoritarian.

a I'd recommend that you join the army.
b It's not for me to say, of course, but I don't suppose you've ever considered looking into the possibility of a military career?
c I wonder if you've ever thought about joining the army?
d You must join the army.
e Perhaps you could join the army.
f My advice is to join the army.
g Well, what do *you* think you should do?
h You pathetic worm! If you had any pride, you'd join the army.
i I think you'd be wise to join the army.
j I strongly recommend that you join the army.
k Join the army.
l I really think that you should join the army.
m It's high time you stopped feeling sorry for yourself, got off your backside and joined the army.

1.2 Giving advice

Someone has a problem, and asks us for advice. But note that this gives us neither a licence to run that person's life nor an opportunity to talk about ourselves and how we solve our own problems. The best advice comes not from someone who has all the answers, but from someone who has listened with care and empathy to the other person's problem.

A Work in a group of four and read the letters below.
1 Discuss each problem. Do you fully understand it? What do you know, and what can you guess about the writer?
2 Discuss the possible solutions.
3 Decide what advice structures you would use.

B Each write an answer to a different one of the letters.

Task bank: Tasks 17, 18 and 32

Dear Katie ...

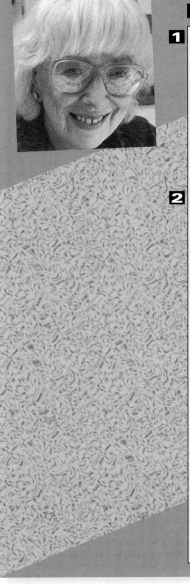

Relationships

1 This may not seem to be a problem, but my flatmate is too tidy. She arranges cans so the labels all face the same way and straightens the bathroom mat every morning. Her mother is the same – she spends hours cleaning and ironing when she visits. I'm not untidy, but this is hard to live with.

2 How can I make my daughter see how unacceptable her boyfriend is? Everyone comments on his appearance and asks what my daughter sees in him. He looks dreadful, unshaven and with long hair. He's unemployed and has a criminal record. My daughter, who's 18, has had everything she's ever wanted and lacks for nothing. After excellent results at college, she now has a good job with prospects.

In the two years she's been going steady with this boy, she's dropped her own friends and only sees his, who are much older.

We've pointed out to her their different lifestyles, but to no avail. We live in an exclusive part of town and my husband is a company director. I don't want to tell my daughter not to see this boy again as I'm afraid she may leave home. Please advise me.

Careers

3 I have just started my first job and do not object to working overtime because I am prepared to put in the effort to get on. But from the beginning I have found that I regularly work till 6.30 at night or later. This is because my boss is completely disorganized and leaves the most important items until very late afternoon. As the most junior person in the department, I feel powerless to change things.

4 I am halfway through a course at college and I'm sick to death of it. My parents bulldozed me into taking this place and I've been unhappy since the beginning. I realize that a degree will stand me in good stead, but I want to give it up. I know that this means I will have wasted the last year, and could also jeopardize any future chances of higher education. But why should I struggle on to please my parents? All I want to do is start work.

PEOPLE AND PLACES

Warm up: register exercise

Read the descriptions (**A–G**), then match them with the contexts (**1–7**) from which they were taken.

A Her features, dark-eyed and pale, have a nervy mobility; her voice, like that of many dancers, gives the false impression of breathlessness. She sits with her long legs disposed beneath her and turns her hands as she speaks

B The taller boy was aged about 13 and 5 ft 1 in tall, slim with short, dark, straight hair. He was clean-looking and very pale with brown eyes, black eyebrows, a long nose and a long face. He was wearing a light-coloured three-quarter-length jacket with no belt, and his trousers were a dark colour. His companion looked younger, and was about 4 ft 9 in. He was chubby but not overweight, with a rounded, cherub-like, flat face and a small nose. His hair was very short and dirty. He was wearing . . .

C My English teacher, Miss P. Wynne, terrified all of us. But she had great presence. She never smiled and hadn't the slightest interest in popularity or even in getting to know us. There was total silence for every lesson. These lessons were inspired. She could take a poem and have us, a class of grubby fourteen-year-olds, completely entranced.

D I am very pleased with the way Jane's character has been developing. There has been no recurrence of the antisocial behaviour of her first year; she is now integrating well and showing a lot more consideration for her peers. She has been very much involved in the Music Department and we believe that, even while her tastes in music remain surprising, her interest in music deserves to be encouraged and supported.

E At the end of the room, a bouncer about my age was counting his knuckles. He didn't wear a clip-on bow-tie like Jack at Modesto's, just grey slacks and a green polo shirt that made his biceps squeeze out from the sleeves like apples in a boa constrictor. On the edge of his jaw was an old ribbed scar the colour of bad hamburger.

F I can commend Andrea's motivation and participation in her English studies. She is a bright, pleasant, hard-working student whose attendance, punctuality and homework are excellent. She would undoubtedly have a lot to contribute on a university course.

G For one thing, she hadn't expected him to be so tall – at least six feet – and the impressive breadth of chest and shoulders suggested a muscular solidity. Yet his face had a lean and hungry look – all sharp angles and hollow cheeks as if he never had enough food. His hair was very dark, almost black, its straight wiry thickness tamed by a stylish cut. But he wasn't tamed. The photograph had made him look like a suave sophisticate, but Tiffany had only to look into those black fathomless eyes to sense the savage in him.

1 A detective story
2 A crime report in a newspaper
3 A reference (written by a teacher, to support a college application)
4 A school report
5 A magazine article
6 A newspaper profile (an article about a person, usually based on an interview)
7 A romantic novel

5A Describing people

A checklist of details to mention

Age

She was in her late teens; he was in his early twenties; she was about thirty years old; his twelve-year-old son; a middle-aged woman; a man in his mid sixties

Height

Estimating someone's height is more useful than describing them as tall, short or average height. Use either metres or feet and inches (12 in = 1 ft).

1 m 50 = 4 ft 11 in   1 m 60 = 5 ft 3 in
1 m 70 = 5 ft 7 in   1 m 80 = 5 ft 11 in

Build

Plump, corpulent, overweight,
muscular, athletic, powerful, stocky, chunky,
broad-shouldered
skinny, slim, long-legged, loose-limbed
a well-built man; a woman of medium, average,
normal build

Hair

length, style and colour (normally in that order)
He's got long curly black hair.
She's got copper-coloured hennaed hair that comes down to her waist, and which she often wears tied with a scarf, hanging loosely down her back.

Eyes

size, shape and colour; eyebrows and eyelashes
My attacker had small round grey eyes.
He's got astonishing bright blue eyes and long dark eyelashes.
You could describe the light in someone's eyes: *sparkling, twinkling, flashing, brilliant*
You can also describe eyes in a way that may be a comment on the person behind them: *cold grey eyes; calm, dreamy eyes; inquisitive, shifty, worried eyes*

Clothes

Describing someone's clothes is sometimes easier but just as effective as describing the rest of their appearance. Using adjectives (see page 41) you could mention your opinion of the garment, its age, shape, colour, origin, material and make (usually in that order).
a romantic low-cut crimson satin Laura Ashley evening dress
sexy skin-tight Italian leather trousers
Mention also jewellery and make-up.

Face

a long thin face with narrow lips and high cheekbones
a round face with a little turned-up nose and chubby pink cheeks
a bald man, with a huge forehead and no chin
a pretty face with small regular features and a pointed chin

Skin

colour: *white, pale, tanned, suntanned, olive, Oriental, dark, black*
a smooth complexion, a pale complexion, a dark complexion
clear skin, greasy skin, a spotty face, a fresh-faced youth
age: *wrinkled, lined, laugh-lines, crow's feet*

Distinguishing features

glasses, scar, beard, birthmark, mole, wooden leg, tattoo
speech : *stutter, stammer, lisp, deep voice, a squeaky voice*

Character

Some aspects of people's character are also part of their physical appearance, betrayed in their expressions or the way they move.
jumpy, highly-strung, anxious
self-assured, confident, determined
smug, self-satisfied, arrogant
cheerful, relaxed, sociable, aggressive, sensual

Impression

He looked like a football hooligan; Keanu Reeves.
He looked as if he was waiting for someone.
She might have been a student.
She seemed very confused.
I got the impression that the child was his accomplice.

<u>1.0</u>   **Model**

This description of laundrymen in Mali, West Africa, doesn't describe any individual person, but gives a lot of specific detail.

A Complete the description by writing the missing words in the gaps. The exercise begins with an example (**0**).

B How many of the categories in the checklist on page 79 can you recognize?

The Laundrymen of Bamako

One thing that had struck many of the travelers throughout the Bambara area was the muscular symmetry of the men's bodies. I (0)_____*had*_____ read over and (1)_____ again something like 'As the oarsmen drove their canoes through the surging current one could not help admiring the strength of biceps and shoulders, (2)_____ gave the dark bodies a kind of rude poetry (3)_____ they leaned into their task . . .'

(4)_____ the incongruity of the work they were doing, the men's bodies had this kind of wiry strength. Most of them (5)_____ tall and wide-shouldered, their upper bodies tapering (6)_____ thin waists. Their skin was very dark, almost black in tone. The exercise they got swinging wet shirts (7)_____ the stones gave (8)_____ the same supple muscularity they had had a hundred years ago (9)_____ warriors. Beyond them I (10)_____ see the same lean, wide-shouldered bodies (11)_____ boatmen as they stood in their log canoes pulling at brushwood tangled in the grass of a small island close (12)_____ the bank. Except (13)_____ all that laundry spread out (14)_____ the grass, the scene resembled the exaggerated romance of (15)_____ 19th century engraving from a travel book.

<u>1.1</u>   **Writing practice**

You were involved in a shipwreck, and your life was saved by another survivor who kept you alive in the water. When you come out of hospital, you want to find your rescuer and thank them, but you realize that you don't even know the person's name. A journalist offers to help you find them: write the description you give to the journalist (about 75 words).

2.0   Describing someone in a picture

You can make a description more interesting by going beyond the surface of the picture. You might speculate about some of these ideas.

- Where was the photo taken (or picture painted)? When? Why? By whom?
- Who is this person? (Character, job, social situation, family, past, future)
- What are they doing? What have they just been doing? What are they just about to do? What are they thinking about?
- What is your personal reaction to this picture / to this person? Do you find them attractive, interesting, depressing? Why? How do you feel about what they are doing in the picture? Why?

Here is a description of one of the pictures on this page.

a   Underline the phrases where the writer is *speculating* about the picture: the phrases where the writer is looking for the story behind the two-dimensional image.

b   Find the paragraphs that describe the writer's *personal reaction* to the picture. Why do these paragraphs come at this stage of the description?

c   Now write your own description of one of the other two photographs.

"It's a black and white photograph of a man holding a trumpet. He's holding it as if he's just waiting for the moment to raise it to his lips. Both the man and the trumpet look like they're old, worn and used: the man's face is very lined and wrinkled, while the enamel is flaking off the trumpet. It's very hard to guess the man's exact age, but I would say he was in his late fifties, early sixties.

Judging by his clothes, he's probably a jazz musician: he's wearing an open shirt and a 'smart but casual' sports jacket. The open shirt reveals a strong neck which appears weather-beaten, as if the man had spent all his life in the sun. We can't see the lower half of his body: apart from his head and shoulders, we can only see his hands. The fingers are surprisingly thick and strong, in contrast to the bony, rather haggard face.

The photo seems to have been taken during a concert: to judge by his tight lips and open mouth he is either just about to play or he could be singing, though we can't see a microphone. The sweat-soaked strands of hair across his forehead and left ear imply that he is on stage and hasn't posed for this photo.

There is a lot of atmosphere, thanks to the way the light has caught the lines on the musician's face. This face and this expression – is he suffering, or is he enraptured? – is, for me, the face of an old man retelling the finest and most tragic moments of his life.

I wish we could hear the music."

2.1   Formative years

This extract is from a magazine article taken from a series where people write about someone who has been influential in their life. Notice the writer's use of physical description: how does this contribute to the description of the new headmaster's personality? Notice, too, that the writer tells stories, which are much more interesting than generalizations.

- Does the story remind you of anything in your life?
- If not, how has your experience of teachers been different?
- Apart from teachers (and parents), who has had the most influence on your life?

The New Headmaster

I can remember my first sight of Dr Hughes; it was on the assembly hall stage. He swept in with his big black gown behind him. This guy meant business. He looked at us all, stared at us silently for quite a few minutes. I remember it clearly, that tight crinkly hair, how it was combed straight back with Brylcreem. He had vicious eyebrows, a cruel, tight mouth, a sharp nose, as though it had been specially formed to make a sting at the end of it, and he was so dark that he always looked ill-shaven. I was intimidated by his very appearance.

One event in his first week put the fear of God into us. There was a dirty poem that had been circulating, as they do in schools, and he caught a girl with it. Her name was Amanda Evans. The whole school was assembled, and he brought her up on stage by her ear, with the poem in his other hand, and he held it out as if it was covered in filth. He humiliated the girl in front of us, turned her round, showed us this creature. It was such a humiliating form of punishment; and we were all guilty, that was the worst thing. If we'd all said we'd read it, would we all have been punished? I wish I had dared stand up in that hall. The girl was expelled and her life was totally crushed by that.

He ran the school with iron authority of a calibre that was much more than the average child could take. We lived in fear of this man.

2.2   Writing

Part 2 writing tasks

A A British magazine runs a regular feature called 'Heroes and Villains'. Each week, someone writes about either a person they very much admire or, on the contrary, a person they detest or despise. The people written about may be either dead or alive, famous people or personal friends of the writer, so long as the writer can show why they are either a 'hero' or a 'villain'.

Your local English-language magazine (or school magazine) has decided to adopt the same feature, and has invited readers to submit their articles of about 250 words. Write your **article**.

B You're on holiday, and in the past few days you've met two people, both of whom have made a strong impression on you – one positive, the other negative. Write a **letter** to a friend of yours, telling about these two people (about 250 words).

Task bank: Tasks 11, 12, 19, 20, 21 and 22

5B Describing places

1.0 Varying your sentences

A Prepositions of position (*behind*, *in front of*, *next to*) can be very useful when describing a scene, but they are not the only way to describe spatial relationships. You can improve your writing by using a variety of structures. Compare these two descriptions.

There is a church next to the river, and below the church there are the last houses in the village. After the houses there are fields, and in the distance there is a lake. There are trees all round the lake.

The river flows down past a church, then snakes around the last house in the village before cutting across the fields towards a lake surrounded by trees.

1 Is there any difference between the two scenes described?
2 What structures are repeated in the first text?
3 Which feature of the landscape is the 'organizing principle' of the second text?
4 What replaces prepositions of place in the second text?

B In this description, the writer describes Officer B's cabin and the other facilities on a transatlantic cargo ship.

His cabin was a roomy studio apartment furnished with bookcases, a refrigerator, a kingsized bed, a comfortable sofa, a long desk of varnished pine, a cabinet for drinks and glasses, a coffee table and his own lavatory and shower.

Just down the hall, Officer B could swim in the heated pool, put in a sweaty half an hour on the squash court, work out in the gym and open his pores in the sauna, before showing up in the officers' Bar and Lounge, where Scotch was 10p a glass, and where a new film was shown on the video at 8.15 each night.

This excellent and economical description is written in two sentences.

1 Are the two sentences structured in the same way?
2 Why are there no prepositions of place in the first sentence?
3 What does the second sentence have in common with the sentence beginning *The river flows down past a church . . .*?
4 Is the writer trying to tell us that Officer B is an athletic film-lover with a taste for strong drink? How do we know the second sentence is not a narrative?

1.1 Writing practice

A Using as your model the example above beginning *The river flows down past a church . . .* write a description, in two sentences, of a landscape organized around something (an animal, a vehicle, the rain, etc.) moving across the landscape.

B Using as your model the 'Officer B' text, write a two-sentence description of a place where you once stayed on holiday. In the first sentence you could, for example, describe your room, and in the second other facilities. Make sure your description does not sound like a narrative.

1.2 Precision

This description of a room comes from a detective story set in ancient China. As so often in murder mysteries, the description of the scene of the crime needs to be clear and precise: it holds a clue which will eventually solve the crime. (This is a 'locked room' mystery. There is no apparent way the murderer could have entered the room, or left. Nevertheless, the victim was murdered, with poison.)

A Read the description and draw a plan of the room. At the same time, try to guess how the murder was committed.

Judge Dee opened the door. Holding his lantern high, he surveyed the small square room, simply but elegantly furnished. On the left was a high narrow window; directly in front of it stood a heavy ebony cupboard, bearing a large copper tea stove. On the stove stood a round pewter pan for boiling the tea water. Next to the stove he saw a small teapot of exquisite blue and white porcelain. The rest of the wall was entirely taken up by bookshelves, as was the wall opposite. The back wall had a low broad window; its paper panes were scrupulously clean. In front of the window stood an antique desk of rosewood with three drawers in either end, and a comfortable armchair, also of rosewood and covered with a red satin cushion. The desk was empty but for two copper candlesticks.

B How is the description organized? In what order are the features of the room mentioned? From left to right? Clockwise? By reference to a key feature?

C The detailed description begins, *On the left was . . . directly in front of it . . .* Underline the other prepositional phrases and the other occasions where *was* and *there was* are used.

D Where the writer doesn't use prepositions, what alternative structures are used? Underline them. (For example, rather than *on top of the cupboard there was a tea stove* he uses the word *bearing*.)
Similarly, the writer doesn't rely on *there was* to list the contents of the room. Underline the alternative structures used, such as *stood*.

1.3 Writing practice

As an exercise to develop your ability to write an interesting, lively description, use what you have learned in this module to write a description (about 150 words) of Vincent Van Gogh's bedroom in Arles (illustrated here). To make the exercise more challenging, don't use the same viewpoint as the painter. Instead, imagine you're looking in through the window. Write your description as if, like the Judge Dee description, it came from a piece of fiction – either literature, detective fiction or romantic fiction.

2.0 **Guide books**

A In this text, from a travel guide to Morocco, the writer describes some of the places in Meknès that a tourist might like to visit. The function of the text is to recommend (on the basis of the writer's opinions) and to inform.

Read through the text and choose the best phrase or sentence, given below, to fill each of the gaps. Write one letter (**A–K**) in each gap. Some of the suggested answers do not fit at all. The exercise begins with an example (**0**).

Meknès

The focus of the old city is the massive gate of Bab el Mansour, the main entrance to Moulay Ismail's 17th century Imperial City. The gate is exceptionally well preserved and is highly decorated, with (faded) zellij tiles and inscriptions which run right across the top.

The gate faces onto the Place el Hedim. (**0**)___*B*___ this square is the Dar Jamai, a palace built in the late 19th century which has recently been turned into a very good museum. (**1**)___E___ museums housed in historic buildings, the building itself is as interesting as the exhibits. The domed reception room upstairs is fully furnished in the style of the time, complete with plush rugs and cushions. It is open daily, except Tuesday, from 9am to 12 noon and 3pm to 6pm. Entry costs Dr 3.

The medina proper stretches away to the north behind the Dar Jamai. The most convenient access is through the arch to the left of the Dar Jamai. (**2**)___H___ as extensive or as interesting as the medina at Fès it is, nevertheless, worth a visit and you won't be hassled by 'guides'. (**3**)___G___ are the carpet souks, which are just off to the left of the main medina streets, about five minutes walk from Dar Jamai. (**4**)___J___ Meknès is not a bad place, as the shopkeepers are a little bit more relaxed than elsewhere. Bargains are still as rare as hen's teeth, but at least the bargaining starts at a reasonable level.

Further along the covered main street is the Bou Inania Medressa. (**5**)___F___ it was built in the mid 14th century. It is not all that conspicuous apart from the dome over the street, which is easy to spot. It has the same layout and features as the Fès medressas. (**6**)___K___ you are allowed up onto the roof, as it has all been restored at one time or another. The Bou Inania Medressa is open daily from 9am to 12 noon and 3pm to 6pm. Entry costs Dr 3.

A One of the most original
B On the far north side of
C Most interesting, perhaps,
D Somewhere in that direction
E As is often the case in
F Like the one of the same name in Fès,
G If you are looking for rugs to buy,
H Though nowhere near
J In some ways, I suppose
K It's about the only one where

B Look again at the content of the Meknès text. Which of the following does the writer mention? Why only these?

a) personal adventures and experiences
b) architecture, mosques, museums
c) layout, geography, distances
d) founding and origins of the city
e) population (size, races, languages)
f) society (industry, jobs, politics)
g) theatre, cinemas, live music
h) restaurants, hotels, discos, bars
i) opening times and admission charges
j) public transport
k) places to watch or play sports
l) sounds, smells, temperatures
m) shopping advice
n) what *not* to do, where *not* to go

C If you were to write a very brief tourist guide to your town, what would you include? Use the headings in **B** to help you choose the most important information.

2.1   Atmosphere

This dramatic description of New York harbour, taken from a travel book by Jonathan Raban entitled *Hunting Mr Heartbreak*, evokes an atmosphere – a very different style from the dry description in a guide book.

A In most lines of the text there is either a spelling or a punctuation error. Write the correctly spelled words or show the correct punctuation in the spaces in the margin. Some lines are correct: indicate these lines with a tick (✓). The exercise begins with two examples (**0**). See pages 9–10 for information and advice about this exercise type.

0	Manhattan was a dozen glittering sticks, of light,	*sticks of*
0	through which livid storm clouds were rolling. *There*	✓
1	was Brooklyn Bridge, a sweeping curve of white lights	_____
2	too the north; *there*, on her rock, was Liberty, weirdly	_____
3	floodlit in leprechaun green. Manhattans freakish	_____
4	heigth and narrowness, rising in front of the low dark	_____
5	industral sprawl of the Jersey shore, defied gravity,	_____
6	proportion, nature. It was brazen in it's disdain for the	_____
7	ordinary limits of human enterprise I watched the	_____
8	storm and the city battling it out, high in the sky. For	_____
9	a few moments, the sailing clouds, exposed a large, low	_____
10	moon. It was drifting over the Boroughs like a huge	_____
11	corroded gilt medallion. Given, the air of high melodrama	_____
12	in the surounding landscape, I would have been only	_____
13	mildy surprised to see the moon come crashing out	_____
14	of heaven and set the hole of Queens on fire.	_____

Note: Manhattan, Brooklyn Bridge, (the Statue of) Liberty, the Jersey shore, the Boroughs, and Queens are all features of New York's geography.

B When you have corrected your answers, look at the style of the description. What details contribute to the sense of drama and atmosphere?

2.2   Writing

Part 2 writing task

Your local Tourist Information Centre is planning a brochure which will introduce the town or region where you live to English-speaking visitors. Other people will be writing articles on tourist facilities such as hotels and restaurants, transport, 'things to do' etc. so you should avoid those areas. You have been asked to write the **physical description**, including the location, layout, geographical and architectural features. Some reference to history may be appropriate. Your description should make your area sound interesting and attractive at the same time as delivering a maximum of precise information in about 250 words.

*Task achievement: which of the points you listed in 2.0C (page 85) must you **not** mention?*

Task bank: Tasks 23, 24, 25, 31, 36 and 46

FORMAL LETTERS

6A Letters of complaint: tact

1.0   Layout of a formal letter

Writing a formal letter is like going to a wedding: there are certain conventions that you should respect. The 'formal dress' of a letter is the layout; you may also be expected to use certain fixed 'politeness' phrases. If you do not respect these conventions, your letter will certainly be taken less seriously and will possibly offend, upset or confuse your correspondent. The letter below illustrates the standard layout. There are notes about the layout on the next page.

1   Open Door School of English

2   Rua Boa Morte 2181
     13400–140 Piracicaba
     Est. de São Paulo
     Brazil

3   tel. (0194) 22–3487

4   The Manager

5   Boatrace International Bookshop
     37 Morse Avenue
     OXFORD OX3 3DP   6   24 August 1996

7   Dear Sir or Madam

8   On 23 June I ordered 16 copies of 'In at the Deep End' by Vicki Hollett, to be sent to me at the above address.

9   Two months later, these books have not yet been received.

10   I would be grateful if you could look into this matter and ensure that the books reach me as soon as possible.

11   Yours faithfully

12   *Celia Silveira Coelho*

13   CELIA SILVEIRA COELHO

14   Director

15

Notes on the layout of a formal letter

1 Your address, but not your name.

2 When writing by hand, make sure your address is legible. To someone who doesn't know your country or language, your address will appear to be a meaningless jumble of letters and numbers.

3 Your telephone number may be important – remember, you're trying to *communicate* with these people.

4 The name of the person you're writing to (if you know it) followed by their position. *The Manager* is a good all-purpose option.

5 The address of the people you're writing to.

6 The date.

7 If you don't know the name of the person you're writing to, you can use *Dear Sir, Dear Madam, Dear Sir or Madam, Dear Sir / Madam.*
If you do know the name, use it. But make sure you spell it correctly. Then use *Dear Mr Blair* (never *Mister*); *Dear Mrs Peacock* (a married woman); *Dear Miss Ball* (an unmarried woman); *Dear Ms Metcalfe* (a woman who chooses not to advertise her marital status, or whose marital status you don't know); *Dear Mr and Mrs Bessin.* If your correspondent has a title other than these, use it.
Dear Dr Jekyll   Dear Professor Heger

8 Reference. This sentence should tell your correspondent exactly what you are writing about. If you are replying to a letter, mention the date of that letter.

9 The substance of your letter.

10 How you want your correspondent to respond to your letter.

11 *Yours sincerely* if you started with a name: *Dear Mr Smith*
Yours faithfully if you didn't know the name: *Dear Sir or Madam*

12 Your signature, always written by hand.

13 Your name, in capitals when writing by hand. It must be legible because this is the *only* place your name is written: it appears neither at the top of the letter nor on the back of the envelope.

14 Position. Only used when writing from a business.

15 On this line you may write:
Enc or *Encs* (followed by a list of enclosures – documents which you are sending together with the letter.)
P.S. (followed by information that you forgot to include in the main body of the letter – not a sign of a well-organized piece of writing!)

1.1 Communication task

This exercise involves writing a letter of complaint, then replying to one. It is best done with a partner, so you can write to each other then reply. If you're working alone, you can reply to your own letter.

Copy the first letter below, laying it out correctly, with addresses. Fill the gaps with any details that your imagination (or your real grievances) might supply.

(Note that this is a very formal letter, appropriate for an employer on the verge of sacking an employee, or a business person about to break off a business relationship. The use of the word *you* is particularly direct, and indicates the writer's anger.)

> Dear _____
> As you will be aware, there have been many occasions during the past _____ (period of time) when I have had cause to complain about your _____. Unfortunately, despite your repeated assurances that the situation would be resolved, you _____.
>   Clearly, this situation cannot be allowed to continue and, unless you can ensure that _____, I shall be obliged to _____. It is my hope that such a drastic step will not be necessary.
>   Yours sincerely

Now, having changed letters with your partner if you have one, write a reply. You may use this 'skeleton' if it is appropriate.

> Dear _____
> Thank you for your letter of _____ (date), drawing my attention to _____. Your dissatisfaction with my apparent _____ is quite understandable. Nevertheless, I can assure you that if my _____ has continued to appear unsatisfactory it is only because _____. Please accept my assurance that I have now _____, and am confident that my _____ will give you no further cause for concern.
>   Yours sincerely

1.2 Models

A Fill the gaps in this letter with words from the list.

convenient   repair   carry out   replaced   bought   faithfully
grateful   guarantee   found   arrange   appears   assured

Dear Sir/Madam

Repair to washing machine

On December 2nd your maintenance man called at my home to (**1**)_____ the washing machine, a Wytaswyt Aquaslosh which I (**2**)_____ from you on January 7th of this year and which is still under (**3**)_____. When your man finished, he (**4**)_____ me that the machine was now working.

  The following day I tried to use the machine but (**5**)_____ that it was still not working properly. Again, it flooded the kitchen. I know little about these machines, but the problem (**6**)_____ to be that the rubber seal around the door needs to be (**7**)_____.

  I should be (**8**)_____ if you would (**9**)_____ for a competent person to call and (**10**)_____ the necessary repairs. A convenient time for me would be Thursday or Friday morning, Dec 11 or 12, any time between 8 and 12.

  Please telephone me immediately if these times are not (**11**)_____.

Yours (**12**)_____

B Fill the gaps in these two letters with words from the list.

*claims   sorry   must   convenience   ordered   response   hearing
recover   returning   refund   ensuring   failure   replace   receiving*

Dear Sir or Madam,

On August 2nd I bought a tin of Miracle Oven Cleaner in (**1**)_____ to your television advertisement, which (**2**)_____ that this product will clean 'all the stains that ordinary oven cleaners leave behind' and leave 'even the dirtiest oven as clean as new'.

In the light of the (**3**)_____ of the Miracle Oven Cleaner to clean my oven in anything resembling the manner you describe, I am (**4**)_____ it to you, and ask you to (**5**)_____ the full cost price of £2.12 plus the postage of 64p.

I look forward to (**6**)_____ a cheque for £2.76 from you at your earliest (**7**)_____.

Yours faithfully,

Dear Sir,

I received today the 'Hendrix Junior' guitar that I (**8**)_____ from you on February 28th.

I am (**9**)_____ to have to tell you that when I opened the parcel I found the guitar broken. The neck was detached from the body, and the body itself was shattered.

I (**10**)_____ ask you, therefore, either to (**11**)_____ the damaged guitar – (**12**)_____, on this occasion, its safe delivery – or to refund the price I paid for it, £59.99. Should you wish to (**13**)_____ the broken guitar, I will hold it at your disposal until the end of next month.

I look forward to (**14**)_____ from you.

Yours faithfully,

C Many of the phrases needed for a wide range of letters of complaint appear in the letters you have read so far in this unit. Here are a few more.

Beginning
I am writing to complain about . . .
Further to my letter of May 13th in connection with . . .
I am writing to express my dissatisfaction with . . .

Demand
I would be grateful to receive a cheque for the outstanding sum without further delay.
I must insist that you deliver the piano with no further delay and at no additional expense to myself.
. . . would be appropriate compensation for the inconvenience caused to my family.
In view of the many ways in which it did not match the claims made for it in your publicity, I expect a substantial refund.
Under the circumstances, I feel that an apology should be offered.

Threat (optional)
I shall have no alternative but to put the matter in the hands of my solicitors should your cheque not be received by May 1st.
Unless I hear from you within ten days, I shall have to take legal advice on the matter.
If I do not hear from you before 3 May, I shall be obliged to take matters a step further.

1.3   Tact: how to influence people

You are a student, and have very little money. You were fortunate enough to find a very cheap and convenient flat to rent. Naturally, the flat has its disadvantages: if it didn't, it would be much too expensive for you. Now, with winter coming on, it is time to try to persuade the landlord to improve the flat (without, of course, increasing the rent).

Read the two letters overleaf (the second one is unfinished) and decide how you would react to each of them if you were the landlord.

1   Are there any differences of *fact* between the two letters, or is the difference only one of *tone*?

2   (a) How is the first sentence of the first letter expressed in the second letter?
     (b) In view of all the facts you are given, would you say the opening of the second letter was:

       (i)   hypocritical?
       (ii) untruthful?
       (iii) deceitful?
       (iv) tactful?

Whichever of the above you decide the fact is that this is an aspect of language, culture and communication, and not a question of morality. This kind of politeness is much the same in all English-speaking countries, and breaking these rules is a much bigger language mistake than breaking grammar rules.

3   In the first letter, Oliver describes the problems as if he was telling a friend about the flat: he uses dramatic and strong words to express his emotions, and perhaps exaggerates a little. In a formal, written complaint, emotive language is inappropriate. Exaggeration must also be avoided because if the landlord can show that something you have said is not factually true, this destroys the credibility of your other claims as well.

Find examples of emotive language and exaggeration in the first letter, and see how it is avoided in the second.

4   A letter like this should not become a personal attack on someone. Find instances in the first letter where Oliver becomes offensive when he addresses his landlord in too personal a way.

5   Write the last paragraph of the second letter. Try, as in the first three paragraphs, to make the landlord:

- think what a polite, reasonable, articulate (and therefore dangerous) person you are.
- believe that your complaints are truthful and accurate.
- believe that your requests are reasonable.
- really want to spend money on the flat.
- act with some urgency.

37 Acorn Street

November 7th

Dear Mr Scrooge,

I've been your tenant here for seven months now, and I've got lots of things to complain about.

First, the gas cooker, which is an absolute death trap. It is an antique model – some would say a museum piece – that leaks gas constantly. Quite apart from the fact that the gas is liable to poison me, there is a good chance the cooker will one day explode and burn your house down. What's more, its meagre two rings are slow and inadequate, while the oven (which doesn't close properly because of the huge dent in the door) is so thick with dirt that it is beyond cleaning. So, as you can see, a new cooker is urgently needed, and it's you who should pay for it since I'm renting the flat as 'furnished'.

Secondly, the heating: two one-kilowatt electric fires in the whole flat. This has been incredibly expensive and totally insufficient throughout the autumn. Now, with winter coming on, I'm in danger of freezing to death while you take a holiday in the Bahamas paid for with my rent money. I shall expect an adequate heating system to be installed before the end of November.

Finally, the windows. They don't shut properly (for that matter, neither do the doors) so there's always a howling draught blowing through the house. Actually, so many of the panes are broken that it wouldn't make much difference if the windows did shut. Please do something about this, preferably by replacing the whole lot with double glazing. If you don't do this before winter sets in, I'll be obliged to spend my rent money on making the house fit for human habitation instead of giving the money directly to you.

Yours sincerely,

Oliver Twist

37 Acorn St

November 7th

Dear Mr Scrooge,

I've been your tenant here for seven months now, and in many ways I'm very happy with the flat. Nevertheless, there are one or two details that I think we should look at.

First, the cooker, which appears to be a significant safety risk. It is a very old model, which seems to leak gas constantly. This represents a real danger, on the one hand of asphyxiation and on the other of fire. The cooker is, in fact, not very satisfactory in other respects as well – the two rings are inadequate when cooking for guests, and the oven is no longer operational as the interior is beyond cleaning, and the door doesn't shut. For these reasons, I would suggest that the cooker needs to be replaced at your earliest convenience.

Secondly, the heating, which at present consists of two one-kilowatt fires. I seriously doubt whether these heaters – themselves a fire risk as well as being both inefficient and uneconomical – will provide adequate heating through the winter for a flat of 35 square metres. I do trust you will be able to provide the flat with adequate means of heating before winter sets in.

(last paragraph missing)

1.4   Writing

Part 2 writing task

You start a new job as a secretary in your local branch of a large but not very modern company whose headquarters are in Britain. Everything at your new workplace is old-fashioned, and much of it is either broken or seriously inefficient. You complain about this to your immediate superior, who tells you that 'if you don't think we're good enough for you here' you should write to the (British) manager. This answer angers you, and you decide that you will write the letter.

Choose either **two** or **three** things about the premises that you would like replaced with more modern equipment or facilities. Describe the deficiencies and inadequacies of the present equipment / facilities, suggest replacements and explain why the expense would be justified. Write about 250 words.

- *Remember, you're new and you're only a secretary in this big company. Unless you're tactful, you could make a very bad impression on your new boss. Conversely, if you can demonstrate the inadequacy of the present equipment without giving offence, and show that the improvements would benefit the company, this could be the start of an important career development.*

- *Suggestions for equipment / facilities you would like replaced: furniture, lighting, computers, typewriters, photocopiers, heating, air-conditioning, toilets, canteen.*

1.5   A holiday complaint

Part 1 writing task

You've just come back from a very disappointing adventure holiday. The holiday did not correspond to the advertisement (below) – the handwritten notes are your own comments on what the holiday was really like. Study the annotated advertisement and the note from your friend Chris, then write:

(a) a **letter** to the holiday company complaining about the holiday and asking for some sort of refund. (about 200 words)

(b) a **note** in reply to Chris's note. (about 50 words)

advertisement

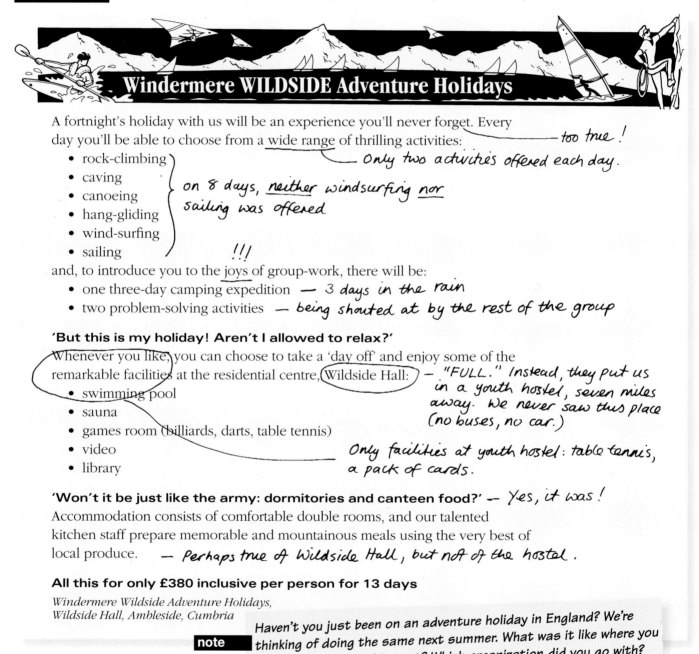

Windermere WILDSIDE Adventure Holidays

A fortnight's holiday with us will be an experience you'll never forget. Every day you'll be able to choose from a wide range of thrilling activities: — *too true!*

— Only two activities offered each day.

- rock-climbing
- caving
- canoeing
- hang-gliding
- wind-surfing
- sailing

on 8 days, neither windsurfing nor sailing was offered

!!!

and, to introduce you to the joys of group-work, there will be:

- one three-day camping expedition — *3 days in the rain*
- two problem-solving activities — *being shouted at by the rest of the group*

'But this is my holiday! Aren't I allowed to relax?'

Whenever you like, you can choose to take a 'day off' and enjoy some of the remarkable facilities at the residential centre, Wildside Hall: — *"FULL." Instead, they put us in a youth hostel, seven miles away. We never saw this place (no buses, no car.)*

- swimming pool
- sauna
- games room (billiards, darts, table tennis)
- video
- library

Only facilities at youth hostel: table tennis, a pack of cards.

'Won't it be just like the army: dormitories and canteen food?' — *Yes, it was!*

Accommodation consists of comfortable double rooms, and our talented kitchen staff prepare memorable and mountainous meals using the very best of local produce. — *Perhaps true of Wildside Hall, but not of the hostel.*

All this for only £380 inclusive per person for 13 days

Windermere Wildside Adventure Holidays,
Wildside Hall, Ambleside, Cumbria

note

Haven't you just been on an adventure holiday in England? We're thinking of doing the same next summer. What was it like where you went? How much did it cost? Which organization did you go with? We're trying to decide between Windermere Wildside and Outward Bound. The agency is putting pressure on us to book now, so could you just drop me a note as soon as poss? All the best, Chris

1.0 A job application

Read the advertisement and the job application. What is the function of each of the three main paragraphs in Carine's letter?

YOUNG COOK required to join a small team in a highly commended Brighton hotel specializing in modern European cooking to the highest standard. Would suit someone with enthusiasm, wishing to develop skills and responsibility. 5-day week, salary in accordance with qualifications and experience. Accommodation available.
Apply with CV to Mrs B H Albion, Restaurant Angélique, The Royal Parade, Brighton BN1 5JS.

79 Rue Daguerre
Paris 75014
France
Tel (00.33) 47.07.83.85

Mrs B H Albion
Restaurant Angélique
The Royal Parade
Brighton BN1 5JS   September 7th 1995

Dear Madam

I would like to apply for the position of cook advertised in this month's issue of The Lady.

As you will see from my CV (enclosed), I served a three-year apprenticeship at the Hotel Meurice in Paris. On completion of my apprenticeship, I left the Meurice to work at La Rotonde, where I stayed for 15 months. I was feeling that my career plans were likely to be hampered by my lack of English, so I left La Rotonde to spend six months studying English in Brighton. My English is now fluent, and adequate to meet any social or professional situation, as my examination results attest.

Having very much enjoyed my time in Brighton, I have decided to look for a job in Britain rather than return to La Rotonde. I am particularly keen to work in Brighton, where I have many good friends. I am available for interview at any time.

I look forward to hearing from you.

Yours faithfully,

Carine Colbert

Enc: CV

1.1   Looking for a job

You are looking for a job where you will have an opportunity to use your English. A friend sends you a cutting from a British newspaper, giving details of two au pair jobs and two in restaurant work; you also find one advertisement in the local paper in your own country. Read through the advertisements. If you had to choose one of these jobs, which would it be?

Jobs for English speakers

Our town has been chosen for our International Summer Camp this year. We require 12 SUMMER HELPERS aged 17–29 who should have a good command of English as well as masses of energy and enthusiasm for working with children aged 12–15 from all over the world. The job is residential, with round-the-clock responsibility for the success of the camp. We also require 4 COMMUNITY COORDINATORS (min. 24 yrs, with a good knowledge of the region and proven organizational ability) to coordinate the sports, social and cultural programmes.

Written applications to: *World Study Tours, 37 Flanagan's Way, Cork, Ireland.*

(your local paper, May 7th)

Situations vacant

Domestic

● Sensible au pair required a.s.a.p. for single working mother and two girls (9 & 12). London SE19. Non-smoker, driver. References. Anna Lee, 12 Hermitage Rd, London SE19.

● Temporary au pair wanted June – Sept. Professional couple, Cambridge, 2 boys (6 & 8). Some experience with children desirable. Steve and Dominique, 99 Harvey Smith Avenue, Cambridge CB3 5SJ.

Hotel And Catering

● High class restaurant requires full-time general assistants. On-the-job training provided as well as the opportunity to attend college for further education. If you are interested and not afraid of hard work, please contact: Mr N. Stiles, The Turkey, High St, Norwich NO4 6FH.

● General assistant required for small 2-star family-run hotel. Position offers experience of waiting, bar and reception work. Good pay, agreeable accommodation. Experience not necessary, but smart appearance and pleasant manner essential. Write: Jean Kerr, Riverside Hotel, Keswick CA12 8DE.

(*The Lady*, May 1st)

A Reading comprehension

1 How many different jobs are advertised altogether?
2 What are the abbreviations for 'as soon as possible', 'per annum' (a year) and 'minimum'?
3 You could send a CV with your application to any of these jobs, but for which two job applications is a CV *most* necessary?
4 In a *business* letter, you put the name and address of the people you are writing to on the left, above the salutation. In a *personal* letter, you don't do this. Which of the job applications require a personal rather than a business layout?

B Writing

Imagine that you are interested in one of the jobs advertised, and that you have suitable qualities and / or experience. Write a letter applying for the job.

You should mention:
- what job you are applying for (get the job title exactly right).
- where you saw the advertisement or where you heard that a job might be available.
- your relevant qualifications and experience.
- why you are interested in the job. Be positive, confident and enthusiastic.
- that your English is good enough.

Do ask questions about any aspects of the job that aren't clear to you – but be careful not to sound completely ignorant of the work the job involves.

It may be appropriate to refer to your enclosed CV. In an exam situation, however, you won't need to produce a CV to support a job application.

Use the letter on page 95 as a model, and adapt phrases from the box below as appropriate.

Useful phrases

Paragraph 1

I wish to apply for the post of . . . which was advertised in today's 'Daily Telegraph'.

With reference to your advertisement in the 'Guardian' of January 5th, I should like to apply for the position of . . .

Paragraph 2

As you will see from my enclosed CV, I have four years' experience in hotels and catering

At present I am employed as a . . . by the local Tourist Office, a position I have held for three years.

In the course of my present job, I have been responsible for the planning and organization of . . .

My duties have included secretarial work as well as . . .

I graduated in Business Administration from Dundee University in 1990.

I was employed as a cashier with Barclays Bank from 1988 to 1992.

I attended the Lycée Paul Bert, where I obtained the baccalauréat in 1989.

During my apprenticeship I obtained practical training in all aspects of the catering trade.

I am used to working under pressure / working to a deadline / working as part of a team.

I am familiar with Word for Windows / recent developments in the industry . . .

I also have some knowledge of accountancy, having kept the books for my father's business . . .

Paragraph 3

I believe the post you offer will give me the opportunity to . . .

I am especially keen to work in an organization such as yours which has a reputation for . . .

I feel that my present position offers little prospect of promotion

I will be glad to supply you with any further information you may need.

. . . have agreed to act as my referees.

Task bank: Task 26

6C Other formal letters

1.0 Letters to the editor

Sometimes people who are not journalists wish to express their opinions in a newspaper or magazine, and they do this by writing a letter to the editor. Although their letters speak to the readers of the paper, the convention is that the letter is actually addressed to the **editor**. This means that the word *you* must be used with care (and courtesy), as it addresses the editor in person.

1 Decide which word (**A**, **B**, **C** or **D**) best fits each space in the model below. Write the letter in the gap. The exercise begins with an example (**0**). See page 9 for information and advice about this exercise type.

2 The writer of this letter has at least two purposes in mind. What are they?

Sir,

Recent letters in your columns about insurance companies prompt me to (**0**) _*B*_ this example. Some months ago a car (**1**)____ to my daughter was (**2**)____ from outside her house in Birmingham.

As a doctor in daily (**3**)____ of her car, she was surprised when her (**4**)____ said she would have to wait six weeks for (**5**)____ .

   To her annoyance they managed, by all kinds of (**6**)____, to drag this out to three months; and then only after a (**7**)____ of lengthy, rather unpleasant phone calls would they pay a penny.

   My daughter was then (**8**)____ to find that there would be no refund, or no extension of the period of insurance, to (**9**)____ the three months lost. A full premium (no (**10**)____ sum for (**11**)____ cover in Birmingham), had to be paid for a quarter of a year, when no cover was (**12**)____ at all.

   Surely this is another example of the way insurance companies (**13**)____ money, perhaps legally but to my mind immorally, which gives them such a bad image.

   If any of your readers know of a way (**14**)____ this difficulty, I would (**15**)____ their advice.

Yours faithfully,

R.R.E. Potter

0	**A** instance	**B** cite	**C** resurrect	**D** say
1	**A** owning	**B** pertaining	**C** trusted	**D** belonging
2	**A** stolen	**B** robbed	**C** nicked	**D** broken
3	**A** use	**B** necessity	**C** utilization	**D** need
4	**A** assurers	**B** insurers	**C** ensurers	**D** insurance
5	**A** retribution	**B** premium	**C** compensation	**D** payment
6	**A** reluctance	**B** slowness	**C** haste	**D** procrastination
7	**A** number	**B** range	**C** lots	**D** heap
8	**A** appalled	**B** intimidated	**C** shocking	**D** impressed
9	**A** refund	**B** cover	**C** return	**D** reward
10	**A** little	**B** bad	**C** lesser	**D** mean
11	**A** complete	**B** integral	**C** comprehensible	**D** comprehensive
12	**A** done	**B** made	**C** provided	**D** affected
13	**A** obtain	**B** extort	**C** earn	**D** win
14	**A** with	**B** round	**C** about	**D** avoiding
15	**A** receive	**B** welcome	**C** take	**D** embrace

Task bank: Tasks 13 and 28

Word formation

Use the words in the box to the right of the text to form **one** word that fits in the same numbered space in the text. Write the new word in the correct box below the text. The exercise begins with an example (**0**).

Dear Dr Wallace,

Thank you very much for your letter of November 5th, (**0**) ... my (**1**) ... to send the (**2**) ... fee for the (**3**) ... talk you gave to our English Society.

I would like to apologize most (**4**) ... for this (**5**) ..., which I must confess was the result of (**6**) ... on my part. I trust this has not been too much of an (**7**) ... for you.

I should also like to take this opportunity to apologize for any (**8**) ... that I may have given in the course of my (**9**) ... speech by my joking remarks about the Scottish. I now realize that my words may have been ill-chosen and (**10**) ... but I can assure you that no (**11**) ... was intended.

Thank you again for your (**12**) ... talk. I know I am speaking on behalf of all our members when I say it was as profound and (**13**) ... as it was (**14**) ... .

Please find (**15**) ... the cheque for £200, together with a copy of the new issue of our English magazine, which I hope you will find of interest.

Yours sincerely,

0 CONCERN	
1 FAIL	
2 AGREE	
3 FASCINATE	
4 SINCERE	
5 OMIT	
6 FORGET	
7 CONVENIENT	
8 OFFEND	
9 INTRODUCE	
10 APPROPRIATE	
11 RESPECT	
12 WONDER	
13 MEMORY	
14 ENTERTAIN	
15 ENCLOSE	

0	*concerning*	8	
1		9	
2		10	
3		11	
4		12	
5		13	
6		14	
7		15	

Task bank: Task 27

1.1   Reservations and bookings

A Model

> Dear Sir or Madam,
>
> This letter is to confirm the reservation I made by telephone this morning, for one single room with shower, for the nights of 11 May to 16 May inclusive.
>
> As agreed, I enclose a cheque for £50 as a deposit. Could you please acknowledge receipt?
>
> Yours faithfully

B Part 1 writing task

You are working in the London office of an international organization called The Happy Planet. You have to make arrangements for a conference at a hotel. Read the note from Julia, the letter from Claus and the message from Paulo, and use the information they contain to write your **letter** to the Royal Hotel (about 250 words).

> Monday Feb 8th, 11 a.m.
>
> I phoned the hotel the tourist board recommended, to check the prices and see if they could take us. They sounded ideal, so I made a provisional booking for the three nights (Sat Sept 3rd – Mon Sept 5th). It's The Royal Hotel, Severn St, Cardiff, and the Conference Manager is called Mrs Lumley.
>
> When you get the rest of the details from Claus, could you write to them and tell them exactly what we need? Save me the room with the biggest bath!
>
> Julia

> I just had a phone call from Chantal who's the French co-ordinator. First of all, one of her delegates (Marcel Blainville) is disabled, so could you mention to the hotel that he'll be coming in his wheelchair? Secondly, six of the French delegates are very keen to see the international rugby football match at Cardiff Arms Park that Saturday afternoon – so could you ask the hotel to try to get them some tickets?
>
> Paulo

7 February 1994

The planning committee has asked me to pass on all the details to you so you can make the booking as soon as you find a suitable hotel in Cardiff.

First, we've finally decided not to start till the Saturday afternoon (that's September 3rd) with a session at 4.30 where all the delegates come together. So we'll need the conference room then. That will finish some time before 7.00, then we'll all have dinner together then maybe go out to explore Cardiff. After breakfast on Sunday morning we'll have seminars from 10.00 till 1.00, then lunch at one o'clock, then seminars again from 2.30 to 4.00, then tea. We'll need four different seminar rooms, so people can choose which talks they go to. Then on Sunday evening we've decided to set off in groups to try out some of the restaurants around the town. After all, we don't want to be stuck in the hotel every evening, especially if their food's not much good.

Monday's programme will be just the same as Sunday's, except we'll eat out again for lunch on Monday. Then in the evening we'll have another big meeting in the conference room with everyone together (same time as Saturday) and then a big dinner together in the hotel in the evening.

Actually, I'm a bit worried about the hotel food. We had enough problems at the East European conference, when all the vegetarian dishes came with either ham or tuna. You'd better tell them that a third of us prefer to eat vegetarian. Then at least we won't all be eating sausages and chips!

I forgot to mention that in the conference room we'll need a video recorder and a TV screen for Dr Schumacher's talk. In the seminar rooms, we'll probably be OK with just whiteboards.

The other thing I haven't told you about is numbers. At the moment, it stands at 36 delegates, six of whom are also bringing husbands or wives who won't be involved in the talks but will take part in every other respect. So that makes a total of 42, in 26 single rooms and 8 double rooms.

I hope this isn't too muddled – I'm glad it's you who's doing the organizing!

All the best,

Claus

1   Part 1 tasks like this often involve a careful selection of information. The following are details from the letters. After careful consideration of the purpose of the letter and the 'target reader', mark whether the details should be mentioned in your letter: are they absolutely essential (A), not essential (B), or completely irrelevant (C).

   1   *the Conference Manager is called Mrs Lumley* _____
   2   *Save me the room with the biggest bath!* _____
   3   *then maybe go out to explore Cardiff* _____
   4   *We'll need four different seminar rooms* _____
   5   *a third of us prefer to eat vegetarian* _____
   6   *at least we won't all be eating sausages and chips!* _____
   7   *a video recorder and a TV screen for Dr Schumacher's talk* _____
   8   *he'll be coming in his wheelchair* _____

2   Write the **letter** to The Royal Hotel (about 250 words). You will probably need to start by re-reading the information and underlining everything you need to include, then making notes. You may lay out your requirements in any suitable way.

Task bank: Task 26

7 INFORMAL LETTERS

7A Technical matters

1.0 Layout of informal letters

The layout of this model is appropriate for any informal letter. It is also appropriate for any *personal* letter, even one that is formal in tone, such as a letter of apology to your boss.

1 *36 Shaston Drive*

2 *Shaftesbury*

3 *Dorset SH2 3AB*
       tel (0747) 5286

4

5 *Mon Sept 4th*

6 *Dear Arantxa,*

7 *Thanks very much for lending me your flat while you were away. I hope you enjoyed your holiday in Morocco as much as I enjoyed my stay in Vitoria. (I'll tell you all about it when I see you at my party on Nov 5th – I do hope you haven't changed your mind about coming!)*

Now you've probably been wondering what has happened to your goldfish. (I'm sorry, I meant to leave a note about this, but I forgot.) You will have noticed that they are a bit smaller and, I think, redder than they used to be. This may have come as a bit of a surprise to you, but I expect you have guessed what happened. It's bad news, I'm afraid. The fish you've got now are a pair I bought to replace yours which, I'm sorry to say, were both dead when I arrived in your flat on Aug 10th.

If I'd arrived on the 8th as planned I don't suppose this tragedy would have happened, but the thing is, I got caught up in the strike and had to spend a couple of days at Heathrow. That's life, I suppose, but I still feel rather bad about it, both for myself (48h at Heathrow is no joke) and for the fish. Perhaps I should sell my story to the newspaper – 'Innocents Suffer In Heartless Strike!', 'Holiday Chaos Hits Heathrow: Two Die!'

8 *Anyway, thanks again for the loan of the flat. I hope I left everything in the right place, and enough money by the phone to cover the few local calls I made – I'm sure you'll tell me if there are any problems. I'm really looking forward to seeing you again, so I do hope you can make it to the party. If not, see you in Bilbao at Christmas.*

9 *Love,*

10 *Rachel*

1 Why did Rachel write this letter? What are the three different subjects she covers?

2 The letter says three different things, or contains three different elements. What are they?

3 What features of informal style can you find in the letter? Consider the following: vocabulary, grammar, punctuation and sentence structure, cohesion / linking words, tone (what aspects of the writing show that Arantxa is a friend?).

Notes

1 Don't write your name here.

2 The house number of a British or American address is written before the name of the street, but write your own address in the way you normally do.

3 Include your postcode and, if you like, your telephone number (not to do so can be a real and unnecessary way of losing a friend).

4 Don't write the name or address of the person you're writing to on the left. This is only done in letters that are formal and impersonal.

5 Date. These abbreviations are commonly used for the days and months: *Mon, Tues, Weds, Thurs, Fri, Sat, Sun; Jan, Feb, Aug, Sept, Oct, Nov, Dec.*

6 *Dear* is always appropriate – for family, intimate friends and even enemies. *My dear* and *Dearest* are also possible, but very affectionate.

7 Most letters start with a reference to the most recent contact you have had with the other person:
Thanks very much for your letter, which came this morning.
It was great to see you again last weekend – and looking so fit and slim!
Some people's letters always begin:
Sorry it's been so long since I last wrote, but . . . followed by the excuses for not having written.

8 Most letters end with a reference to the next contact with the other person:
I'm looking forward to seeing you / hearing from you.
Do write again soon.
I hope to see you again in June, if not before.

9 *Love* is a suitable ending for an intimate friend of either sex.
More affectionate: *All my love, Love and kisses, Lots of love*
For a friend or colleague (not intimate): *All the best, Best wishes*
For a personal letter, but not to a personal friend: *Yours, Regards*

10 Remember that this is the only place either on the letter or the envelope that your name appears. Does your correspondent know who you are? Make sure your signature is legible. You may even need to write your surname.

Task bank: Task 27

1.1 Layout of a note

In the letter above, Rachel says 'I meant to leave a note, but I forgot'. This is the note she might have left.

---

1 *Friday morning, Sept 1st*

2 *Arantxa –*

Just a quick note to say thank you. Staying in your flat has been fantastic.

I'm afraid I got here 2 days late (strike at Heathrow) & both your goldfish had died. Very sorry, but hope that you like the new fish.

3 *Don't forget my party on Nov 5th – I'm so looking forward to seeing you & hearing all about Morocco.*

I'm off now to the airport. See you soon.

4 *Rachel*

PS I'll leave the keys with Josune.

---

1 Where did Rachel leave this note?
2 Why is the note shorter than the letter?
3 How did Rachel manage to include all the important points of the letter in a short note? What did she leave out in terms of (a) information (b) grammar?

Notes
- It is often appropriate to put the time rather than the date, especially when you expect the person to read the note the same day.
- It is acceptable, but not necessary, to write *Dear*.
- It is acceptable, but not necessary, to write *Love, Best wishes, Yours*, etc.

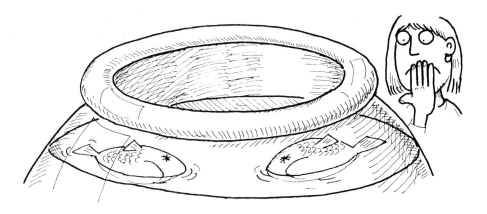

2.0 Technical devices

A How to sound informal

Your writing will sound much more informal if you:

1 remember you're writing to a friend. Imagine a real person.

- Be friendly and jokey.
  How's your diet going?

- Refer to common friends.
  Have you heard from Sybilla?
  Say hello to Edward for me.
  Give my love to the baby.

- Refer to things your friend already knows.
  I'm sure you'll remember . . .
  As you know . . .
  Just like you said . . .

2 write in 'spoken' English.

- Use personal constructions (phrases with *I* and *you*).
  I know this sounds silly, but . . .
  I hope you don't mind my saying this, but . . .
  You'll never guess . . .
  . . . if you know what I mean.

3 use informal vocabulary, including phrasal verbs and informal linking words such as those below.

- Expressing your opinion

To be quite honest	*To tell you the truth*	*As I see it*
To my mind	*From my point of view*	*In my experience*
Frankly	*Actually*	*I'd say*

- Expressing surprise

Believe it or not	*Funnily enough*
To my surprise	*You'll never believe this, but*
This may surprise you, but	*Guess what!*

- Changing the subject

Anyway, . . .	*Talking of which, . . .*	*That reminds me, . . .*
Incidentally, . . .	*By the way, . . .*	*Before I forget, . . .*

- Listing reasons

To start with	*First of all*	*What's more*
And another thing	*And besides*	*Plus*

B Find examples of these technical devices in Rachel's letter and note. Can you find any other techniques which Rachel uses to sound informal?

C Practice

Read the formal letter, written by a job applicant to the head teacher of a school, and use the information to fill the gaps in the informal letter to a friend who works in that school. Use **no more than two words** for each gap. The exercise begins with an example (**0**). The words you need do **not** occur in the informal letter. See page 11 for information and advice about this exercise type.

Formal letter

Dear Dr Cox,

I very much regret that, as the result of an injury, I shall not be able to attend the interview on August 15th for the post of Sports Teacher.

Having suffered an injury on July 1st while playing tennis in the Wimbledon tournament, I am at present undergoing hospital treatment to my knee. Consequently, I fear that I shall not be sufficiently mobile to make the journey to Sevenoaks until late August.

Doubtless this will be most inconvenient for you, and I will of course understand if you are unable to await my recovery before appointing someone to the post. Nevertheless, should you remain interested in my application, I fully expect to be available for interview by September 1st at the latest.

I look forward to hearing from you.

Yours sincerely,

Informal letter

Dear Pat,

I'm (0)_____really sorry_____ but it looks as if I won't be able to

(1)_____ to the job interview at your school in August.

(2)_____ I'll see if I can persuade them to interview me in September instead. A pity if I've missed my chance, because I'm sure it would've been fun working with you. The thing is, I (3)_____ hurt playing tennis at Wimbledon, and (4)_____. I'm in hospital (5)_____ my knee sorted out – (6)_____ I'm (7)_____ I'm not going to be fit (8)_____ to come down to Sevenoaks till the end of August.

    As far as the interview goes, this is obviously going to be a (9)_____ for them. I expect they'll (10)_____ someone else the (11)_____ without waiting to see me.

(12)_____, I'll try and persuade your Dr Cox to interview me in Sept – at worst, she'll say no.

    See you at Christmas if not before.

    (13)_____,

2.1 ## Informal punctuation

A Exclamation marks

Formal English is written in sentences, not in a series of exclamations. Thus exclamation marks are used almost exclusively when presenting direct speech.

'Get lost!' she shouted.

In informal writing, exclamation marks are much more widely used and are characteristic of a very chatty, conversational style:

No wonder she left him!
How awful!

B Dashes

Dashes are highly characteristic of informal writing; they are used in two different ways.

a A pair of dashes – as in this sentence – is used for parenthesis.
In formal writing, a pair of brackets (like this) or a pair of commas, like this, are usually preferred.

b A single dash can have the same function as the (more formal) colon, and can mean *because*, *so*, *namely*, etc. (see page 35).

Look at the examples below which show how a single dash is used. In the first sentence of each pair, the dash is followed by an exclamation or a surprising statement (hence the exclamation mark). In the second sentence no exclamation mark is required.

Don't bother to bring an overcoat – it's 40° in the shade out here!
Don't bother to bring an overcoat – I've got a spare one you can use.

Her teeth are like stars – they come out at night!
Her teeth are like stars – they are white and shiny.

After studying the examples above, punctuate the sentences below, using dashes and exclamation marks as and where appropriate.

1 I'm fed up with this stupid job my new boss is even worse than the last one
2 I'm fed up with this stupid job I want to live
3 I was amazed to see John at the party I thought he was in prison
4 I was amazed to see John at the party he's normally very unsociable
5 The wild pig didn't attack Emily it was Emily who attacked the wild pig
6 The wild pig didn't attack Emily it was just trying to escape

Complete the following sentences, using the examples above as models.

7a He's always badly dressed –_____
_____ !

7b He's always badly dressed –_____
_____ .

8a She's had too much to drink –_____
_____ !

8b She's had too much to drink – _____
_____ .

9a It's too cold to go camping –_____
_____ !

9b It's too cold to go camping –_____
_____ .

C Practice
Punctuate this informal letter.

dear mum guess what youll never believe this but im going to be famous at last my new life starts tomorrow in poland on tour with U2[1] it all happened so suddenly we were just doing a gig[2] in a small town in the north when bono walked in you should have seen the look on kemals face anyway to cut a long story short bono loved our music and it just happened that he needed a support band for U2s east european tour so were all off to poland next week by the way hows your polish can you still speak the language if so why dont you come with us im sure youd really enjoy it its not all sex drugs and rock n roll you know must dash weve got a rehearsal in half an hour and my bagpipes are out of tune your loving son edmund.

[1] U2 – a rock band, led by Bono
[2] concert

2.2 Abbreviations, contractions and ellipsis
Ellipsis, abbreviations and contractions are three features of informal writing. They all involve writing less.

A Abbreviations
. . . the Vatican and all the other important sights.   *. . . the Vatican, etc.*
From Monday morning until Tuesday afternoon   *Mon a.m. – Tues p.m.*
Many people abbreviate their names in informal contexts: Michael → *Mike.*

B Contractions
I will; she will not; we did not   *I'll; she won't; we didn't*

C Ellipsis
It was nice to hear from you   *Nice to hear from you*
I've just read your note   *Just read your note.*
I was glad you could come.   *Glad you could come.*
Do you remember me?   *Remember me?*

D Examples
Find examples of abbreviations, contractions and ellipsis in the letter from Rachel to Arantxa on page 102.

E Practice: a covering note
This covering note was included with a report describing what happened at an anti-racist demonstration. *Punctuate* it, and introduce *abbreviations* and *contractions* where appropriate. There is also one occasion where you should use *ellipsis*.

michael here is my account of what happened at the demonstration i have described everything i saw from when we set off from oxford street to the moment we arrived in trafalgar square i know you will not agree with me about everything especially the order of events i am pretty sure i saw people throwing stones before the first baton charge but the important thing is to clear jennifer of the charges against her and i think my evidence here will help a lot i hope to see you again at next months meeting of fight racism penelope

2.3 Writing
Write a **letter** (about 250 words) to an English-speaking friend, telling them of your recent problems and successes in your work / studies and in your private life and inviting them to go on holiday with you.

Task bank: Tasks 4, 9, 10, 18, 25, 29 and 47

7B Diplomacy and tact

1.0 Introduction

Whether you're asking for money or declaring your love, you never write without a purpose. Sometimes the purpose is simple, but often it is complex:

- refusing an invitation without offending someone.
- cancelling something you've arranged with a friend without damaging your friendship.
- expressing your anger with a friend without losing them.

The following writing task also calls for a certain degree of tact. Read it, then work through the exercises that follow before writing the letter.

You looked after a friend's pet animal, Attila, while she was away on holiday last summer, but the two weeks were one disaster after the other, so you are not at all keen to look after the creature again this year. You have told your friend this, so she has asked someone else (someone you don't know, called Agatha) to take care of it while she is away this summer. Unfortunately Agatha has heard something about the problems you had with the animal, and has written to you:

> . . . I'm sure it wasn't really as awful as I heard. I wonder if you could put my mind at rest by telling me exactly what happened when you were looking after Attila last summer? And please do tell me if you think I'm letting myself in for too much trouble . . .

Write a **letter** to Agatha (about 250 words), giving an objectively true account of the disastrous two weeks, but describing your experience in a sufficiently positive way so that she doesn't change her mind about taking the animal.

1.1 Planning the effect of your letter on the reader

You are an honest person, and you know that you must not tell lies. Nevertheless, you do want Agatha to look after Attila, otherwise you might be asked to do so again. What effect would letters giving each of these impressions have on Agatha?

1 The animal is very easy to look after and a pleasure at all times.
2 The animal is a dangerous monster that should be kept in a zoo.
3 The animal wasn't always easy, but any trouble was well worth while.
4 You did have problems with Attila, but they were all your own fault – the animal is certain to behave better for someone who understands him.

Which would persuade her to take the animal?
Which would be completely dishonest (and therefore unacceptable, both in society and within the terms of this writing task)?

1.2 Being economical with the truth

It is obvious that Agatha has heard some true stories about what happened last summer. You don't know what she has heard, and you cannot deny the stories (because they are true) but you can present them in a much more positive light.

A Understatement – the opposite of exaggeration

1 *He is incredibly noisy.* (True, but tactless.)
2 *He is not the quietest of animals.* (An understatement, but true.)

1 *He ate three pairs of my most expensive shoes.*
2 *He showed an interest in my footwear.*

B Look on the bright side

1 *Looking after Attila was a full-time job and caused me a number of problems.*
2 *Despite some small inconveniences, I can truly say that I never had a dull moment while Attila was around.*

1 *He kept jumping up on me with his dirty paws and knocking me over.*
2 *He's so affectionate – sometimes it takes your breath away!*

There is no factual difference between sentences 1 and 2. The only difference is that sentence 2 describes the same facts in a more positive light.

C Think positive!

Stress all the animal's qualities (big brown eyes, good temper, good appetite, courage) or, if the animal has no qualities, think of the vices it *doesn't* have (doesn't bite, doesn't smell bad).

D Practice

Rewrite the following problems, using the ideas in **A–C**, to make them more appropriate for your letter.

1 He destroyed the garden.
2 He was always getting into fights with other animals.
3 He was very noisy at nights.
4 He insisted on sleeping on my bed.
5 He was very tiring, and always doing stupid things.
6 If he wasn't taken for two long runs every day he became unmanageable.
7 If I didn't let him out as soon as he wanted, he made a mess on the carpet.

1.3 Planning the content

Either on your own or with a partner, invent a list of the problems you had with Attila, and which Agatha may have heard about. You can use ideas from the preceding exercises or invent your own. Then decide how you are going to describe them to Agatha.

1.4 Starting the letter

The following are the first paragraphs of four CAE students' attempts at this writing task. Which one is best? What is wrong with each of the others?

A

I am an honest person, and I know that I must not tell lies. Nevertheless, I do want you to look after the animal. So here is an objectively true account of the two weeks Attila stayed with me last summer. I'm sure that you'll see you have nothing to worry about, and so you won't change your mind about taking the animal.

B Thanks for your letter. I don't know what you've heard about my experience with Attila last summer, which certainly wasn't 'awful' – I can't imagine who you've been talking to! Admittedly, those two weeks were eventful, but all in all I think it would be fair to say that Attila and I spent a memorable and at times enjoyable fortnight together. So let me tell you exactly what happened – I'm sure you will realize that Attila could not possibly be held to blame either for my father's heart attack or for the damage to the police car.

C *Thanks very much for your letter asking for advice about how to look after Attila. I think you'll find he's no problem at all once you get used to him, even though this may take two or three days. Just so that you don't have any surprises, I'd better tell you everything you need to know about all his habits: eating, sleeping, exercise and, above all, his sense of humour.*

D Thank you very much for your letter, which I received this morning. In reply to your question concerning the fortnight during which I looked after Attila last summer, I hasten to reassure you that the experience was by no means as 'awful' as it would appear to have been painted by some; please allow me to clarify the situation by describing in full the events of those two weeks.

1.5 Writing

Write your reply to Agatha (about 250 words).

Task bank: Tasks 17 and 32

REPORTS

8A Information reports: people

1.0 Appraisal report

A Read the following conversation, in which a hospital administrator, Gary, gives an informal, spoken report on a clerical worker. Use the information in the conversation to fill the numbered gaps in the more formal report written by his colleague Annette. Use **no more than two words** for each gap. The words you need do **not** occur in the spoken version. The exercise begins with an example (**0**).

Annette I wonder if you can help me, Gary, I've been asked to write a report on one of our new clerical workers, but I've been away for three months and I hardly know where to start. She's called Chan Kit Yu. I think she came in January.

Gary Well, first of all I'd say Kit's been fantastic, especially in the circumstances. I mean, I think you'll remember that, what with the epidemic, then the nurses' strike, there have been a lot of problems; so everyone in the hospital's been getting pretty tired and fed up, and there's been a lot of lateness and absenteeism. Anyway, Kit's been one of the few who hasn't let the pressures affect her. She's always on time, and she's never been off sick. I've even managed to get her to work overtime once or twice, on the rare occasion when she didn't have any rehearsals to go to.

Annette I remember now. Isn't she some kind of pop singer?

Gary Something like that. She used to talk about it all the time, but I had to put a stop to it. In her first few weeks she'd spend the whole morning telling everyone about her music and her adventures – everybody loved it, of course, and nobody got any work done, so I had a word with her and now she toes the line.

Annette And her work?

Gary As I say, she's serious and hardworking. Oh yes, we did have one teething problem. At first she was pretty hopeless on the computer and she didn't seem to know any of the software. But we sent her on a course, and now she's fine.

Appraisal Report: Chan Kit Yu

I am pleased to report that Kit has performed
(0)___*exceptionally*___ well in her duties as Administrative
Assistant since (1)_____ us on 5 January.
The hospital has been beset with a (2)_____
of difficulties during this time and I have been particularly
impressed by the manner in which Kit has not
(3)_____ these to affect the quality of her
work.

Kit was quick to develop a good working relationship with
(4)_____, and if at first her
(5)_____ life threatened to intrude into the
workplace, she soon learned where to draw the line.

So far as her administrative skills are concerned, the only
question mark has been over (6)_____ of
familiarity with some of our computer software. This has,
(7)_____, been remedied by a recent training
course.

Her (8)_____ and attendance have been
excellent, and she has been (9)_____ to work
overtime when the situation has required it.

In sum, a most satisfactory start.

B Language study

To understand the difference in style between the two versions, you must bear in mind that the written report is a permanent record which will have an important influence on the employee's career. It will be referred to when promotion or dismissal are being considered, or as the basis for a reference.

1 What aspects of Gary's assessment would be inappropriate in a written report?

2 What changes has Annette made?
   Consider (a) the choice of details to be included / omitted
             (b) the vocabulary
             (c) the organization
             (d) the length
             (e) the 'tone': what impression do we get of the writer?
                              what makes this report sound formal?

1.1 Character references

When writing a character reference, whether as an employer, as a teacher or as a friend, the first thing to mention is how long you have known the person and in what capacity. After that, there are a number of areas that may be worth mentioning, depending on the job or course your employee, student or friend has applied for. This list suggests some of those areas, together with a few adjectives and phrases describing positive qualities. In a written reference these qualities will be illustrated with concrete examples and facts.

Reliability
punctual, her timekeeping is good
reliable, dependable, conscientious
  responsible

Attitude to people
works well in a team
a natural leader
competitive
considerate, understanding
friendly, helpful, generous
tolerant, patient, considerate
gets on well with those around her,
  sociable, integrates well

Disposition / Personality
easy-going, relaxed, laid-back
self-confident, self-assured
good-humoured, good-natured
self-reliant, independent
shows initiative
positive, enthusiastic, optimistic
quiet, introverted,
outgoing, extroverted

The spoken word
articulate, eloquent, persuasive
well-spoken
discreet, diplomatic, tactful

Personal appearance
tidy, neat, presentable
well-dressed

Attitude to work
meticulous, thorough, methodical
diligent, industrious, assiduous
ambitious, determined
adaptable, flexible
willing, keen, enthusiastic

Thinking
imaginative, creative, has a capacity
  for original ideas, innovative
rational, logical
intelligent, brilliant

Honesty
truthful, sincere
trustworthy, honest
a person of great integrity

Deciding and Doing
confident, decisive, dynamic
energetic, adventurous, spontaneous
competent, practical
well-organized, level-headed

Other areas that may be worth considering include **academic ability, practical skills, qualifications, interests**.

Practice

A Negative aspects of a person's character must also be mentioned, whether as a matter of honesty or in order to give more credibility to an otherwise implausibly glowing reference. In either case, negative points are usually expressed in as positive a way as possible. The following phrases, all taken from character references, describe negative qualities. For each phrase, find a word or words in the list above that expresses *the opposite*. The first has been done as an example.

Attitude to people

1 can be a little impatient with other people's weaknesses   (OPPOSITE: *tolerant*)
2 although her critics see her as a bit of a troublemaker,

Disposition

3 as yet, she is lacking in self-confidence, but
4 he takes himself very seriously
5 while it is true that she is easily led,
6 he tends to keep himself to himself

Attitude to work

7 though he doesn't always show a total commitment to his work.
8 can give the impression of carelessness when finishing a piece of work

The spoken word

9 has a very frank way of expressing himself
10 though occasionally she has trouble expressing herself clearly.
11 her regional accent and occasional use of dialect may not be immediately comprehensible to some

Thinking

12 his arguments are not always entirely coherent
13 though he has been accused of a lack of imagination.
14 rather slow at times / not especially quick-witted

B Study the example below, as well as those in **A**, then write similar positive descriptions of five of the ten negative qualities given in the list below.

impulsive, impetuous
When it comes to taking decisions, no one could accuse her of being hesitant.

dresses very casually
His clothes, while unconventional, are always interesting.

has a criminal record
Although she may, in the past, have found herself on the wrong side of the law, . . .

1 fussy / a perfectionist
2 a workaholic
3 unscrupulous / ruthless
4 authoritarian / bossy
5 arrogant
6 impatient
7 a clock-watcher
8 unsociable and disruptive

1.2 Writing

Part 1 writing task

You have just completed a three-year academic course at a college in Britain. A friend of yours, John Kino, has now applied for the same course, and he has asked you to write a character reference for him. You are willing to write the reference because you think the course would be a wonderful opportunity for him and you feel that, despite his faults, he has a reasonable chance of successfully completing it.

Read the extracts from three letters: the first from John, the second from someone who took the course with you, and the third from the college, then write:

(a) your reply to Dr Flode, a **letter** in which you write a (sufficiently positive) character reference for John (about 175 words).

(b) a **short letter** in reply to John (about 75 words).

From John

Do you think you could write a reference for me? I'm not sure exactly what they'll want to know, so I suggest you just tell them the whole truth about my magnetic personality, intellectual genius, impeccable manners, magnificent physique, endearing modesty, etc.!

Actually I'm counting on you, because I've already given them your name as a referee. The thing is, there was a deadline for the applications, and yours was the first name I thought of, since you've just finished the course and you've always been such a good friend to me. I would've asked you first but I'd lost your phone number.

From a classmate

Have you heard that John is hoping to get onto the course next year? He must be mad – I mean, it was much too hard for me, and even you found it difficult. He asked me if I'd write him a reference, but how could I? Frankly, I think he'd be a disaster in Britain. His English isn't very good so he'd have problems with the course. And for all his intelligence, I'm sure he'd be too lazy to get through all the work. I mean, we're talking about a guy who gets out of bed around midday, but doesn't wake up until the discos open . . .

Anyway, I suggested he ask you to write the reference instead, firstly because you're a better liar than me, and secondly because your opinion of John has always been a lot higher than mine. I know there are a lot of things to admire about him: his voluntary work in Rwanda, his physical courage, the way he always wants to be the best, his brains, the way he can talk himself out of any difficult situation, his ability to 'always look on the bright side', his smile, his guitar-playing, and most of all his dazzling displays on the dance floor! But for all this, I just see him as a waster: arrogant, lazy, spoilt and vain!

From the college

. . . We are considering Mr John Kino for a place on the course which you have just completed so successfully. He has given us your name as a reference and I would be most grateful for your opinion of his suitability for the course.

Every year, as you yourself will be aware, a high percentage of students from abroad drop out of this course for a number of reasons: problems of adaptation to the British environment and culture; the difficulty of finding new friends and building a social life in Britain, and the consequent loneliness and homesickness; the heavy workload on the course and the frequent exams; the difficulty of studying exclusively in English. For this reason – to minimise wastage and suffering on our courses – we particularly appreciate character references that are a fair assessment of an individual's potential.

Yours sincerely,

L Flode

Dr L. Flode

Task bank: Task 33

8B   Recommendation reports

1.0   A consumer report

This recommendation report from a consumer magazine is based on tests of five cars. In most lines of the text there is **one** unnecessary word. It is **either** grammatically incorrect **or** does not fit in with the sense of the text. Write the unnecessary words in the space in the margin. Some lines are correct: indicate these lines with a tick (✓). The exercise begins with two examples (**0**).

0	The Peugeot struck the best balance between ~~the~~ performance and	*the*
0	being easy to live with. It was very rewarding to drive and practical	✓
1	for everyday use. It wasn't so good drive at low speeds, but this was	_____
2	easily outweighed by the car's too many virtues. The Ford Fiesta and	_____
3	Rover Metro rated both well in our secondary safety assessments.	_____
4	The Metro is £1,000 pounds cheaper than the Fiesta and is the better	_____
5	buy if always you don't often carry passengers in the back. If you	_____
6	need the extra space and can put up with the bumpy ride, the	_____
7	Fiesta is worth a look. We can't to recommend the Fiat: it didn't have	_____
8	the handling to complement the high performance. The Suzuki was	_____
9	noisy and uncomfortable and, though cheap, but can't be recommended	_____
10	either. We cannot recommend any of all these cars for those with	_____
11	little or limited in driving experience. They require a higher degree	_____
12	of responsibility, skill and experience than you have need just to pass the driving test.	_____

1.1   Organizing a recommendation report

The first paragraph of this recommendation report is missing. Read the report, then choose the most appropriate first paragraph from the three given.

PROPOSED SUBSCRIPTION TO A BRITISH NEWSPAPER

(First paragraph missing: choose from a, b and c below)

Tabloids

There was general agreement that, despite their low price, none of the tabloid newspapers (also known as the 'popular' press) could be recommended, for the following reasons:

1 the inappropriacy of the prose as a model of written English.
2 the limited coverage of international news, the arts, business, etc.
3 a tendency towards sexism, racism and insularity.

Quality press

It was unanimously agreed that only the *Independent* and the *Guardian* merited close scrutiny, the other quality papers holding too little appeal for a readership of students and young professional people.

The *Independent*

(Monday–Saturday, £93.47 for 13 weeks)
All agreed to commend
• the quality of the writing.
• the proportion of international news.
• the broad spectrum of arts coverage.
• the independence of the political stance.

The air mail price appeared to be good value, but there was some disappointment that the Saturday colour supplement was not included.

The *Guardian*

(Monday–Saturday, £127 for 13 weeks)
It was felt that the *Guardian*, although comparable to the *Independent* in most other respects, had a significant advantage in the strength of its Tuesday supplement, *Guardian Education*. This supplement is written in tabloid form and includes excellent articles written to be of interest to secondary school students; there are also articles addressing matters of interest to teachers. The *Guardian's* other advantage was the inclusion on Saturday of a supplement entitled *Guardian Weekend*, more than eighty pages long and illustrated in colour.

Recommendation

Both the *Guardian* and the *Independent* contain a wealth of reading matter that would be a most valuable resource for teachers and students alike. The question was raised whether they would in fact contain too much: would the students and teachers find time to read them? Should this be seen to be a problem, the cheaper and apparently thinner *Independent* may be preferred. If, however, the students and teachers have a large appetite for quality journalism, and if the price of the *Guardian* is within a school's budget, then a subscription to the *Guardian* is recommended.

a   There are many newspapers in Britain, but not all of them would be useful for foreign students. Some of them contain little other than scandal and football, while others are only read by stockbrokers or the landed gentry. We're going to look at the different papers and see which would be best for your school.

b   This report is the product of a working party of five members of the ELT Department of Wessex University whose brief was to identify which British daily newspaper would be most appropriate as a resource for CAE students at language schools in Alava. After a week of individual research, a meeting was held in order to share findings and reach a conclusion.

c   A working party led by James Bigglesworth (myself) was requested, on 3 February 1993, to undertake a survey of the current daily press in Britain and to report their findings to the English Language Teaching Association of Alava. After a long and fascinating week's work during which we ploughed through an enormous quantity of newsprint, here is what we decided.

1.2   Writing

Part 2 writing task

You are studying English in a school where there are a number of classes, ranging from beginners to advanced. The school has been given an exceptional grant of £2,500 to spend on new resources. The decision as to how the money should be spent will be taken by a committee of five, including one representative of the students – yourself.

You have been asked to conduct a survey of the students' wishes and to submit to the committee a **report** based on your findings. Write the report (about 250 words).

You might like to conduct the survey in class before writing this report.

Task bank: Tasks 34, 35 and 36

8C   Eye-witness and narrative reports

1.0   Two styles of eye-witness report

News stories in newspapers are also described as *reports*, but are written in a very different style from the other reports in this unit; the style of newspaper and magazine writing is examined in the next unit.

A Newspaper report

One of the objectives of an eye-witness account in a newspaper is to bring the events to life in the imagination of the reader. This is achieved by the tight organization of the narrative and the inclusion of 'concrete' details that help the reader visualize the scene. What details in the following text contribute to the success of the writer's description of the Los Angeles riots of 1992?

He was about 15 years old, a good-looking boy in a blue woollen hat. He had jumped out of a yellow Cadillac next to my rental car at a traffic light. Now he was standing at my window pointing a shiny, new-looking revolver at my head. 'Open the door', he said.

The car radio had just announced: 'It's a bright, breezy day in Los Angeles, apart from the smoke drifting over the Hollywood hills.' I mumbled the first foolish thing that came into my mind. 'I can't open the door.'

This was Manchester Boulevard and Van Ness Avenue in the epicentre of the riots. On every second corner a building burned. But the cars were still stopping for red lights. We were hopelessly boxed in. All over town white motorists were being dragged from cars and beaten or shot.

The boy, looking puzzled and scared, smashed the window with the gun butt, covering me in glass splinters. My companions shouted, 'Get out of here', which is exactly what you should not do when a scared child points a gun at your head.

I pressed the accelerator and rammed the car in front; turned the wheel and, bumping into another car, jerked forward into the oncoming traffic.

B Writing practice: a statement to the police

If the writer of the piece of journalism above had to describe the incident in a statement to the police, the statement might begin like this.

I stopped my car at a traffic light in the centre of the riot zone. While I was waiting at the lights, a boy got out of a yellow Cadillac next to my car and pointed a gun at me.

Complete the statement, using the relevant information from the newspaper article but omitting any details that would not be of interest to the police.

1.1 Planning a formal eye-witness report
Part 1 writing task

Yesterday you and a friend set off for a stay in Britain. Your friend was due to begin an English course in Oxford, whereas you are on an ecological study visit to the remote Shetland Islands. You both travelled on the same plane, but had to separate on arrival in Britain: you were in a hurry to catch your connection, but your friend was held up in Customs.

Just after you had checked in at the airport in your own country, a stranger, apparently an American student on the same flight, had started a conversation with your friend. This is part of the conversation you heard.

Stranger Have you bought any duty-free goods yet?
Friend What do you mean?
Stranger Well, alcohol and tobacco are very expensive in Britain, so you can save a lot of money by taking some with you. Even if you yourself don't smoke or drink, it's a good idea to take some as a present.
Friend I don't think I'll bother. I've got enough to carry already.
Stranger You're crazy! Don't you know that cigarettes are about $5 a packet in Britain? I'm going to be staying four weeks, so that's more than $100. And I'm only a student.
Friend Well if you smoke that much, you'd better bring your own cigarettes with you.
Stranger That's just the problem. They only let you carry 200 duty-free cigarettes in. I've taken a risk, I've got 400. But if they catch me at Customs I'll have to pay a fine, and I couldn't afford that.
Friend Look, why don't you give me 200 of them and I'll take them through Customs for you . . .

A British lawyer representing your friend has just phoned you at your hotel in the Shetlands to tell you that your friend is being held by the police in London: the package your friend offered to carry contained not cigarettes but drugs. The stranger has not been caught; indeed, the police have no reason to believe your friend's story.

The lawyer asks you to fax him a statement within the next hour in which you report what happened. Write the **statement** (about 250 words).

A Planning

As with every CAE writing task,
1 be certain not to change any of the facts you are given.
2 remember what you are trying to achieve – in this case, to get your friend out of a police cell.
3 don't include irrelevant details, and don't write too much.

What should you include in your report and in what order? Consider the following list, and delete anything irrelevant.

a your opinion of drug dealers
b what you think happened
c description of your feelings about your friend's arrest
d a plea to the British authorities' sense of fair play and justice
e a heading or title
f direct quotation of the dialogue
g descriptive details that bring your narrative to life
h a sentence testifying to your friend's good character

i what you saw and what you heard
j a description of the stranger
k an explanation of who you are and why you are writing this
l a description of the airport

Having deleted everything irrelevant, put the remaining elements in a suitable order and arrange them in paragraphs. Compare your paragraph plan with the one suggested in the key on page 159.

B Vocabulary

In this type of task, it is particularly important to distinguish between *facts* (which are known) and *suspicions*, *accusations*, etc. There are a number of words that can be used to achieve this, whether in the form of a verb, an adjective or an adverb.

*The stranger **appeared** to be an American.*
*My friend's **apparent** involvement in drug-smuggling . . .*
***Apparently**, the stranger tricked my friend . . .*

Supply the adjectival and adverbial forms in the table below.

Verb	Adjective	Adverb
to appear	apparent	apparently
to suspect	suspected	—
to seem	_____	_____
to presume	_____	_____
to suppose	_____	_____
to allege	_____	_____
to be certain	_____	_____

C Writing

Write your **statement** (about 250 words).

Task bank: Tasks 10, 28 and 37

ARTICLES AND REVIEWS

At least one of the tasks in Paper 2 can be expected to involve writing for publication. Such tasks include *an article*, *a review* and a piece of writing for *a competition*, all for publication in an English-language magazine. The publication is sometimes described not as a magazine but as a newspaper, or sometimes as a *newsletter* (a thin, home-made magazine, sent to members of a club or society). Always read the instructions for the task carefully to get a clear idea of **who** you are writing for.

Other writing tasks for publication include articles for guide books and tourist brochures, and leaflets and information sheets: these are all dealt with in Unit 10.

9A Openings and closings

1.0 Model

The following article appeared in the *Radio Times* magazine, to introduce a TV season of British films from the 1960s. The first and last paragraph have been removed. Read the article, then choose the best first paragraph and last paragraph from those printed opposite. Make sure that the opening, the text and the closing all fit together.

1 *(First paragraph missing)*

2 There was a sudden flowering of new acting talent; there were new writers and directors; there was an outbreak of movies that looked, sharply and wittily, at aspects of British working-class life that had rarely been explored before. Films were churned out in remarkable numbers – 76 of them in 1968, for example, compared with the annual 25 or so that we can manage these days.

3 Before the 1960s British actors were, or anyway had to appear to be, middle-class unless they were content to play servants or provide comic relief. But now this was no longer true, and we saw the burgeoning of stars from other sectors of society, people like Michael Caine and Terence Stamp. Along with them came an energetic generation of directors and writers to introduce strong elements of social consciousness into British films.

4 The great flurry of activity that such people provoked brought its artistic rewards. *Darling*, for instance, won Oscars for its star, Julie Christie, and writer, Frederick Raphael, and a nomination for its director, John Schlesinger. Oh, believe me, optimism, confidence and euphoria ran high – until the very end of the decade when, all at once, the whole house of cards collapsed.

5 What we had failed to realize was that this apparent rebirth of the British film industry was funded almost entirely by American money. And though the movies did pretty well in Britain and were greatly respected throughout the world, they fared rather badly where it really counted – at the American box office.

6 Some films succeeded there, of course – *Darling* and *Tom Jones* among them, to say nothing of the James Bond pictures,

which presented Sean Connery to an appreciative international audience. Generally speaking, however, the returns were less than the bean counters had expected.

7 All in all, then, backing Britain had not been a very lucrative venture for the Hollywood studios, and in the end they withdrew their financial support, leaving us to reflect ruefully that what had once seemed a new awakening was after all no more than a false dawn.

8 The cinema here has never really recovered from that setback. True, the '60s unearthed a rich crop of people, many of whom are still around, but no British money was forthcoming to make up for the loss of American backing, and so the indigenous movie industry began its slide towards the sorry state we see today.

9 *(Last paragraph missing)*

Openings (first paragraph)

A It was at some time near the end of the '60s that the Americans stopped investing money in British films, and that was more or less the end of the British film industry. A pity, because the '60s had been a good time for British cinema. Today, we are only making about a third of the number of films we were making then.

B The 1960s were, from the British film industry's point of view, the best of times and yet, in the end, close to being the worst of times as well.

C The purpose of this article is to look briefly at the way in which British cinema in the 1960s enjoyed a renaissance which continued until the end of the decade, when the Americans ceased to invest in the industry. The article will go on to look at the negative effect that the '60s collapse of the industry has had up to the present day.

Closings (last paragraph)

A To sum up, the '60s seemed to be good for the British cinema until the very end of the decade: many good films were made, acting became a more 'classless' profession, and morale was high. On the other hand, the decade ended with the collapse of the industry, from which it has never recovered. In conclusion, then, perhaps the '60s were not such a good time for the British film industry.

B Throughout the '90s we have been making fewer and fewer movies in Britain. Fortunately, many British directors are very successful in the USA, and British television too is a success, both commercially and artistically, around the world.

C A fascinating decade, certainly. Such a pity that for film-makers, as perhaps for many others, it all turned out to be a fool's paradise.

1.1   Writing for magazines: things to remember

Don't talk about yourself
You're writing for the public, not for your friends. Your opinions are only interesting if you can explain them, justify them, or make them entertaining.

Be interesting
People don't buy magazines in order to be bored. If your article isn't interesting, they won't read it – and the magazine won't publish your writing again. To be interesting, you should:
- give your article a good title.
- start with a good opening.
- use concrete images and facts, not concepts and generalizations.
- use precise and interesting vocabulary.
- surprise the reader – or at least say something new.
- know when to finish – and finish in style.

Remember who you're writing for
Who reads this magazine? How old are they? What nationality? What do they already know about the subject of the article, and what will you need to explain?

What are you trying to achieve?
Are you trying to persuade the reader to do something? To inform? To advise? To recommend? To entertain? Or a combination of these?

Layout
Your article should normally have a title and be written in paragraphs. Some magazine articles include lists – lists of instructions, lists of 'tips' or advice – which require a graphic layout such as that used in 'Be interesting' above. Note also the use of subtitles on this page and in certain magazine articles.

Organization and planning
Try to say just one thing in a 250-word article. Make notes, then summarize what you want to say in one sentence. You could write a plan based on that one sentence; the rest of the article would explain and illustrate what you want to say.

Relevance
Make sure that your article is relevant to the title, and that everything within the article is relevant to your main idea.

Length
If a magazine or an English exam asks for 'about 250 words', don't write 500. The magazine wouldn't print the article; the examiner may only read the first half of it, and you will certainly be penalised, perhaps severely.

Accuracy and libel
Don't present opinions, guesses and rumours as if they were facts. Such carelessness, apart from making your article inaccurate, untrustworthy and valueless, can also be illegal when printed in a magazine. Distinguish between fact and rumour by adding a simple word or phrase: the alleged murderer, the suspected mafioso, I've heard it said that . . ., there is a rumour that . . ., the minister is said to have / rumoured to have / supposed to have taken bribes.

2.0 Openings

A Which of these eight openings would you choose to begin an article entitled 'Openings and Closings of Magazine Articles'?

1

The 'opening' is the beginning of a piece of writing (either the first sentence or the first paragraph); the 'closing' is the way the piece of writing ends (the last sentence, or the last paragraph).

2

Two students of mine used to be great rivals at tennis, but recently Laura has become too good for her rival. 'The only difference is my service', she confided in me. 'Helena's service is so predictable that I can always return it. But mine is now stronger and more varied. She never knows what to expect.' The service in tennis has a similar role to the opening of a piece of writing – and many writers could 'improve their game' by developing a range of different openings.

3 *Doo-be-doo-be-doo-wa, shawop bam boom! Does it matter how a magazine article starts?*

4

To light a fire, take a few big logs and a box of matches. Strike a match and the logs will easily catch fire. Later, when the fire is burning well, add some smaller wood, which must be very dry. Finally, for a big blaze that will last all evening, throw a small twist of paper on top of the fire.

Is that how to light a fire? Of course not. Yet how few writers start their articles with the 'twist of paper', the inflammable opening that would bring it to life!

5 This article is about how to begin and how to end a piece of writing.

6 There are at least 15 different ways of beginning a magazine article, and a good dozen ways of ending. Not all of them are possible in every style of writing, but the ability to choose interesting and appropriate openings and closings is a very useful skill for a writer to have.

7 Kane and Peters, in their authoritative work *Writing Prose*, include a five-page essay entitled 'Beginnings and Closings'. The essay begins 'The British essayist Hilaire Belloc – who knew, if anyone did, how to begin and how to end an essay – once wrote that "To begin at the beginning is, next to ending at the end, the whole art of writing."' Kane and Peters close their essay with an epigram of their own: 'Anyone can stop writing. Only writers can finish.'

8

'Just take the horn out of your mouth.' This was Miles Davis's advice to a fellow jazz musician who didn't seem to know how to end his lengthy solos. But when you want to end a piece of writing, is it enough to 'just put your pen down'?

B Purpose

The opening of a magazine article has one or more purposes, in descending order of importance.

- to catch readers' attention and make them want to read the rest.
- to tell readers what the article is going to be about (the topic).
- to tell readers what the article is going to say (the content).
- to tell readers how the article is going to be organized (the structure).

1 Which of the openings in **A** best achieves the first purpose? (In other words, which one would you most want to read?)
2 Do any of the openings leave you in doubt about the topic of the article?
3 Which of the openings gives you the clearest idea of what the writer is going to say and how the article is going to be organized?

C Nine ways of opening an article

1 Match the openings 1–8 in **A** with the following categories a–i. Some of the categories may have more than one example; others may have none.

a **A surprising fact**, perhaps including statistics.

b **A surprising, shocking or bizarre statement**. The reader keeps reading out of curiosity: how are you going to continue? Do you really believe that? What on earth are you talking about?

c **A question**. This helps to define the subject of a piece of writing. It also starts readers thinking about the subject, making them want to read what you have to say.

d **A quotation**.

e **A story** that illustrates what you are going to say. It may be a story about the subject itself; it may be a story about another topic that has something in common with the subject of your article.

f **A statement of the topic**. The statement mentions what the topic is, and often summarizes what you are going to say. This opening is often the key to the organization and paragraphing of the article.

g **A definition of the topic** (sometimes a dictionary definition). This opening may be appropriate, but is one of the least interesting.

h **A description or image** that evokes a suitable atmosphere or symbolizes the whole question.

i **A reference to a well-known phrase** from literature, a song, a proverb, etc.; an allusion or 'rewritten' quotation.

2 Here are five more openings, all of them introducing an article on the same subject. What subject?

9

As Mark Twain might have put it, reports of the death of the family have been greatly exaggerated.

10

It's 6.00 in the evening and Jason has just cooked dinner for two. He's sitting in the kitchen, waiting. He's had a long day. He got up at 7.30, ate breakfast alone, did the washing-up and made his bed. He still hadn't seen or spoken to anybody when he left home at 8.30. Jason is 12 years old. He's waiting for his dad to come home from work.

11

Jane Smith is a junkie because both her parents are in the police force. She had problems at school, but when she got home she found no one to talk to. The day she broke up with her boyfriend, both her parents were working late. Jane's parents were never there when she wanted them. If they had been, would she have needed to turn to drugs?

12 Forty years ago, 75% of wives in Britain were 'housewives' whose husbands were working: today only 20% of British families fit this model. What factors have led to this change, and what effect has it had on society, in particular the upbringing of children?

13

In theory women are free, yet everywhere they are still in domestic chains.

3 Match these openings to the categories a–i above.

4 Which of the openings 1–13 use quotations or direct speech? Would these openings be just as good without the quotations or direct speech?

5 Some of the openings (e.g. 8) only use words and ideas. Would you agree that it is more interesting to use *images* and *pictures*? Which openings do this, and which of them is most successful?

D Writing practice

At a time when many people are taking exams, your college's English-language newsletter invites you to submit a 250-word article on the subject of exams. Are they useful? Are they necessary? Do exams help students to study, or do they obstruct a student's wider education?

Do Not Write the Article. Just write **two openings** for your article, of no more than two sentences each

      a) a very bad one, so that no one will read beyond the opening

      b) a very good one, so that everyone will want to read the rest of your article

Task bank: Task 38

2.1   Closings

A piece of writing is like a film: a weak or unsatisfying ending spoils all the good things that went before. The ending of a good film gives you a feeling of satisfaction. The film feels whole, complete.

How do we always recognize the end of the film before the words THE END come up on the screen? What signals does the film give out to tell us it is finishing? What makes a film feel complete? Think of the plot, the musical score and the images.

Referring to specific films you have seen, how many different kinds of ending can you think of?

A Six ways of closing an article

1 *Return to the beginning*: a conclusion paraphrasing the opening, or a return to the imagery or words of the opening.
2 *A Summary or conclusion*.
3 *A Question*.
4 *A Quotation*.
5 *An Image / picture*, symbolizing the end (sunset, death) or a new beginning (dawn, birth).
6 *A short sentence* to signal a break with what went before, or to indicate the intention to finish.

The closing of a piece of writing is also often signalled by certain linking words: *All in all; then; to sum up*. There is a list on page 23.

B Examples

Here is the opening of an article attacking education.

> I don't believe in education. In most cases it does more harm than good. In the words of Oscar Wilde, 'Ignorance is like a delicate exotic fruit – touch it, and the bloom is gone.'

Here are some possible closings for the same article. Match them with the six different types of closing referred to on page 126. Some of the closings (a–g) may illustrate more than one of the categories (1–6); some of the categories may be illustrated by more than one closing.

A

They say that education promotes civilized values, tolerance and understanding. They say that education opens the doors to happiness and success. Education, as I have shown, does precious little of this. School education does even less.

B

To quote from the song by Pink Floyd, 'Teacher! Leave those kids alone!"

C

And in this brave new world that I envisage, education will be a minority interest, rather like the hobby of growing stunted bonsai trees. A new generation will spring up, a virgin rainforest bearing the exotic fruit of blissful ignorance.

D

In short, it is high time we questioned the law requiring all children to be educated. This law is an abuse of a fundamental human right, the right to innocence and individuality.

E

In the light of all this evidence, who could still believe in education? Who but an educated fool?

F   No, I do not believe in education.

G   As the poet so rightly says, 'Where ignorance is bliss, 'tis folly to be wise.'

C Practice

This is the opening of an article. Choosing from the six ways of closing an article, write **two** different closings. You will have to imagine the five short paragraphs that haven't been written.

'The best things in life are free,' they used to say, but for most of us having fun usually means spending money. And yet, even in a city, there are at least five ways you can enjoy yourself without putting your hand in your pocket.

2.2   Writing

Using the opening given at the top of the page and one of the seven closings above, write an **article** attacking education. Your article should have four or five paragraphs, and be about 250 words long. Alternatively, write an article **defending** education, using your own opening and closing. The article is for publication in the magazine of your school, university or language school.

Task bank: Tasks 14, 15, 39 and 40

9B Reviews

Magazines and newspapers publish a wide range of reviews, covering all the arts as well as other areas. Most reviews have two functions: description and information on the one hand, judgement, opinions and recommendations on the other.

Reviews are generally based on the following structure.

1 The subject of the review is clearly identified, with all the essential information (What? Who? Where? When? How much?) This is done either in the heading or the first lines of the review, or both.
2 A detailed description and analysis, including the reviewer's opinions. A review of a book or a film should summarize the plot, telling the story *in the present tense*, but should not reveal the ending.
3 A conclusion in which the reviewer makes either a judgement or a recommendation.

1.0 Reviews – punctuating and writing conclusions

Capital letters Capital letters are used for the first letter of every word in the title of a film, book, play, opera, record, etc. The only words that do not have to start with a capital are small words like *a*, *the*, *of*, *to*, when they come in the middle of the title: you can write either *The Discreet Charm Of The Bourgeoisie* or *The Discreet Charm of the Bourgeoisie*.

Inverted Commas In handwriting, it is necessary to put inverted commas around the title.

Have you seen 'The Jungle Book'?

Brackets When telling the story of a film or play, are you going to use the names of the actors / actresses or the names of the characters they portray?

When Jack Sommersby returns to his wife and son in rural Tennessee after fighting in the Civil War, he seems a changed man. The question is whether Sommersby (Richard Gere) is or is not the man that Laurel (Jodie Foster) married years ago. His transformation has been so great that many people wonder whether Sommersby* is an impostor. Laurel*, too, is bewildered by her rediscovered husband, who seems too good to be true.

* In a film review, *Gere* and *Foster* could be written instead of the names of the characters. This is not done in theatre reviews.

Practice
These are all conclusions of film reviews. Punctuate them.

1 this is a film for every age bracket and is highly recommended for all those who enjoyed julie andrews earlier film the sound of music
2 if you like your thrillers moody atmospheric pessimistic and spine chillingly bloodthirsty then this is the film for you
3 the piano is essential viewing as diverse and tuneful as the instrument of its title
4 youll laugh youll cry youll love every second of sleepless in seattle sentimental who cares
5 this is the most tedious of road movies and when the fugitive lovers finally come to the end of the road shot dead by cynical detective eddie mars clint eastwood the few people in the cinema still awake applauded recommended for insomniacs only
6 overall however the films faults do not spoil an exciting and stylish piece of film making well served by an intense script and fine performances from its cast

1.1 Book review

Some lines in this review have **one** unnecessary word. Delete it and write it in the margin. Some lines are correct. Indicate each of these lines with a tick (✓). The exercise begins with two examples (**0**).

Katharina Hedinger's *Christmas Cookbook* (Goose Press)

0	Christmas is coming soon with all its secrets, festivities and ~~the~~	*the*
0	traditional dishes. Right on time, Goose Press have published	✓
1	Katharina Hedinger's sumptuously illustrated book, which containing	_____
2	many a suggestions for the preparation of gifts, decorations and	_____
3	food. In each case, step-by-step instructions and detailed lists of	_____
4	ingredients are given, making Christmas preparations easy even for the beginner.	_____
5	The first chapter, 'Early Preparations', starts with explain all the	_____
6	things that can to be prepared about two months before Christmas,	_____
7	such as homemade gifts, candles, wrapping paper and Christmas puddings.	_____
8	In the second hand chapter, 'Countdown to Christmas', Hedinger	_____
9	describes how to make decorations that need with fresh ingredients	_____
10	such as leaves, twigs and flowers. Here you will also have find	_____
11	suggestions on how to get decorate the tree. The last chapter – 'Last	_____
12	Minute Preparations' – again concentrates on all sorts of gift	_____
13	wrappings, special Christmas dishes and table of decorations.	_____
14	You will enjoy reading this marvellously illustrated book and as much as	_____
15	you enjoy Christmas itself. Well worth at the price of £12.99, it turns	_____
16	to preparation for Christmas into an art form.	_____

Book reviews

Non-fiction	*biography, autobiography, history, reference book, manual*
Fiction	*novel, short story, play, best-seller, sequel*
Stories	*setting, plot, climax, theme*
Genre	*romantic novel, detective story, science fiction, spy story, thriller*
Technical	*paperback, hardback, cover, chapters, illustrations, preface*
People	*novelist, playwright, biographer, author, writer, poet, editor, publisher*

You may also need to write reviews about music. These follow the same structure.

Music reviews

Classical	*concert, recital, chamber / symphony orchestra, concert hall, opera house*
Rock	*concert, live performance, gig* *jazz band, blues band, rock band, folk group, pop group*
Bad music	*sharp, flat, out of tune, discordant, tuneless, inaudible, out of time*
Recordings	*CD (compact disc), video disc, cassette, single, album*

1.2   Film review

Complete the review by writing the missing words in the gaps. Use only **one** word for each space. The exercise begins with an example (**0**).

Howard's End

The partnership of James Ivory, director, and Ismail Merchant, producer, has been making films for almost 30 years. But (**0**)_____*it*_____ has seldom managed a more successful literary adaptation (**1**)_____ that of E. M. Forster's *Howard's End*.

It is (**2**)_____ of those elegant period pieces (**3**)_____ which the Merchant–Ivory team is famous (the book (**4**)_____ written in 1910) and is their third Forster adaptation, following *Room With A View* (**5**)_____ *Maurice*. It is also their best – beautiful to look (**6**)_____ , subtly scripted by Ruth Prawer Jhabvala, the novelist (**7**)_____ is their regular collaborator, and acted with panache by a distinguished cast.

The book is (**8**)_____ story of two families: the Schlegels are cultured and liberal, the Wilcox family prosperous and conventional. Its theme concerns the breaking (**9**)_____ of barriers between people who find it impossible to understand (**10**)_____ other in normal circumstances.

Emma Thompson and Helena Bonham Carter play the two Schlegel sisters whose fates become inextricably linked with (**11**)_____ of Mr and Mrs Wilcox (Anthony Hopkins and Vanessa Redgrave). Helen (Bonham Carter) falls in love (**12**)_____ their son; Margaret (Thompson) is befriended by Mrs Wilcox and, (**13**)_____ she dies, marries Mr Wilcox.

Each performance makes its mark. James Wilby, Prunella Scales and Samuel West are also involved, but it is Hopkins, (**14**)_____ the puritanical Wilcox, (**15**)_____ heart is softened by Margaret, who is most notable.

Film reviews

Types of film	*feature film, documentary, box office success / failure, blockbuster, art movie, thriller, Western, horror film, comedy (romantic, black), cartoon, love story*
People	*director, producer, cameraman, cast, actor / actress (the lead, star, co-star),*
Technical	*camerawork, camera angles, on location, in the studio, subtitled, dubbed, screenplay, script, soundtrack, special effects, stunts*
Narrative	*storyline (plot), final scene, climax, flashback*

Theatre reviews

Shows	*play, tragedy, comedy, farce, musical, cabaret, ballet, modern dance*
People	*director, set designer, costume designer, stage manager, audience, prima ballerina, principal dancer, choreographer*
Roles	*the title role, a leading part, a walk-on part*
Words	*a speech, a monologue / soliloquy, dialogue*
Things	*stage, scenery, backstage, box office*
Organization	The curtain rises on Act 1 Scene 1; it falls at the interval and at the end – *the final curtain.*

Television reviews

Programmes	*current affairs, nature programme, the news, a documentary, an educational programme, a soap opera, situation comedy, drama, game show, chat show, variety show, children's programmes*

1.3 Restaurant review

Restaurant reviews use the same structure.

A Read the review and choose the best phrase given below to fill each of the blanks. Write one letter (**A–J**) in each gap (**1–6**). The exercise begins with an example (**0**).

STIR CRAZY

31 Camden High St, London.

The Concise Oxford Dictionary defines stir-crazy as 'mentally deranged from long imprisonment'. Dave, the slightly balding manager of Stir Crazy, didn't look off his head. The only clue that he might have been out of circulation for a while was (**0**) _C_ . But perhaps the tacky cartoons on a duck theme, the incredibly bright lighting and the gingham tablecloths were just irresistibly cheap.

OK, so Dave's not the enfant terrible of Camden cuisine. But he has got a trick up his sleeve: a Mongolian barbecue. A flat, semi-circular hotplate the size of a small sofa adorns (**1**)_____. Diners pick up a bowl and choose raw ingredients from the buffet: bamboo shoots, chick peas, mushrooms, pineapple and peppers lie adjacent to (**2**)_____. Herbs, spices and chopped nuts sit in tiny pots, while tall vessels hold ladles and a selection of sauces. You pick and mix – a blackboard recommends what goes with what – and Dave slaps the selection onto the barbecue. In two minutes you've got a stir fry. One trip up and down costs £4.95, while £8.95 buys you (**3**)_____.

The stir fry retains its flavour and crispness, is really tasty and for some reason feels healthy. The starters (all £1.75) are mediocre, but (**4**)_____. Dave's mum makes the pancakes with hot cherries and ice cream. The cherries are not too sweet, the vanilla ice cream is as good as Haägen-Dazs and (**5**)_____.

There's something to be said for picking raw ingredients, seeing them cooked before you and (**6**)_____. What Dave lacks in taste he's made up for in common sense. He's given something back to the diners of Camden. He's empowered the people. ∎

A the back of the restaurant
B that sort of thing
C the restaurant's glaringly tasteless decor
D carrying them back to your table
E more than half as much
F the desserts are something else
G finely sliced raw beef and chicken, prawns and fish
H unlimited servings
I the pancakes are fresh
J they made me feel sleepy

B Read the review again then answer these questions.

1 Why do you think the restaurant is called 'Stir Crazy' if the phrase means 'mad from being in prison'?
2 What kind of opening and what kind of closing does the reviewer use?
3 How does she express her opinions without using the words *I* or *me*?

1.4 Writing

Part 2 writing task

For an English-language magazine for students in your country, write a **review** of **one** of the following (about 250 words). Make use of the three models you have just studied.

a book (either fiction or non-fiction) that you have read recently
a film, play, dance performance or other show that you have seen recently
a restaurant where you have eaten recently
a record or CD you have heard recently

Task bank: Tasks 16, 42, 43 and 44

PUBLIC INFORMATION

10A Leaflets, brochures and information sheets

Leaflets and brochures are printed documents, usually illustrated, distributed free. Their functions can include commercial advertising, persuasion (political, religious, etc.) and information.

Brochures tend to be thicker, highly illustrated booklets.

Leaflets are often single sheets of paper, often folded in three, with a balance of text and illustrations.

Information sheets are also usually single sheets of paper, not folded, with few or no illustrations.

The word **handout** can refer to a leaflet or an information sheet.

For the purposes of the exam, you are not required to illustrate your work. In real life, however, illustrations and diagrams can, of course, be very appropriate.

1.0 Model

A Read this model information sheet and choose the best phrase given below it to fill in each of the blanks. Write one letter (**A–L**) in the gaps. Some of the suggested answers do not fit at all. The exercise begins with an example (**0**).

Homeopathy simply explained

HOMEOPATHY is an effective and scientific system of healing which assists the natural tendency of the body to heal itself. It recognizes that all symptoms of ill health are expressions of disharmony (0) __*B*__ , and that it is the patient who needs treatment not the disease.

What is homeopathy?

In 1796 a German doctor, Samuel Hahnemann, discovered a different approach to the cure of the sick which he called homeopathy (from the Greek words meaning 'similar suffering'). Like Hippocrates two thousand years earlier, he realized that there were two ways (1)_____, the way of opposites and the way of similars.

Take, for example, a case of insomnia. The way of opposites is to treat this by giving a drug (2)_____. This frequently involves the use of large or regular doses of drugs which can sometimes cause side-effects or addiction.

The way of similars, the homeopathic way, is (3)_____ a minute dose of a substance which in large doses causes sleeplessness in a healthy person. Surprisingly, this will enable the patient to sleep naturally. Because of the minute dosage, no side-effects or addiction will result.

How does it work?

Homeopathic remedies work by stimulating the body's own healing power. This power is very great (4)_____, but when the healing process is faulty, blocked, or slow, the homeopathic remedy acts as a stimulus to the curative powers of the body. To provide this stimulus, your homeopath must prescribe (5)_____ the right dosage for you.

What will my homeopath need to know?

In order to find the right remedy, your homeopath will want to know all about you. You will be asked many questions about yourself as well as your illness (6)_____, both present and past. The initial consultation will probably last an hour or more.

What will the treatment be like?

Your homeopath will give you a remedy, often in the form of pills which should be allowed to dissolve under the tongue. Nothing else should be put in the mouth for at least 20 minutes (7)_____, not even toothpaste or cigarettes.

What can I expect to happen?

After taking the remedy, you should notice some changes. For instance, (8)_____ your symptoms appear worse for a short time. This is the remedy taking effect, and you should feel the beginnings of recovery when this period has passed. Alternatively, patients often experience a period of exceptional well-being and optimism.

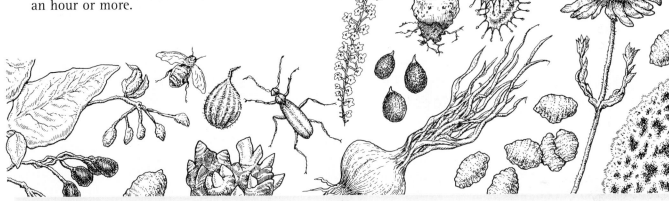

A what you personally need
B within the whole person
C the right remedy and
D before or after taking the remedy
E some people complain
F to give the patient
G to bring on an artificial sleep
H of treating ill health
I it occasionally happens that
J to achieve the desired effect
K and also about the health of your family
L and many complaints heal themselves unaided

B What was the purpose of the homeopathy information sheet? Who do you think the target reader is, and where would the information sheet be distributed?

<u>**1.1**</u>   # How to write a leaflet

A This advice is written and set out in the manner of a leaflet.

How to write a leaflet

What makes a good leaflet?

A good leaflet is one that makes people want to pick it up and read it.
So it must look good.

* TITLE AND HEADINGS – give your leaflet an eye-catching title; break the text into short sections with appropriate headings.
* TEXT – short and light; avoid very heavy, complex sentences and long blocks of prose.
* LETTERING – headings and titles should be BIG and attractive.
* LAYOUT – should be visual. Lists can be presented in columns, with items either numbered or marked, as here, with an asterisk.

Before you write

Make sure you know who you're writing the leaflet for, and why.
Are you trying
* to sell them something?
* to persuade them to do something?
* to warn them about something?

Making notes and writing

1 Write down everything you want to include.
2 Group these ideas into sections.
3 Give each section a heading; reject any ideas that don't fit.
4 Decide on the order of the sections.
5 Think of a good title (or do this at the end – but leave space!).
6 Write.
7 Check and revise. If you have time, rewrite.

B This is the text of an appeal by the British charity *War on Want*, which campaigns against world poverty. Copy the text, punctuating it and adopting the layout of a leaflet.

human rights begin with breakfast at a time when the world community is considering how to promote universal human rights war on want is launching a new campaign called a human right to development war on want believes that it is time that equal attention should be given to social cultural and economic rights alongside civil and political rights universal human rights will never exist while one in three of the world's children are malnourished one in four people worldwide are without adequate homes lack of decent healthcare means every year 40 million children worldwide never see their first birthday 80% of all sickness and disease is due to unsafe water and sanitation globally £1.5 million is spent every minute of every day on arms and armies for more information on war on wants work please contact us at

War on Want, Fenner Brockway House, 37–39 Great Guildford St,
London SE1 0YU

1.2 Writing

Part 2 writing task

Next year, for the first time, a large group of English-speaking people will be joining your school / college / workplace for one year. On behalf of the students / workers, write an **information sheet** (about 250 words) that welcomes them and tells them briefly something about the organization and the facilities it has to offer. Include some advice about how they can best fit in and enjoy their stay.

Task bank: Task 45

10B Tourism

1.0 Writing for a tourist brochure

A A tourist brochure combines *information* with *advertising*. The brochure informs tourists about a town or region, but above all it aims to persuade tourists to come and, when they have come, to enjoy themselves (and spend their money). Which of these two texts is the introduction to a tourist brochure?

1

Welcome to Oxford

❖

Oxford has many old buildings (in one square mile, there are over 900) but no tall monuments from which you can see the whole city. The University consists of 35 colleges in different parts of the town. Many good bits of architecture, as well as the entrances to some of the colleges, may be hard to find.

2

Welcome to Oxford

Many periods of English history are impressively documented in Oxford's streets, houses, colleges and chapels. Within one square mile alone, the city has more than 900 buildings of architectural or historical interest.

For the visitor this presents a challenge – there is no single building that dominates Oxford, no famous fortress or huge cathedral that will give you a short-cut view of the city. Even Oxford's famous University is spread amidst a tangle of 35 different colleges and halls in various parts of the city centre, side by side with shops and offices. Nor does Oxford flaunt its treasures; behind department stores lurk grand Palladian doorways or half-hidden crannies of medieval architecture. The entrance to a college may be tucked down a narrow alleyway, and even then is unlikely to be signposted.

Persevere, and you will be amply rewarded . . .

a What is the difference between the first and the second text?
b Does the second text include any *facts* that are absent in the first text?
c Why is the second text so much longer than the first?

B Now read the following text, welcoming visitors to Rovaniemi (in Finland, on the Arctic Circle) and rewrite it in a purely *factual* style – that is, in the style of the first Oxford text.

The Warm Embrace of the North

In a sheltered spot among hills and rivers nestles Rovaniemi. A place to relax in contentment; between the hills of Ounasvaara and Korkalovaara, enclosed by the rivers Ounasjoki and Kemijoki. Close to the heart of Mother Nature.

The countryside around Rovaniemi releases warmth, or reddens the cheeks in the winter frost. At the height of summer the sun shines, sultry, for a whole month, and the never-ending light confuses night with day. Towards Christmas Eve the sun offers only the briefest glimpse of itself, but the light of the stars and the Northern Lights glisten in the pure white snow. Even throughout the winter darkness, nature cares for its children.

What is there to be found in the shelter of these hills, by the murmuring streams, right in the heart of nature? Electricity, traffic, the bustle of people, the laughter of children, the greetings of friends.

An expressive, vital city and its inhabitants bid you welcome. Rovaniemi offers you a place in its heart.

Rovaniemi – a winter wonderland

1.1 Making the most of your region

A In most lines of the text, there is **either** a spelling **or** a punctuation error. For each numbered line **1–15**, write the correctly spelt words or show the correct punctuation in the margin. Some lines are correct. Indicate these lines with a tick(✓). The exercise begins with three examples (**0**).

Welcome to the Landes!

A limitless coast

0 Seventy sun drenched miles of fine sand. Wide-open spaces of natural   *sun-drenched*
0 countryside and freedom. Peacefull freshwater lakes for the enjoyment   *Peaceful*
0 of all the family. Recently-built resorts in perfect harmony with the   ✓
1 surrounding landscape. The coast of the Landes, unique in Europe.   _____

All the emotions

2 The festivals which give rythm to the year in the Landes find new   _____
3 conoisseurs each year. From the flamenco art festival to the festival   _____
4 of the abbeys, emotions can be guarantee. Likewise, in the numerous   _____
5 inns, whether highly reputed or little, known, the visitor is offered all   _____
6 the genrosity of the Landes, the hospitality of a region which has maintained _____
    the ancient traditions.

Space for action

7 The open spaces, available here have everything for those who are   _____
8 looking for action. The ocean offers some of the best waves in Europe,   _____
9 where fans of the surfboard can surf along side the champions. Golfers   _____
10 will find outstanding courses desinged by the best architects. And the   _____
11 countless forest paths, invite the visitor to explore the forest on foot or by bicycle. _____

A culture to savour

12 In the Landes, culture can be found at every turning The marks of   _____
13 history are to be seen and felt at the heart of each town and village.   _____
14 And the unique charm of the culture is enhanced as the froce of the   _____
15 ocean, the calm off the Adour river and the tranquillity of the forest mingle _____
    together in a harmonious landscape.

B Who was this leaflet produced by? Who was it written for? What is its purpose?

In what ways is it different from the homeopathy information sheet on page 132? (Think of the grammar the sentence structure, and the choice of vocabulary.)

1.2 Word formation

Use the words in the box to the right of the text to form **one** word that fits in the same numbered space in the text. Write the new word in the correct box below the text. The exercise begins with an example (**0**).

TRINIDAD AND TOBAGO

0 DEPEND

1 CULTURE

2 CENTRE

3 SWEEP

4 CONTINUE

5 CULTURE

6 EUROPE

7 RACE

8 TOLERANT

9 NATURE

10 SPAIN

11 SLAVE

12 LABOUR

13 DEVELOP

14 POPULATE

15 DECIDE

16 COMBINE

15 DECIDE

16 COMBINE

17 DEPEND

The nation of Trinidad and Tobago nestles close by the coast of South America – either the first among Caribbean islands, or the last word, (**0**) … on your direction.

Once part of the mainland, these islands decided they wanted their own identity and drifted north. Geologically, they remained as exotic as Brazil. (**1**) …, they became a law unto themselves!

A mere 21 miles separates Trinidad and Tobago, daily spanned by plane and ferry. Trinidad is the larger of the twins – a riot of nature's exuberance, from the mountains of the Northern Range, to the (**2**) … plains, to the soft, green hills of the south. Tobago is a masterpiece in minature, with a spine of forested hills steepling down to wind-(**3**) … shorelines.

Visit a rainbow

T & T is ethnic diversity. Name a people, and they're probably here, (**4**) … creating and re-creating their rich (**5**) … stew. African and Indian descendants dominate the mix but throw in Chinese, Lebanese, (**6**) … and Amerindian, and you have a very special blend. (**7**) … and religious (**8**) … comes (**9**) … . All are proud citizens of a place known, since the earliest times, as 'The Land of the Hummingbird'.

Two histories, one destiny

Amerindian spirits linger at Guayaguayare, Tunapuna, and Cocorite. 'Trinidad', itself, was Columbus' name for the island with three hills that he espied in 1498. The (**10**) … settled in Sangre Grande, San Fernando and Port of Spain. French planters, uprooted by the Revolution in 1789, gave us Sans Souci, Blanchisseuse, Matelot.

With the evil of (**11**) … abolished in 1833, indentured (**12**) … were brought to Trinidad, predominantly from India. As the irrepressible African and Indian influences permeated, modern Trinidad was born.

Tobago's biography, too, is told by names. British rule gave us towns called Scarborough, Plymouth and Roxborough, while its (**13**) … into the richest sugar island in the Caribbean led to a modern (**14**) … of mostly African descent.

It was the inspired (**15**) … of a British bureaucrat that created the magic (**16**) … we are blessed with today. Thus, it was as one nation that Trinidad and Tobago gained (**17**) … from Britain in 1962, and, in 1976, declared itself a republic.

0	*depending*	9	
1		10	
2		11	
3		12	
4		13	
5		14	
6		15	
7		16	
8		17	

1.3 Writing

Your local tourist board produces an eight-page **brochure** which presents your town (or region) to English-speaking tourists. The brochure comprises **eight** sections, **each** of 250 words.

1 *A general introduction* to the town, mentioning one or two key features but above all describing the whole town in very positive terms.
2 *A 'walking tour'* – a guided tour following a route around the town and pointing out some of the monuments, churches and places of interest. This section may include architectural information.
3 *Hotels, restaurants, pubs, discos and clubs* – a brief guide to accommodation and entertainment. The Arts are not mentioned in this section.
4 *The Performing Arts* – a brief guide to music, theatre, dance and cinema.
5 *The Visual Arts* – a brief guide to museums, galleries, public sculpture.
6 *Traditions and customs* that the tourist can enjoy.
7 *Famous local people*, either historical or living – a brief article summarizing the person's life, achievements and contribution to the town.
8 *Industry and employment* – a brief article written for two purposes: to paint a picture of a modern town which is thriving economically and not just living in the past; to attract industry and investment to the town.

Task 1 Write section 1 (a general introduction).

Task 2 Write one other section.

Class activity Produce the whole brochure. You may think of alternatives to the above plan.

If you are studying in Britain, research and then write the brochure for the town / region / country you are studying in. Your target readers are foreign students coming to study there, like you, in the future.

Task bank: Tasks 7 and 46

TASK BANK

Task 1

You saw a car leaving the scene of a crime at high speed. You got a good view of the car, but you saw neither the number plate nor the people inside. The police have asked you to write a description of the car. Write 100–150 words.

Task 2

An English-language magazine is running a series entitled *The Eye of the Beholder*. Each week an article is published in which a reader describes an object or a work of art that they find particularly beautiful. In the articles that have been published so far, the writers have usually included a physical description of the object before giving a personal commentary on why they find the object beautiful. Write about 250 words.

Task 3

You have arranged a house (or flat) exchange with someone from New Zealand. This means that, for the month of July, you will be living in their home in New Zealand, and they will be living in your home.

The New Zealanders have just written to you, telling you everything you need to know about the house you will be staying in (including the plumbing problems, and how to turn off the water supply in an emergency; the broken washing machine, and where to find the launderette; the cat, what it eats and where it hides; the local shops and facilities).

Reply, in about 250 words, telling the New Zealanders what they need to know about your house.

Task 4

You are on holiday and next week some friends are coming to join you, but you are not staying where you had expected to be, as you have found somewhere much better. Write a short letter to your friends, (about 250 words) telling them that you have moved and persuading them that you have made a good choice. Then explain where they will find you, giving them instructions how to get there by public transport.

Task 5

An American couple, friends of friends of yours, will be passing through your town one day next July. You will be away on holiday when they come, but nevertheless you have promised to write them a brief guided tour. They are only planning to be in your town from mid morning to early evening, so they just want to see a few of the most interesting sights, have lunch somewhere and maybe a coffee or a drink later. You have never met them before, their names are Walter and Phyllis and they are in their early thirties. In about 250 words, write the couple a letter in which you give them directions for a guided tour of your city / town / village.

Task 6

For a young people's English-language magazine in your country, write an article of about 250 words giving advice on the following subject:

Healthy eating: some sensible advice for teenagers

Task 7

People in your country are frequently upset by the behaviour of some tourists. Tourists sometimes do things that are acceptable in their country, but shock, surprise or offend in your country; conversely, they sometimes fail to do things that in your society they are expected to do. Your local tourist office asks you to produce a sheet of advice addressed to English-speaking tourists giving them advice on how to behave in your country. Write the sheet of advice, suggesting what the tourists should and should not do if they wish to be well received in your country. Write about 250 words.

Task 8

For an educational magazine aimed at 16–18 year olds in Britain, describe either the educational or the political system in your country (250 words).

Task 9

An English-speaking friend living in your country, impressed by the amount of enjoyment you get out of your favourite sport (and possibly by your skill and success), has decided to take up the same sport. A complete beginner, your friend writes asking you to explain the rules / techniques of the sport, where to do it and who with, to detail all the necessary equipment and to give any other advice that may be appropriate. Write a letter answering your friend's request (250 words).

Task 10

As a result of a misunderstanding, you were arrested by the police (either in your own country or abroad) and kept prisoner for three days. You have a friend who is a lawyer. Write a letter to your friend (about 250 words), describing exactly what happened – why you were arrested, and how you were treated by the police – and asking if you are entitled to any kind of apology or compensation.

Task 11

A local English-language magazine runs a regular feature entitled *No One Is An Island* in which readers are invited to describe a relationship that has been important in their life. Write an article (about 250 words) for publication in this series.

Task 12

For the English-language edition of a tourist guide to your town / region, write the life story (about 250 words) of one of the famous people associated with your town / region.

Task 13

An American national newspaper has invited people from around the world to write an 'open letter' to the President of the United States, for publication in the newspaper. Write your letter (about 250 words).

- The content and style of your letter is left very open here, giving you a lot of scope to demonstrate your skills and creativity. To succeed in this task you should write a letter that the people who buy the newspaper would enjoy reading. You might criticize the President, or you might praise him. More constructively, you might draw his attention to one or more of the many ways in which he could use his immense power to make the world a better place. Are there any injustices in the world, or threats to the future of the world, that you would like him to do something about?

Task 14

NO JOKING MATTER!

Unemployment is increasing throughout the developed world, and its effect on individuals and families can be tragic. Do you have a solution to the problem of unemployment? Consider the causes of unemployment, and how work could be better shared.

Write an article (about 250 words) entitled 'A Solution to the Problem of Unemployment'. *P.S.* Magazine will publish the best article received.

Task 15

The problem of famine in the Third World is ever present – but easily forgotten from the comfort of our homes. What should we be doing as individuals to help the people who are dying of hunger? What should our governments be doing? Write an article of about 250 words for your school magazine.

Task 16

For your school magazine, write a review (250 words) of the worst film, concert or TV programme you have seen recently.

- You have a good reputation as a critic, and you will maintain this reputation by offering a balanced judgement. Mention the positive points as well as the negative aspects, and justify your opinions.

Task 17

You have just received the following letter from a 19-year-old friend who is working in New Zealand. Write a reply to her letter (about 250 words).

Help! I need your advice!

Things with Gary just got worse and worse, and I'm not going out with him any more. I can't believe I came all this way just to be near him! The trouble is, I'm still working in his parents' factory, so I still see him most days, and he always makes sarcastic, hurtful comments. I've been offered two other jobs, one in a bar and the other in a pharmaceutical factory. But as you know, I don't approve of drinking or drugs, so I turned them both down. Oh yes, one more job offer (much more interesting!) I met a man who is looking for crew to sail around the Pacific in his yacht. But I haven't seen him again.

Anyway, without Gary and his friends I don't know anybody here. I never go out any more, but spend my evenings at home thinking of the good times we all had together last summer.

I had so wanted to explore these islands, the mountains, the beaches, the Maori culture. But that dream has gone now, together with my hopes of improving my spoken English (I hope you don't mind my practising my written English on you, by the way). There are only two reasons why I haven't come home already. First, I'm having trouble changing the date of my flight. And second, I haven't really got a lot to go back to: when I came out here I had to give up my job and my flat, and it cost me all my savings.

Please write and tell me what I should do! Your advice would bring a ray of sunshine into my confused life!

Love,
Anita

Task 18a

You are sharing a flat with two other people, and the arrangement isn't working very well. Write a letter to a friend (about 250 words) describing some of the problems you are having with your two flatmates and asking for advice on how to improve things.

Task 18b

Exchange letters with another student. Reply to your friend's letter (about 250 words).

Task 19

Just before setting off by train on a foreign holiday, you see someone leave a bag underneath a bench in the railway station. The following day, you learn that a bomb exploded in the station at about that time. You feel it is just possible, though very unlikely, that the bomb was in the bag you saw being left under the bench – in which case, you also saw the terrorist who planted the bomb, and would be able to describe them to the police. You write a letter to the police describing what you saw. Don't write the whole letter. Write only your description of the person who left the bag, the bag itself, and the location of the bench. (About 150 words.)

Task 20

Your good friend Alex is flying to Britain, and will be picked up by another friend of yours (who lives there). The two have never met, but Alex has a photo of the one in Britain; unfortunately, you haven't got a photo of Alex. So write the description of Alex that you send to your friend in Britain in order to help them find each other at the airport. (About 100 words.)

Task 21

P.S. **Magazine Writing Competition:
A Dinner Party**

If you could invite any two famous people to dinner at your house one night, who would you choose? The people may be dead or alive, from history or from fiction.
- Say why you choose these people
- You may also briefly discuss your plans for the evening

LENGTH   about 250 words
PRIZE $100 cash plus a dinner for four at the restaurant of your choice.

Task 22

You are either a private detective, a secret agent, a political extremist or an outlaw. One of your contacts needs to get a false passport made, in a hurry. You know that there is only one person in town who can do it. This person can always be found at a certain time in a certain bar, and will be prepared to negotiate the job with a stranger so long as they can give the password. Write a note for your contact, telling them where to go, when, how to recognize the forger, and the password. (Having written the note, you will, of course, put the note inside a folded copy of the *Herald Tribune*, and throw the newspaper into the rubbish bin beside the park gates at midday precisely.) (About 150 words.)

Task 23

Write a magazine article that takes a critical look at your town as seen through the eyes of a dissatisfied tourist. Your article should be enjoyable to read, but make a number of valid criticisms.
- Suggested approaches:
  - Write the article in the form of a letter written by a dissatisfied tourist.
  - Write the article in your own voice, after hearing from a dissatisfied tourist.

Task 24

P.S. **Magazine Competition: memories that take you back!**

Our memories and dreams often return to a beautiful place we once visited – childhood memories of visits to a farm or to the city, adolescent settings of first romances, adult memories of beauty spots, holidays in the mountains, beaches . . . In about 250 words, describe that place, and P.S. Magazine will take you back there, as well as giving you a £250 cash prize, if your article is selected for publication in our April edition.

Task 25

You are on holiday and the place you have come to is extremely disappointing. An English-speaking friend of yours is planning to come to the same place next month. Write a letter to your friend (about 250 words), describing the unsatisfactory accommodation, amenities and facilities, and suggesting that they change their holiday plans.

Task 26

You spent last summer working on a fruit farm in England. The farmer, John Ambridge, has written to you asking you to come and work for him again next summer, this time as a 'team leader'. You would like to accept the job, but only if he makes some improvements to the conditions. You have also received a letter from James, an English boy you worked with last summer who feels the same way as you do.

Read the job advertisement below, and the extract (right) from James' letter. Then, using the information given, write the letter and the note listed below.

JOB ADVERTISEMENT

LOOKING FOR A WORKING HOLIDAY IN BRITAIN?

Then spend July and August
PICKING FRUIT
at Archer Farm, Evesham

FREE ACCOMMODATION in the 'bunk house' – one dormitory for the boys, and one for the girls – with good washing and cooking facilities.

MINIMUM AGE 16. Fruit pickers are organised in 3 teams of 6, each with a team leader. The team leader is responsible for the welfare of the younger members of the team.

PAY is by piece work: you are paid according to the amount of fruit you pick.

SOCIAL LIFE – meet and work with people your own age from all over the world. Your team leaders will help organize games and activities on rainy days, and there's a mini-bus for excursions and cinema trips.

PLUS ALL THE FRUIT YOU CAN EAT!

Write (a) your reply to the farmer's letter mentioning the points suggested by James (about 200 words).

(b) a note to James that you include when you send him a copy of your letter to the farmer (about 50 words).

You must lay these out in an appropriate way but it is not necessary to include addresses.

EXTRACT FROM JAMES'S LETTER

'... I just got a letter from John Ambridge – I expect you have too. He says he wants us both back again next summer ...

These are the notes I've been making about the things I want to mention – I think it'll be really effective if you put the same things in your letter:

<u>The bunk house</u>: two cookers not enough for 18 people to cook on. We need 4 – & one more big fridge. One shower not enough – at least 2 needed (preferably 3).

<u>Social</u>: mini-bus not working all last summer – must be repaired. More games and activities needed: disco in bunk house? table tennis for rainy days? volleyball?

<u>Young people</u>: too many aged 14 & 15 last summer (you remember the problems!) Minimum age 16 to be enforced if I'm in charge of the little darlings!

Actually, I'd be really grateful if you sent me a copy of your letter – to make sure we're both asking for the same things, and also to help me write mine!'

Task 27

Is there an English-speaker that you have offended at any time in the past, but you have never apologized to them? Did you ever do something wrong, and it's still on your conscience today? Have you ever (accidentally or otherwise) caused problems for someone, and you would like to apologize to them?

(With a partner) Explain to your partner exactly who you would like to apologize to, and for what. Your partner must write the letter for you; you will write the letter your partner asks for. Then read the letters together and decide whether they are good enough apologies – and whether to send them!

(Working alone) Write that letter of apology in English. Kill two birds with one stone! Practise your writing at the same time as getting something off your chest!

Task 28

You were on holiday with a friend in the USA three weeks ago when your friend had his wallet stolen by a pickpocket. The two of you, obstructed by an old man, chased after the thief, and finally your friend caught him in a side-street, bringing him down by diving and catching his legs. Unfortunately, the thief was carrying an open knife in his trouser pocket which cut him when he fell. You were joined by a young American woman who had seen the robbery and called the police. You recovered the wallet from the thief's pocket and waited for the police. The thief was taken to hospital, while you all went with the police to make a statement.

This morning, you receive a letter from the American woman. Here is an extract from her letter.

'... Do you remember me? I'm Annie, the one who called the police when your friend had his wallet stolen. Anyway, I'm writing to tell you that last week I read a letter in our local paper from that old man who saw your friend catch the pickpocket. He obviously misunderstood everything. These are the things he claims we did:
• attack an innocent victim (three against one)
• stab him in the leg
• rob him of all his money
• leave him to die.

He even thinks I was an accomplice, when we'd never even met before. He says were were scruffily dressed and looked like professional thieves. He reckons that tourists visit places to attack and steal before moving on. The trouble is, now lots of people have been writing to the paper in support of his letter, complaining about tourists. I'd be really grateful if you could write to the newspaper saying what really happened. In a small way, your letter would help fight against ignorance and prejudice.'

Write a letter to the newspaper setting the record straight (about 200 words) and an appropriate post-card to the American woman (about 50 words).

Task 29

You are alone at home, waiting for your two English-speaking guests to come back with the shopping. When they arrive, you are going to show them how to prepare a special meal that is traditional in your country. Suddenly the phone rings, and you are unexpectedly called out for a couple of hours. Before you go out, write a note for your friends giving them instructions on how to cook the meal you were planning (including any necessary advice on where to find everything necessary in your kitchen, and how to use your kitchen equipment).

Write the note (100–200 words).

Task 30

Last time you saw a friend, they did something that made you very angry. You haven't spoken to them since. Now, two months later, you're still a bit angry but you want to renew your friendship. Write your friend a letter (about 250 words) that succeeds in both expressing your anger (and ensuring that your friend doesn't behave that way again) and renewing your friendship.

Task 31

You are on holiday and you have discovered a wonderful place and a wonderful person. You want to stay in this place for the rest of your holiday, but you had promised to spend a week with an English-speaking friend of yours. Write a letter to your friend (about 250 words) describing the place you have discovered and the person you have met, and trying to persuade your friend to come and join you. Tell your friend what a difficult choice you will have if they don't come to join you. At the same time, be careful not to offend them.

Task 32

Here is an extract from a letter written to you by Shane, an Australian friend who is at present living in Britain:

'... Next month is my 19th birthday, and I'm going to have to take a big decision. In fact, I'd really appreciate it if you wrote and gave me your advice. You see, I'm in the position of having to choose between three things. First, I could realize my dream of becoming a professional footballer – I've been offered a contract by Bristol Rovers! OK, so they're only in the Fourth Division, but everyone has to start somewhere. Alternatively, I could go to University: I've got a place to study Engineering at Leicester, and I would get a small scholarship to enable me to complete the course in three years. My third choice is to do what my father really wants me to do – to go back to Alice Springs and help him run the family hotel there. (He'd probably also like me to marry the Willards' daughter from next door – and give up all my other girls!) Do write and tell me what you think, because whichever I choose, I'm sure to lose the other two opportunities.'

Write your reply (about 250 words).

Task 33

You recently spent six months in an English-speaking country working as an au-pair. Now a friend of yours wants to go and work for the same family. The family have written to you asking if you think your friend would be suitable for the job. (The work involves child-minding for three children aged 3, 6 and 8; some housework, including vacuuming and washing-up; and the choice of either gardening, cooking or walking the dog.)

Write a letter to the family, recommending your friend. Your letter should be sufficiently positive to ensure that your friend gets the job, but you should at least pretend to give a balanced judgement. Write about 150 words, of which about 100 words should be the 'reference'.

Task 34

The International Health Council is collecting information about eating habits around the world. They invite you to submit a report of about 250 words to cover:

- the availability and affordability of fresh vegetables, fruit, fish and meat in your area.
- the typical diet of people in your area and the factors (financial, seasonal, traditional, advertising, etc.) influencing that diet. If appropriate, this section should be subdivided to cover different social groups within your society.
- any observations you may have as to how people in your area could take better advantage of the available resources to improve their diets.

Write your report.

Task 35

The British Centre is researching English language teaching in schools around the world. They already have information supplied by the teachers and management of schools, but recognize that this information is only half the story. In order to obtain a more balanced picture of the schools, the British Centre invites all advanced students to write a 250-word report on their school. As an incentive, the Centre is offering study grants worth £2,000 each to the writers of the best three reports.

Your report should cover all the relevant aspects of your school/English Department, from classrooms and facilities to teachers, management and methodology. You should also mention what you perceive to be the strengths and weaknesses of your school.

Task 36

You work for a multinational company whose head office is in an English-speaking country. Every year in the first week in July an international training week is held in a different country from among the twelve countries where the company operates. A total of 200 employees attend, from all 12 countries. Activities include lectures, seminars and workshops, but recreation (including nightlife, swimming, sightseeing, eating out, etc.) is in fact the most important aspect of the week, as selection to attend the week is seen as a reward for the company's outstanding employees.

Next year the training week is to be held in your country, but it remains to be decided in which city. You are asked to prepare a report on possible venues. Write the report (about 250 words) recommending two suitable locations and showing the advantages and disadvantages of each.

Task 37

Write a magazine report of 250 words describing a major disaster, either natural (fire, flood, earthquake, volcanic eruption), or man-made. You may write from experience or use your imagination, but the report is to be written as an eye-witness account.

Task 38

You have been invited to write a 250-word article for an international English-language magazine in your country. The subject of the article is *Television in my country today*. The editor has asked you to:

- give your article an interesting title.
- briefly summarize the TV channels available and the kind of programmes they show.
- comment on the positive and negative effects of TV, whether on society or on the individual or both.
- suggest ways in which TV programming could be improved in the future.

DO NOT WRITE THE ARTICLE.

1 Write three different first paragraphs for the article, all of them good. Each first paragraph should use a different kind of opening from the nine listed on page 125.
2 Write three different titles for the article, to match the three openings. The title, like the opening, should do two things: indicate the content of the article, and make people want to read it.

Task 39

Your local English-language magazine is running a series entitled *Formative years*, in which readers are invited to write about someone who had an important influence (for good or bad) on the way they grew up. Write your article (about 250 words).

- Beware of self-indulgence. The reader of the magazine doesn't know you, and probably doesn't want to hear about your teacher or your family *unless you have something interesting to say about them*. In particular, try to start your article in a way that will make the reader want to read more.

Task 40

In Britain, there is some debate about whether the political system is a good example of democracy. For instance, there is a democratic body ('The House of Commons') elected to govern the country – but any decisions that the Commons make must be approved by an unelected body of aristocrats, bishops and former politicians ('The House of Lords') and also by the Queen. Similarly, the electoral system is sometimes criticised, as is the reluctance of the government to hold referendums. As a contribution to this debate, a British newspaper has invited you to submit, for its weekly supplement aimed at 17–18 year-olds, a 250-word article in which you describe your own country's political system and comment on its strengths and weaknesses. Write the article.

Task 41a

For a young people's English-language magazine in your country, write an article giving advice on one of the following subjects:

- How to make the most of your time as a student.
- 'The best things in life are free' – five ways of enjoying life for free.

Task 41b

For a national English-language magazine targeting the 18–36 age range, write an article giving advice on one of the following subjects:

- Things to remember when buying clothes: tips for successful shopping.
- How to succeed at work: tips for the office worker and the young executive.

Task 42

An English-language magazine is running a series of articles in which famous people choose 3 records that they would take with them if they were going to spend the rest of their life living alone on a desert island. Some weeks, the article is written by someone who is not so famous. This week, it's your turn (if your article is interesting enough). Write the article (250 words) explaining which three records you would take, and why.

- It will probably be more appropriate to tell interesting stories about your personal reasons for choosing the records than to write the whole article as if you were a music critic.

Task 43

P.S. **Magazine Writing Competition: Win a Free Holiday in the U.S.A.**

Imagine that next summer you are going to spend a month touring the U.S.A. You will be travelling with a friend. You don't want to carry much luggage so you decide that, apart from any maps, dictionaries, grammars and religious books, you will take just three books with you. What books will you take, and why?

Write a 250-word article for this magazine, answering that question. The writer of the article we publish will win a holiday travelling around the U.S.A.

Task 44

An Australian media company is offering to donate 40 English-language videos to your school, for use in or out of class, and also a scholarship for one student to study for a month in the States. In order to decide what videos to send, the Australian company has invited every student in the school to choose two videos that they think would be interesting and suitable, and to write an article of about 250 words explaining their choice. The videos should be of any feature film, documentary or TV programme that you have seen: preferably they should have been made in English. The articles will be read by the representative of the Australian company, who will send 40 of the videos chosen and award the scholarship to the writer of the best article. The article itself will be printed in the company's magazine, in Australia. Write your article.

Task 45

You are working at an International Summer Camp for children aged 12–16. Every member of staff has been put in charge of one sport or activity and asked to write a short leaflet in English introducing the children to the sport/activity, describing the equipment, rules, techniques and safety procedures, and giving any appropriate advice to beginners. You are lucky enough to be able to choose a sport/activity that you know a lot about. Write the leaflet (about 250 words).

Task 46

A small travel company specializing in holidays for British people over 65 years old is planning to expand its operation to include your country. You have been asked to help prepare the holiday brochure. Since many of the old people may still have an image of your country that they formed 20 or more years ago, you are asked to write a 250-word article for the brochure describing the ways your country has improved as a place for tourists.

- You will probably aim to show, as far as possible, that your country has retained all the positive qualities it used to have, lost any negative qualities, and created wonderful new opportunities and facilities for tourism.

Task 47

You are going away on holiday for three weeks. You have a pet animal at home, and a friend of yours is going to look after it while you're away. You don't get a chance to see your friend personally before you go away, so you write a set of instructions in the form of a note for your friend, explaining how to feed and look after the animal. You will leave this note on the kitchen table: your friend has a key.

Write the note (75–100 words).

ANSWER KEY

PAPERS 2 AND 3

2.0 page 7

1 register 2 content 3 accuracy
4 cohesion 5 organization 6 target reader
7 range

STYLE AND REGISTER

A Introduction

1.0 page 12

Business letter	D
Tourist brochure	–
Newspaper review of restaurant	A
Spoken: job interview	C
Short newspaper report	G
Spoken: polite conversation	F
Back cover of a novel	J
Informal telephone conversation	E
Advertisement	–
Love letter	H
Police officer's report	I
Recipe	B

Name and job	Motive	On the other hand	Opportunity
Miss Lee Job: Waitress (Text I)	Grudge against Stefan's company I.D.S. (Text C)	Shouldn't have been serving Stefan's table (Text I)	Could have slipped something into the food (Text I)
Maximilien Job: Restaurateur (Texts A,J)	*His wife was having an affair with Stefan (Text H)*	Doesn't want a death from poisoning in his own restaurant (Text A)	Could have put something into the cooking rabbit (Texts A, B, F)
Colonel Lamont Job: Arms Dealer (Text D,G)	Something to do with the arms trade (Text D,G)	Can't risk damaging his career, which depends on appearing totally trustworthy (Text D)	*Could easily have poisoned Stefan's food while dining with him (Text J)*
Kevin Truckle Job: Waiter (Text G)	None – unless he was paid by someone else (Text E)	*Was poisoned himself (Text G)*	Served Stefan's food (Text I)
Henry Hungerford Job: Kevin's dog			

Kevin Truckle is the murderer. It isn't hard to imagine someone paying him to poison Stefan, considering Stefan's line of business. Kevin first tried out the poison on his dog to assess the strength, then ate a small amount himself to simulate food poisoning and clear himself of suspicion.

B Formal and Informal

1.0 page 14

A

VERBS		NOUNS	
to depart	to go	carnivore	meat-eater
to retain	to keep	putrefaction	rot
to cease	to stop	deficiency	lack
to function	to work	vision	sight
to masticate	to chew	residence	home
to demonstrate	to show	respiration	breathing
to reside	to live	somnambulist	sleep-walker
to appear	to seem	comprehension	understanding
to abbreviate	to shorten	perspiration	sweat
to terminate	to end		
to assist/aid	to help	ADJECTIVES	
commence/initiate	to begin	incorrect	wrong
to desire/require	to want	amiable	friendly
to obtain	to get	vacant	empty
to liberate/release	to free	insane	mad
to consume	to eat	inexpensive	cheap
		vivacious/animated	lively
ADVERBIALS		superior/improved	better
subsequently	next/later	infantile/ juvenile	childish
principally	mostly/mainly	immature/puerile	
consequently/therefore	so	sufficient	enough
initially	at first	entire/complete	whole
ultimately/finally	in the end	senior	older

B a 1 arrived 2 irritated 3 despaired
4 becoming 5 provoking 6 discussed
7 contacted 8 lodging 9 connected
10 investigate 11 came 12 arranged
13 postponed 14 visited 15 refer

b 1 got 2 put up with 3 bring back
4 gone by 5 got 6 got 7 joined in
8 get on with 9 fell out 10 turned out
11 making out

c Connecting words in informal spoken English are usually one-syllable words such as *and, but, so,* which are used repetitiously. In formal speech the connecting words are more complex.

1.1 page 16

1 a The best place to spend an autumn afternoon in Paris is probably the Jardins de Luxembourg.

b The actress playing his lover is Juliette Binoche, and her (*or* whose) performance is very good.

c This guidebook is very helpful. It tells about many little-known places, and is the right guidebook for tourists who don't like to be part of the crowd.

2 a Those marrying now, in the '90s, only stand half a chance ...

b One easily forgets ... (or, It is easy to forget ...)

c It's incredible how much they spend (better, "is spent") on the army, especially in view of all the poor and homeless people.

d ... is a good way for beginners to improve their vocabulary.

e As one reads this book, one gradually becomes less ignorant about what it is like to belong to an ethnic minority that suffers from racial discrimination and abuse.

f ... create a homely atmosphere.

g This book tells the layman (the ordinary person) everything he needs ...

h ... made me think / makes one think.

i In my home town, we're always seeing violence in the streets, but we ... / one is always ... but one learns ...

j ... when people are desperate, they ... / when one is desperate, one ...

3 a ... not enough activities for young people are offered.

b Something must be done about these problems.

c Greater customer satisfaction could be achieved if the promises made in the brochure were respected.

1.2   page 17

Job advertisement in a newspaper
1 maternity leave   2 candidate / applicant
3 skills   4 command   5 desirable
6 appointed   7 have   8 manner   9 further
10 available   11 Completed
12 considered / accepted

1.3   page 18

Tues 9am

Jane –

Thanks for phoning to say when you'd be back. Sorry I won't be in when you arrive - I'm going out to lunch, and then I've got to go to the dentist's. But me and the others are dying to hear about your holidays (especially about Adonis!), so perhaps we could get together as soon as possible after you get back. Maybe we could all meet up for a drink in the Café des Sports at 6, then go out for a bite to eat? Give us a ring and say if that's O.K.

– Nicole

---

37 Rue du Vieux Faubourg
59002
Lille

April 4th

Dear Miss Kurosawa,

I write with reference to your letter of April 1st.

I sincerely regret that I shall be unable to meet you at the airport on Thursday: unfortunately I have previous commitments, namely a luncheon engagement and a dental appointment.

Nevertheless, please allow me to assure you that not only myself but also a number of my colleagues are very much looking forward to meeting you. In view of this, might I suggest a meeting at your earliest convenience? Could we perhaps meet at your hotel at 8pm and take you out to dinner in one of the finest restaurants in Lille? I should be very grateful if you would phone to confirm.

I look forward to hearing from you.

Yours sincerely,

Nicole Renault

p.p. Jean Émar, Export Manager

COHESION

A Introduction   page 19

A The good writer
  – writes in sentences and uses punctuation
  – writes in paragraphs
  – organises the writing by putting the ideas in order
  – connects the ideas by using:
    a conjunction (*When*)
    a reporting verb (*replied*)

B Mick and Keith were two bed-ridden old men sharing a room in an old people's home. Mick had the bed next to the window, from which he used to describe in loving detail to his friend the children playing in the sunshine, the dogs running in the park and any really nasty street fights.

At first, Keith loved the descriptions, but soon he became sick with jealousy.

This went on for years until one night (when) Mick was very ill and called out, 'Please, Keith, ring for the nurse. I don't think I'll last the night.'

His friend reached for the alarm, but then thought, 'If he dies, I'll get the bed next to the window.' So he ignored the calls, pretending to be asleep.

C 1 in   2 but   3 On   4 At   5 so   6 soon
7 and

B Linking words

1.0   page 20

A 2b By that time / By then

3b Meanwhile / In the meantime / At the same time

4b As a result / Because of this / Consequently / For this reason / On account of this / Therefore

5b Accordingly (the words suggested for 4b are also possible)

6b Despite this / In spite of this / Nevertheless / Nonetheless / All the same / Even so / Be that as it may / However

7b on the other hand / by comparison / by contrast / however / though

8b What is more / Also / In addition / On top of that / As well as that (*also possible:* Furthermore *and* Moreover, *but these words are a bit formal*)

B (*The punctuation suggested is what this book recommends, but is not always the only possibility. The commas in brackets (,) are optional.*)

1 We are advised to do this exercise very
  a carefully, otherwise we will make a lot of *mistakes.*
  b carefully(,) while our teacher *is in the pub.*
  c carefully, even though it looks *easy.*

2 My weeks in captivity weren't too
  a unpleasant(,) considering the terrible reputation of my *kidnappers.*
  b unpleasant once I got used to *the conditions.*
  c unpleasant, even if the *food* was terrible.

3 The tigers ran away from the
  a Englishwoman as if she *was going to eat them.*
  b Englishwoman the way *mice* run away from a *cat.*
  c Englishwoman the moment they saw *her.*

4 Her Olympic gold medal was
  a remarkable, though many people *criticized her for her arrogance.*
  b remarkable, not that she didn't deserve *it.*
  c remarkable in view of the fact that she had just *had a baby.*

5 His clothes smelled of Chanel
  a Number 5, just as *she* had expected.
  b Number 5, besides which he had lipstick on his *collar.*
  c Number 5 now that he was going out with *Vanessa.*

6 I'll look after your crocodiles while you're on
  a holiday provided that you look after *my grandparents next August.*
  b holiday as though they were my *very own children.*
  c holiday(,) as well as watering the *pineapple plants.*

7 I told him I had decided to break off our
  a engagement, much as I regretted losing *the opportunity to live in a castle.*

b engagement, whereupon he started to *cry*.

c engagement, so he made me *give him back the ring*.

8 The FBI took the

a photographs so that they could put pressure on *the minister*.

b photographs in case evidence against *the President* was needed.

c photographs in spite of *the CIA* asking them not to.

9 I've decided to do two hours of aerobics every

a day in order to lose weight and *look good on the beach*.

b day as soon as I can afford *the clothes*.

c day as long as *my boyfriend* comes with me.

10 a By the time we arrived in Barbados, I was sorry I had *married him*.

b No sooner had we got to Barbados than I discovered *his secret*.

c Whenever I return to Barbados, I am filled with *nostalgia*.

11 a Hardly had Ana entered the room when everyone started to *applaud*.

b As a result of Ana's recent *Hollywood success*, everyone wanted to meet her.

c Despite her reputation, Ana didn't seem to *be interested in the men*.

12 a Not only was their relationship happy, but it also produced *two children*.

b Since she has been with Bruno, she has forgotten *all her old friends*.

c So as to celebrate their anniversary, they returned to *Barbados*.

1.1 page 22

1

A Suggested answers

Immediately – At once, Instantly, Now

At the same time – Simultaneously, Meanwhile, In the meantime

Finally – At last, Eventually, In the end

At Last implies a feeling of relief

B Suggested answers

1 I've been waiting an eternity for this moment. *At last* I can hold you in my arms, Clementine.

2 A friend of mine got a job on a ranch near Buenos Aires. *At first* (,) he found the life very hard, but it didn't take him long to find his feet.

3 The food's in the oven and dinner will be ready in an hour. *In the meantime* let's go and do some gardening.

4 We are always looking for bright young men to join our staff. However, there are no vacancies *at present*.

5 The police received the bomb threat at 6.15pm and arrived at the scene six minutes later. *By then*, the cinema had been evacuated and the adjoining streets cordoned off.

6 On my twelfth birthday, I was finally told where babies come from. *Until then*, I had imagined they came from the supermarket like everything else.

2

A Suggested answers

First – Firstly, First of all, In the first place

Second – Secondly, Next, In addition

Lastly – Finally, Furthermore, On top of that

B Suggested answers

1 It's luxurious, it's not too expensive, and the food's out of this world. *On top of that* there's the Italian barman: my friends think he's the real reason I always go there.

2 I don't want to have a drink with you, because it's too early in the day and also I don't like you very much. *Besides*, I'm not thirsty.

3 We are not wholly satisfied with your work to date, particularly in terms of productivity. *Moreover*, on more than one occasion your poor timekeeping record has been brought to our attention.

3

A That is (to say), To put it another way, I mean

B It came as a surprise to hear that Clea was married. *In fact*, it came as a shock.

The only thing Chantal wants for her birthday is a new English grammar book. *At least*, I think that's all she wants.

Our hotel was what the travel agents describe as 'lively and colourful'. *In other words*, it was in the red light district.

I don't know how you can listen to that music. *I mean*, it sounds like Rambo's foreign policy: no harmony but lots of explosions.

4

A 1 Similarly – Equally, In the same way, Likewise, By the same token

2 By contrast – By comparison, Conversely, In comparison, On the contrary, On the other hand.

3 But – All the same, And yet, Be that as it may, Despite this, Even so, However, Nevertheless, Nonetheless, Still, Then again, Though, Yet

B Suggested answers

1 All three films give an extremely fine grained result. Delta, *however*, cannot quite match T-Max 100 for the fineness of its grain structure°.

2 The Delco freezer is cheap and efficient. Sometimes, *though*, it can be difficult to open.

3 'Batman Returns' is surely Hollywood at its most original. *Nevertheless*, the film has its faults.

4 He's not much to look at, and he's certainly no hero. *But* I love him.

5 Managers are advised to avoid confrontation. *Instead*, they should encourage staff to discuss their problems°.

6 Professional cyclists do not get stomach pains, even though they eat and drink while competing. *Likewise*, swimmers rarely suffer.

7 You say I was driving fast and dangerously. *On the contrary,* I was observing the speed limit and driving with great care.

5

A In brief – In short, In conclusion, To sum up

In general – As a rule, Generally, Broadly speaking, By and large

B Suggested answers

1 The earnings gap between men and women in Europe is at its highest in Britain. *On average*, women in British industry receive 69 per cent of men's earnings.

2 The Personnel Manager interviews all job applicants here. *On the whole*, she looks for potential rather than experience or qualifications.

3 And what was worse, it was raining all the time. *All in all,* it was a disastrous weekend.

4 (430 students voted in favour of the motion to ban smoking on the college premises, while 462 voted against.) *Overall*, students at the college are against a smoking ban.

5 At the back of the bookshelf, I found the cassettes of the telephone calls. It was Barbara, *then*, who had been tapping the palace phone lines.

6

A For example – For instance, Among others

Mainly – Primarily, Principally

B Suggested answers

1 My cat seems to think she's a dog. Yesterday, *for instance*, she bit the postman, and this morning she jumped up and started licking my face.

2 Yes, I am studying English at the moment. It's *primarily* for my job, but it also means that I'll find it a lot easier to travel.

3 His parents said I was a bad influence on him. *In particular* they accused me° of taking him drinking last Sunday morning; they didn't mention any other ways in which I was supposed to have corrupted him.

7

A Anyway - Anyhow, At any rate

By the way - Incidentally

B Suggested answers

1 I spent the rest of the day watching the cycling on television. *Talking about* bikes, have you got yours mended yet?

2 Darlene is still as miserable as ever, and Jackie never comes to visit us. *Anyway,* I'm sure you don't want to hear about my problems, so let's get back to those holiday plans.

3 I had a letter from Patrick Eggli the other day. *By the way,* I don't suppose you remember Carine Imhof?

4 Education is still way behind the rest of Europe, and the Health Service is in crisis. *As for* the economy, there's no immediate sign of an end to the recession.

8

A As a result   – informal: So
　　　　　　　　– formal: Accordingly, Consequently, Hence, Thus

In that case   – For this / that reason, Because of this

B Suggested answers

1 It is not advisable to drink beer after vigorous exercise because alcohol is a diuretic – it makes you urinate. *Thus* rather than replacing what you have lost in sweat, it promotes dehydration.

2 Finally, I found the pricing to be as attractive as the other features detailed above. *Accordingly* I recommend purchase of the AW/EU/4CAE Mark 1.

3 With 'The Last of the Mohicans', Day-Lewis has found that vital element – star quality. *As a result,* he is a strong candidate for an Oscar.

4 Sorry I didn't come out last night, but I was feeling a bit under the weather. *That's why* I stayed at home and watched telly.

5 Don't forget to pack insect repellent. *Otherwise,* you may find yourself eaten alive by the local mosquitoes.

6 'She's only inviting you because you've got a car.' '*In that case* I won't go.'

1.2 page 26

A	admittedly	true	granted
B	astonishingly	incredibly	surprisingly
C	fortunately	luckily	happily
D	strangely enough	funnily enough	curiously enough
E	naturally	of course	predictably
F	apparently	it seems	supposedly
G	in my opinion	to my mind	frankly

C Reference

1.1 page 27

Suggested answers

a ... often refuse *to; to go / to move*, etc

b *This* means ...

c *These* concern ...

d I think *this research* is ...

e ... *my working conditions*

f ... need *rescuing* (from the sea) / *to be rescued / lifesaving*

g ... have *one,* there ...

1.2 page 28

A
1 Some years ago *I* came across a copy of the 1906 edition of Prince Peter

2 Kropotkin's 'Memoirs of a Revolutionist' in a second-hand bookshop. I bought

3 it for £3. As soon as I started to read it I recognized a hero.

4 Being myself a coward and a pessimist, and having been *so* as long as I can

5 remember (and I can remember falling out of my pram, which confirmed me in

6 *my views*), the people I most admire are the bold and the optimistic - unless of

7 course they are very stupid as well. Kropotkin, however, was as clever as he

8 was kind, and he had a sincere faith in the absolute importance of reading

9 books. In *this* he was encouraged by his beloved elder brother, *who* wrote to

10 him when they were separated by the exigencies of their harsh education,

11 'Read poetry; *poetry* makes men better.'

12 Kropotkin was an explorer who mapped some of the wildest and most majestic

13 rivers in the world. He was an anarchist *who,* when he was imprisoned in the

14 dreaded fortress of St Peter and St Paul in Moscow, escaped by dashing out of

15 the gate into a waiting carriage and galloping through the streets waving to his

16 friends who were waiting at every corner to see that the way was clear; then he

17 shaved off his beard and spent the evening at a smart restaurant, *where* no-one

18 thought of looking for him. He was a pioneer of the ecological movement, and in

19 his book 'Mutual Aid' he uses his own observations of nature to support his

20 view that altruism has an important role in evolution; he was also fond of

21 quoting Darwin's description of the blind pelican *which* was fed by its fellows.

22 'Memoirs of a Revolutionist' is a wonderful adventure *story,* redolent of the

23 generous spirit and vigorous mind of *its author;* if it has not already been

24 reprinted, *it should be.*

PUNCTUATION

A Full stops, sentences, paragraphs

1.0 page 29

A Sentence 2 is correctly punctuated. The others should read:

1 One day he married a cabaret dancer. This woman already had two daughters.

3 I think that a teacher's method is very important. Would I have learned as much with another teacher?

4 I seem to have lost Naomi's address. I wonder if you could have a look to see if you've got it.

5 Cinderella was in her room. She couldn't help thinking about the boy who had bought her the Coke. Her father came in and asked her how the disco had been. She told him about the boy, and how she didn't even know his name. Finally she told her father the worst of it, that she had forgotten her bicycle when she left the disco some time around midnight. Suddenly there was a ring at the doorbell. It was the boy who had bought her the Coke, and he had her bicycle with him. 'This bike's much too small for you,' he said. 'Shall I adjust the saddle? Or better still, if you'll be my girlfriend, I'll buy you a new mountain bike.'

B The Fakirs of India are distinguished by their attempts to demonstrate their resistance to pain and privation. Some have been frauds, and some have shown remarkable powers of mind over matter, demonstrating that all pleasure and pain is *Maya*, or illusion.

At the end of the 19th century, Fakir Agastiya of Bengal proved the mental control he possessed over his body by raising his left arm above his head and leaving it in that position until he died in 1912. Gradually, the blood circulation diminished to almost nothing and rendered the arm completely numb and rigid. Even the joint locked, and Agastiya was laid to rest with his arm in the same position. The only poetic touch to an otherwise pointless exercise was the decision by a bird to nest in the palm of his hand.

Whether the accumulating bird-lime set solid over the years and helped to support his arm is unknown and open to after-dinner speculation.

1.1 page 30

A Suggested answers

2a Looking for an adventure, Lucy answered the advertisement.

2b Since she was looking for an adventure, Lucy answered the advertisement.

2c Lucy, who was looking for an adventure, answered the advertisement.

3a Approaching the desert island, she was impressed by its beauty.

3b As she approached the desert island, she was impressed by its beauty.

3c She approached the island, whose beauty impressed her.

4a Finding a good place to camp, they pitched the tent.

4b When they found a good place to camp, they pitched the tent.

4c They found a good place to camp, where they pitched the tent.

5a Needing to find food in order to survive, Lucy learned to fish.

5b Since she needed to find food in order to survive, Lucy learned to fish.

5c Lucy, who needed to find food in order to survive, learned to fish.

B 2 Frightened by the anonymous phone calls, he went to the police.

3 The stamps collected by my father are worth a fortune.

4 Children not accompanied by an adult will be refused admission.

5 Bored by the film, I left the cinema and went to a café.

6 A woman attacked by a dog received no compensation for her injuries.

7 Diana is wearing the expensive coat worn by Lauren Bacall in 'The Big Sleep'.

8 I won the game of chess by using a clever gambit learnt from Nigel Short.

B Commas

1.0 page 30

A 1a We all agreed that we would spend the next day touring the villages.

1b The deer were not disturbed by our presence.

1c My brother Matthew finally became a good enough trumpet player to join the army.

1a She was, however, tired after her expedition.

2b Politicians have, to be fair, lied less this year.

3b He told me, when his company was going to be taken over by a multinational, that he was drinking too much.

4a Jenny, told the story of her husband's accident, was angry with him.
(The other sentences are correct.)

B 1 However, I decided to spend the day in the mountain refuge.

2 We found deer near the top of the mountain, the highest in Catalonia.

3 On hearing about the deer, Fabiana decided that she would climb the mountain.

4 High in the sky, an eagle soared effortlessly, enjoying the sunshine.

D 1 My birthday, which had begun with sunshine, ended with rain.

2 Cleopatra, Henry's dog, or rather bitch, was a nuisance the whole day.

3 Norway being a bit cold in January, I've decided to go to Morocco.

4 Marion, who was frightened of spiders, begged us, crying, to turn back.

5 What's happened to the car you used to drive when you were in California?

6 Henry's brother the doctor was unable to accompany us(,) but his brother the guitarist did come.

7 However, old as she is, she has entered the London Marathon again.

8 He told me, and I know you're not going to like this(,) after all the drinks you've bought him and all the energy you've put into your attempt to sell him a Jaguar, that he's bought a Fiat.

1.1 page 32

A 1 I asked her what time her mother expected her home.

2 I couldn't persuade him to tell me when he had started to indulge in this habit.

3 I told her, to simplify matters, that I was the boss.

4 There was no way we could have guessed who was going to be at the party.

B 1b She promised, to keep her mother happy, to leave the ball before midnight.

2b If only you'd told Helen, she wouldn't have been shocked when she saw it.

3a She asked me, to cut a long story short, to mend her car.

4b I can remember, whether you can or not.

5a It was she who chose, which was unusual for her.

1.2 page 32

A 1b When he started to play polo, Kate stopped loving him.

2b Whether or not you're going, I certainly am.

3a Where there used to be a factory, now there were fields of wild flowers.

B 1 Wasn't it Churchill who said that power corrupts and absolute power corrupts absolutely?

2 Many of the students and their friends and supporters were shot at by the police, who later claimed that they were only obeying orders.

3 My youngest sister, who was a baby during the time I spent in the 'House of the Rising Sun', was strongly advised not to do what I had done.

4 A large number of fairly successful trials had already been completed with laboratory animals before any change in the behaviour of the professor who was responsible for the project was noted.

1.3 page 33

To avoid giving the impression, half way through the sentence, that both the cat and the dog go in the box.

A 1 Australian footballers can kick the ball or throw it.

2 The burglars ate all our food, and the baby never woke up.

3 She thought Miss Verner was going to be furious and she waited all morning to be summoned to the 5th floor, but the call never came.

4 She squashed a grapefruit in Cagney's face and walked out of his life.

B 1 Before he took off, Lindberg made himself some sandwiches.

2 Much as I admire his paintings, I wouldn't trust him with my daughters.

3 I bought this bicycle so I could go to the beach every morning.

4 Footballers dream of scoring goals, and philosophy students dream of finding the meaning of life.

1.5 page 34

CHARLES CHARLESWORTH, Who Died of Old Age at the Age of Seven.

The ageing process affects us all at different rates. Some people of 53, like the esteemed author, look a mere 35, with sparkling brown eyes and a handsome gait. Others, like the author's friend Colin, look like little middle-aged men at 21(,) with middle-aged outlooks, set ways and planned futures. In women the former condition is common, but women rarely suffer from the latter, being fired with the insatiable drive of ambition for either an independent and distinguished career in a still male-dominated world, or a home and seven children by the time they are 30.

No such luck for Charles Charlesworth, who was born on the 14th of March 1829 in Stafford. At the age of four(,) Charles had a beard and was sexually mature.

In the final three years of his life(,) his skin wrinkled and he developed varicose veins, shortness of breath, grey hair, senile dementia and incontinence. Some time in his seventh year(,) he fainted and never regained consciousness.

The coroner returned a verdict of natural causes due to old age.

(N.B. The commas in brackets are possible but not very useful.)

C Semicolons

1.0 page 34

1, 4, 5.

1.1 page 34

1 ... tournament: six women including myself; Peter Bates and John Wade; the twins; and, of course, the team captain with his partner.

2 While working at the hospital she was overworked, exploited and constantly criticized at the same time as being underpaid, undervalued and taken for granted.

3 ... activities: music and singing; circus skills, including juggling; vegetarian cooking; mime and acrobatics; improvisation; and, above all, a warm group experience.

D Colons

1.0 page 35

Suggested answers

1 I think Mary is in love: she hasn't bitten anybody today.

2 I'm sure I'll pass my exams: I'm going out with the examiner.

3 Silvia is interested in animals: she has hundreds of wildlife videos.

4 The dress was elegant, sensual and provocative: tonight she would be irresistible.

5 He was bitten by a cobra: he died at once.

6 I had a terrible hangover this morning: I stayed in bed till midday.

7 Suddenly I remembered my grandmother's advice: never trust a man whose eyebrows meet in the middle.

8 She thinks she's a model: she spends all her time dressing up and posing in front of the mirror.

1.3 page 36

1 Rosewall no longer had the strength and energy of his youth and so his game became more economical: nothing was wasted.

2 The string quartet I play with comprises two violins, a viola and a cello, but my jazz quartet has rather an unusual line-up: double bass, violin, piano and tenor saxophone.

3 But now, after a bath, a change of clothes and a drink, the thought returned to me: how was Foxton going to react when he found that I had escaped?

4 I've just decided to emigrate to Canada: it sounds like the perfect solution.

5 There are four things we would need to know more about before we could offer you a job: we would need to question you further about your education, your family background, your experience(,) and your plans for the future.

E Dashes

Practice page 36

1 Now at last – here in my hands – was a book whose entire subject was railway trains in India in the 1940s.

2 The people here are always happy and smiling – which is more than can be said for Edward.

3 Binoculars must be held steadily, which means resting them – or your elbows – on a solid support.

4 The writer of this novel is trying to tell us how important it is for us to keep in touch with our own violence and aggression – at least(,) I think that's what she's trying to say.

5 On the brink of a total breakdown, he met Laurie – his fourth and greatest love – who was to inspire some of his most moving compositions.

F Hyphens

Practice   page 37

PORSCHE-DRIVING ARMY CHIEF IN ANTI-NUCLEAR PROTEST

Local anger was revealed yesterday when a cross-section of the population was questioned about plans for a new gas-cooled nuclear reactor just twenty-three miles north-west of the city centre. The opinion poll revealed strong anti-nuclear feelings among three-fifths of the population. Indeed, the coexistence of two pressure groups in the valley came to light: one a small-time affair led by a dog-loving cat food factory-owner cohabiting with a used-car saleswoman in a twenty-storey high-rise block, the other a more threatening operation with left-wing Marxist-Leninist sympathies. This latter group, co-ordinated by Lieutenant-Colonel James Fox-Talbot, the red-haired Porsche-driving managing director of an ultra-modern high explosive factory, is already suspected of having committed a number of acts of low-level sabotage. Lady Fox-Talbot, the Lieutenant-Colonel's university-educated wife and co-coordinator of the group, has described these accusations as far-fetched.

'We are simply reminding the democratically-elected government of its democratic responsibilities,' the Fox-Talbots said in a joint statement issued yesterday. 'As parents with a three-year-old son, we are deeply worried about the government's happy-go-lucky attitude to radiation. We urge all our fellow valley-dwellers to join us and take advantage of this once-in-a-lifetime opportunity to prevent the mistakes of twentieth-century technology being carried over into the twenty-first century.'

1 DESCRIPTION

Warm up: register exercise

1 and 2   page 38

A A dictionary definition. (heading, e.g., 'also...')

B An extract from a 'consumer advice' article in a magazine. (details, figures, 'our tests')

C An extract from a letter of complaint. ('I'm having problems', 'I'm writing', 'firstly' ...)

D A magazine advertisement. (adjectives – 'classic', 'attractive', 'ideal', 'practical' ...)

E A description, taken from a letter to a lost property office. (factual description)

F A personal advertisement, either from the 'small ads' column of a newspaper or from a card pinned on a noticeboard or in a shop window. (name and tel. no.)

G An extract from a description of a painting. ('reds and greens', 'strokes', 'canvas' ...)

1B Describing pictures and objects

1.0   page 41

A Use a dictionary to check that the compounds you have written exist.

1.1   page 42

1 been   2 the   3 he   4 slowly   5 it
6 ✓   7 too   8 also   9 ✓   10 has
11 both   12 such   13 after   14 ✓
15 and
Three senses described – sight, sound and smell

1.2 Describing a photograph   page 43

Just for your own interest, the following words are the original ones from both texts.
1 impish   2 black   3 fur   4 plummy
5 annoying   6 happy   7 independent
8 frightened   9 tiny   10 forbidding
11 bright   12 polluted

1C Describing products

1.0   page 44

A The theme of freedom and escape is introduced in the title ('Getaway car'), continued in paragraph 1 (*freedom*), paragraph 2 (*liberation*), paragraph 6 (*far away*) and paragraph 10 (*in the wild*), and in paragraph 14 (*getting away to the back of beyond*).

B paragraph 7 - '*Steal* a day's sailboarding'

C 1 The word 'forerunner' is given the strange spelling 4Runner in order to convey a second meaning, that it is a 4-wheel-drive vehicle (and presumably *runs* well, or fast).

   2 • A car which city people can drive to get away from the city; a car used for escape by criminals.
   • mentally taken to another place / world; physically taken to another place.
   • an exciting life, full of adventure; strip of road marked out for fast traffic.
   • a caravan or trailer is 'hitched' (attached) to a car; a 'hitch' is a disadvantage.

D get in; turn on / switch on / start; climbing / driving over

F Paragraph 5 – 'more power and torque than anything else in its class'

G • Paragraph 7 – 'It will *relish* the climb' – cars are not in fact capable of enjoyment.
   • Paragraph 11 – 'this car will never make heavy weather of it' – cars are not capable of making a task more difficult than it is.

H • Because no-one would read them.

I • Paragraph 12 – 'Which is why it comes with ... warranty.' A relative clause, not a 'grammatical' sentence.
   • Paragraph 3 – 'Including the window on the tailgate.' A participle clause, not a 'grammatical' sentence.

1.1   Practice   page 46

1 C   2 J   3 G   4 I   5 H   6 A

1.2   page 47

A The missing information is 'It can tow a load of over one and a half tons.'

B Stoves have produced ovens in Merseyside since the 1920s. They spend a lot of money on market research and product development. The ovens they make can be single or double, gas or electric, and with or without a fan; all have a system to keep the door cool. The gas ovens have a grill that gives an even heat. All the ovens are designed to stay clean. (Stoves ovens are the best in Europe.)

2 ACTION

Warm up register exercise   page 48

Suggested answers

A Article about surfing – people interested in sport

B Packet of cocoa – consumer

C Business advice – businessman, administrator

D Article, advice leaflet – parents

E Article about coffee – student

F Christmas cracker, cigarette packet – general audience

G First Aid advice – people learning First Aid techniques

H Recipe – people interested in cooking

I Direct speech from teacher – students

J Article about massage – people interested in massage techniques

K Shampoo bottle – consumer

Telling you to do something – F, I
Telling you how to do something – B, H, J, K
Giving advice on how to do something – C, D
Describing a process – A, E, G

2A Instructions and directions

1.0   page 49

A The first set is much more detailed, and would be adequate to explain the exercise even to someone who had never done the exercise before and who didn't have the picture.

Stand upright with your bottom tucked in, your knees slightly bent and your hips slightly forward. Bending sideways at the waist to your left, bring your right arm up, letting your left arm slide slowly down your leg as you breathe out. Hold and start going upright as you breathe in. Repeat five times and then on the other side five times.

Hello magazine - 'Beauty: Focus on Exercise', ed. Vickie Bramwell.

1.3 page 50

B Paragraph 1: Telling you what you are going to do
Paragraph 2: How to get started
Paragraph 3: How to draw the glass
Paragraph 4: How to draw the face and the straw
Paragraph 5: How to draw the fish and its straw
There is no conclusion.

C woman, her, show, straw, glass

D He gives very precise instructions: 'one third of the width', 'eighty five per cent full', 'behind it, in the middle ..., at the bottom'.

2B Advice

1.0 page 51

1 and 2 of 3 ✔ 4 all 5 try 6 ✔
7 though 8 after 9 ✔ 10 them 11 to
12 or 13 yourself 14 happens 15 ✔

1.2 page 52

A There are somewhat different methods of picking up a baby or half-grown rabbit as opposed to an adult. A young rabbit can be easily picked up by sliding a hand under the belly(,)° and lifting bodily before it has a chance of jumping away. The trick is to have the animal's body nicely balanced in the palm of the hand. A very young rabbit being picked up for the first time may struggle a little, so transfer it to your chest and soothe it by gentle stroking.

Alternatively, bring up the other hand and cuddle it gently. Hold the animal firmly but not tightly, otherwise it may struggle all the more vigorously.

Most young rabbits quickly adapt to being picked up in this manner and, correctly held, rarely struggle. However, they must have the opportunity to become accustomed to the human hand(,)° and it is advisable to handle youngsters of about five to six weeks onwards on a regular basis. Spare a few moments at feeding time to fondle the youngsters while they are eager for food.

° The commas in brackets are possible, but not necessary. If you have used any commas apart from those shown above, return to the section on commas on pages 30 to 34.

B 1 To go right, move the steering wheel clockwise. / (You can) go right by moving the steering wheel clockwise.
2 To make it work (To get it to work), kick it. / (You can) make it work by kicking it.
3 To avoid this problem, use cold milk. / (You can) avoid this problem by using cold milk.
4 To interrupt the speaker, raise your hand. / (You can) interrupt the speaker by raising your hand.
5 To get a higher note, blow harder. / (You can) get a higher note by blowing harder.
6 To avoid getting burnt, let go as soon as it gets hot. / (You can) avoid getting burnt by letting go as soon as it gets hot.

7 To improve your handwriting, write more slowly. / (You can) improve your handwriting by writing more slowly.

2.0 page 52

Suggested answers
1 A Read as much as possible
  B Use a good dictionary
  C Visit an English-speaking country
  D Use the language
  E Get used to the exam

2 Introduction should include acknowledgement of the difficulties of the exam, but be positive that students can do a lot to improve their chances of passing.

3 Suggested answers
Paragraph 2: You're probably ... perfectly.
Paragraph 3: Babies ...
Paragraph 4: It's possible ... dictionary.
Paragraph 7: In some ... CAE.

2C Processes and systems

1.0 page 54

A A water-filled fire extinguisher comprises a red-painted steel cylinder connected to a hose and controlled by an operating lever. The cylinder is filled almost to the top with water. Inside the cylinder is a cartridge containing CO_2 gas at high pressure.

When the safety pin is removed, the operating lever can be squeezed, pushing a pin down to pierce the CO_2 cartridge. The high-pressure gas is released into the space above the water in the cylinder. The gas pushes down on the water, which is forced up the discharge tube to a hose connected to a nozzle.

The nozzle is narrower than the discharge tube, so the speed at which the water leaves is increased. The water is thrown far enough so that the operator can stand back from the fire.

B 1 As you can see / This lever here / this safety pin here / And that / of course
2 the passive voice / in the last sentence, 'the operator'

1.1 page 55

A 1C 2I 3H 4A 5F 6B

B nicely, slopped, stuff

2.0 page 56

A The order of the paragraphs: apart from the first paragraph, which summarises the whole process, the paragraphs reflect the order of the process. Within each paragraph, a similar order is respected.

B its (1.9) – sugar; solution (1.10) – the mixed sugar and water; the syrup (1.12) – the heated solution; it (1.16) – the hot, sticky, clear solution; it (1.19) – the reheated fondant; which (1.31) – the indentations in the cornflour (or, the shapes stamped into the cornflour); the liquid fondant (1.32) – the fondant which has now been further reheated; it (1.32) – the liquid fondant; This (1.37) – the conveyor; which (1.38) – the bath of melted chocolate; the covered sweets (1.42) –

the fondant centres covered in chocolate; which (1.43) – 30°C; These (1.49) – glucose and fructose.

C In the first paragraph, the writer summarizes the process in a simple way. This makes the more detailed process description much easier to follow, as we already have a general idea of what is happening and why. The first sentence of paragraph 4 has a similar function in relation to the rest of paragraph 4.

D The version in the text is better because it is equally clear and precise even though it uses fewer words. Here, as in most writing, economy is a great virtue.

2.1 page 57

1 the / that / this 2 to 3 An
4 As / Since / (Because) 5 which / that
6 this / it / that 7 These / Such / Those
8 then / (immediately) 9 But / However
10 has / needs 11 then

3 NARRATIVE

Warm up: register exercise page 58

A 4 B 2 C 6 D 1 E 8 F 3 G 5
H 7

3A Narratives and connecting words

1.0 page 59

1 had 2 he 3 are 4 ✔ 5 there 6 ✔
7 being 8 were 9 off 10 after 11 these
12 first

3B Biographical narratives

1.0 page 62

1 F 2 G 3 B 4 E 5 A 6 C

1.1 page 62

B
3 1 Having heard / hearing what his daughter had done, he was proud.
2 Singing 'Flower of Scotland', the soldiers marched through the blizzard.
3 Visiting the Sudan last year, I was shocked by what I saw.
4 Born in 1975 and educated at Hirst, Susan Gallon became a star in 1996.
5 Having pulled a muscle yesterday, I can't do any training today.
6 Not having been to the States, I don't know what you're talking about.
7 Having insisted that we should all be punctual, he himself was half an hour late.
8 Not having opened the letter, I hadn't realised that I had won first prize.
9 Looking around old houses, some people get a sense of history.
10 Not being fluent in their language, I had to use a lot of mime.
11 Inspired by the concert, her son started to learn the piano.

12 Having assumed / Assuming that August would be hot, I had only brought T-shirts and beach clothes.

13 Having been bitten by snakes many times before, I wasn't frightened of the cobra.

14 Having just read an article about the life of Francis James, I wouldn't be surprised if you told me that he spent three years in prison in China.

15 Delighted about winning the prize, I took all my friends out to celebrate.

1.2 page 64

Suggested answer

31 Coleridge Road
Cambridge CBX 1TT

The Editor
The Daily Correspondent
77 Fleet Street
London WC 1PP

12 February 1996

Dear Sir

I was very surprised to read the ill-informed references to the musician, actress and writer Cindy Vitale in the review of 'Turn of the Century: 6 Stories for the '90s' which appeared in your issue of February 12th. Writing as someone who knew Cindy in her post-punk days – we met in 1981 in Bali where she was studying gamelan, and remained in touch till her tragic death in a car accident in 1994 – I would like to correct the very false impression of Cindy that your readers may have after reading Eric Bacon's review.

Your reviewer, who for a literary critic is surprisingly willing to assess the artistic ability of a musician, claims that Cindy's musical career was 'far from distinguished'. He also claims that, because Cindy showed great ability as a writer, she was wasting her talents in the years before she started to write. A more responsible journalist would not have made such sweeping statements without first ascertaining the facts, which paint a very different picture.

Cindy was a woman of many parts who, after an early start as a classical pianist (she was playing Chopin and Liszt on Brazilian TV at the age of 16), developed a passion for drums and percussion which took her around the world during a distinguished career as a performer, teacher and student of her chosen instruments. She was also an accomplished actress who trained at LAMDA, spent 18 months with the RSC, achieved critical success with her film role in Derek Agios's 'Street Party', and found regular TV work throughout the '80s in Cuba.

Not content with reducing Cindy's entire artistic career to 'punk rocker', your reviewer describes even that period as 'unsuccessful' – if 5 Top 40 singles and 2 albums in just two and a half years is unsuccessful, then who needs success! Mr Bacon further claims that she was 'disappointed' not to land the leading role in the film 'Broken English': she was, in fact, offered the role, but refused to participate in the commercial exploitation of a culture she believed in; she chose to make 'Street Party' instead.

By publishing this letter, you will restore both the reputation of a remarkable woman and this reader's faith in the integrity of your newspaper.

Yours faithfully,

Judit Szilbereky

3C Newspaper stories

1.0 page 66

A doctor who came across a mock rail disaster exercise thought it was the real thing and joined in the rescue effort.

Robert Lambourn realised his mistake when he gave one of the injured a painkilling injection and the surprised actor looked up to ask, 'Do we really have to go that far?'

The volunteer patient explained to the doctor that the 40 casualties lying around the crash scene were all acting, then he was stretchered away to sleep off the effects of the injection in hospital.

Doctor Lambourn had inadvertently joined in an exercise with police, fire and ambulance services at Choppington, Northumberland. He was thought to be part of the medical team and was allowed through the police cordon.

Doctor Lambourn was not available for comment yesterday, but his colleague in Ashington, Northumberland, Dr John Campbell, said, ' My colleague acted with the very best intentions.'

1.1 page 66

A 1 d, i, a, c, e, h, g, f, b (g, h also possible)
  2 'had taken' makes the order of events clear / 'were heading' helps set the scene.
  3 Suggested answers
    Absent-minded runaway found safe at home – having tea!
    73-year-old Tom abandons wife, 84, for a cuppa.

B Suggested answer
  A Swedish au pair has been sent back home – for being a man.

C Middle paragraphs should include:
  • the name of the gardener
  • when, where and how he discovered the hoard
  • how much it is worth
  • details of the problems it has caused

4 GIVING YOUR OPINION

Warm up: register exercise page 68

A 5 B 3 C 1 D 7 E 6 F 2 G 4

4A Argument

1.0 page 69

A Students often wonder whether it's worth going to Britain to study English. **I would say it depends on** how much money you have, and whether or not you have a taste for adventure. **Some students** make very good progress when studying in Britain, and enjoy themselves enormously. **Others, however,** acquire near-perfect English without ever visiting an English-speaking country. **All in all**, it depends very much on the individual.

B This is only the third time I've been to a football match, and I still don't know if I really enjoy it. **In some ways**, being part of such a big crowd is rather a frightening experience. **Also**, I must admit that I don't understand all the rules. **But at the same time**, it is an exciting and fairly inexpensive way of spending an afternoon. **By and large, I think** I do find football matches enjoyable, and I probably will go again.

C I'm often told I'm lucky to be a woman, but in fact it's a mixed blessing. **While it is true to say that** women are stronger than men in many ways, **I nevertheless** feel that society tends to be prejudiced in favour of men. **On balance, I suppose** that although I am both proud and happy to be a woman, I think that it is the men who are 'lucky'.

D Many young actors and actresses dream of becoming stars, but in reality stardom has its drawbacks as well as its attractions. **On the one hand**, stars can earn a lot of money. **Also**, they can travel a lot and have an exciting social life. **On the other hand**, stars become public property, and lose a lot of their privacy. **Not only that, but** they **also** lose much of their freedom: they can no longer walk in the streets without having to talk to strangers and sign autographs. **Ultimately**, the young actor who dreams of stardom is in danger of becoming a star who dreams of the wonderful freedom he enjoyed when he was anonymous.

E As an Olympic Gold Medallist, I am often asked what is the best way to spend the night before a big race. **On the one hand**, it's a good idea to stick to your normal routine. **On the other hand**, some athletes find they cannot sleep properly unless they use some special relaxation techniques. **Personally, though**, I like to go out for a meal with my husband, then get an early night.

F There are many reasons why I love chocolate. **One reason is** that I have a sweet tooth. **Another** is that chocolate gives me energy when I'm feeling tired. **What is more**, they say that chocolate contains a drug that acts on the brain like morphine: I don't know if I believe this, but I am certainly addicted. **Above all**, I love chocolate because I know I could never be happy without it.

G Of all the soap powders in the world, I would recommend that you use Halo. **In the first place**, it is concentrated, so you only have to use very little of it. **More importantly**, it is 100% biodegradable, and therefore does no harm to the environment. **On top of that**, as everyone knows, Halo washes whitest. **In short**, Halo is your wisest washday choice.

1.1   page 71

A 1   a, d, g, i
      2   c, f, h, k
      3   b, e, j, l

B Paragraph 1: Introduces the subject with examples
Paragraph 2: Disadvantages of lying
Paragraph 3: Disadvantages of telling the truth
Paragraph 4: Conclusion

4B   Reviews

1.0   page 72

A 1   The first sentence informs the reader that two different points of view follow.
      2   It offers the critic's view.
      3   It offers the advocate's view.

B There are two schools of thought about mountain bikes such as the Lamia Anboto. Critics dismiss them as expensive toys with no

real justification. Why buy a mountain bike with 21 gears if you're only ever going to use it in the city? Why spend £400 on a bike that you will seldom use, knowing that if ever you park it in the street it is liable to be stolen?

Advocates point to the Anboto mountain bike's urban advantages. The shock absorbers and thick tyres are very effective at coping with the rough surface and potholes between the car lane and the pavement, for instance. With it being able to climb rocks, you can always get out of trouble by mounting the pavement. Ecology comes into the reckoning too, especially when car owners can be tempted into cycling by the styling and technology of this fashionable and prestigious machine.

1.1   page 73

A Suggested answers
1 however   2 which   3 which   4 Such
5 also   6 their   7 same   8 nor   9 In
10 too   11 Despite   12 it   13 hardly
14 But   15 by

B Using understatement, and by contrasting this film to previous films by the same director.

1.2   page 74

A 1 D   2 F   3 B   4 H   5 A   6 E

B It began as expected ... extraordinary ... triumphant; Not great songs ... as ever; ... speed ... thoughtful lyrics; ... rolling and slick; ... unbearably painful.

1.3   page 74

A Personally, I can't see what distinguishes; in my opinion; but I for one; what really annoys me; I don't know about you; the impression I get; the plot too is corny.

B It can't be her prose, surely: although the words 'heat' and 'dust' appear frequently, no impression of heat or dust is given. Indeed, the careful, well-organized sentences convey instead the impression of a very literary, upper-class woman sitting at her typewriter drinking tea.

Finally, what is particularly annoying about this book is the writer's morality. She's a romantic and a moralist: she looks down on her narrator with a patronizing attitude, and paints a degrading picture of modern love by giving her narrator a kind of abject promiscuity in the place of a love life. And incredibly, the message of the book seems to be that the best thing that can happen to a woman – even an unmarried woman, without a boyfriend, travelling abroad – is to get pregnant. It is not just that Jhabvala is writing about a different continent: it would appear that she's also living in a different world.

1.0   page 76

The problem is that the boyfriend is unhappy with the woman's success. He's lost confidence in himself.

1.1   page 76

1 b, c, g   2 e, i, l   3 a, f, j   4 d, k   5 h, m

5 PEOPLE AND PLACES

Warm up: register exercise   page 78

A 6   B 2   C 5   D 4   E 1   F 3   G 7

5A   Describing people

1.0   page 80

The laundrymen of Bamako

A 1 over   2 which   3 as   4 Despite
   5 were   6 into   7 against / onto   8 them
   9 as   10 could   11 of   12 to   13 for
   14 on   15 a

B height, build, skin, character

2.0   page 81

A a Suggested answers
      as if he's just waiting; look like they're old; I would say he was in; he's probably; as if the man had spent; The photo seems to have been taken; he is either just about to play or he could be; sweat-soaked strands ... imply that
   b Paragraphs 4 and 5 describe the writer's personal reaction. Personal reactions are often used as a method of summing up.

5B   Describing places

1.0   page 83

A 1   No   2   there is / are   3   The river
      4   'then' / 'before'

B 1   Both are lists.
      2   It's a description of a room and its contents. Position of the contents is not important.
      3   It focuses on the 'organizing principle' of the description and sets the scene.
      4   No. The sentence says 'Officer B *could* swim' and 'at 8.15 *each* night'.

1.2   page 84

B The left hand side is described in detail first then very brief mention of the right hand wall is made and finally a detailed description of the back wall.

C Next to ... In front of ...
   The rest of the wall was ... The desk was ...

D Taken up by ... but for two ...
   he saw ... The back wall had ...

2.0   page 85

A 1 E   2 H   3 C   4 G   5 F   6 K

B b, c, d, i, m
The other details are not appropriate here; they are not relevant, not factual etc.

2.1   page 86

A 1 ✓   2 to   3 Manhattan's   4 height
      5 industrial   6 its   7 enterprise.   8 ✓
      9 clouds exposed   10 ✓   11 Given the
      12 surrounding   13 ✓   14 Whole

B glittering sticks; livid storm clouds ... rolling; sweeping curve; weirdly; freakish; defied gravity ...; brazen; battling; large, low moon; huge ... medallion; high melodrama; crashing; set ... on fire.

6 FORMAL LETTERS

6A Letters of complaint: tact

1.2 page 89

A 1 repair 2 bought 3 guarantee
4 assured 5 found 6 appears
7 replaced 8 grateful 9 arrange
10 carry out 11 convenient 12 faithfully

B 1 response 2 claims 3 failure
4 returning 5 refund 6 receiving
7 convenience 8 ordered 9 sorry
10 must 11 replace 12 ensuring
13 recover 14 hearing

1.3 page 91

A 1 There are no differences of fact between the two letters.
2 (a) Positively and politely
3 Suggested answers
'an absolute death trap'
'A museum piece'
'Liable to poison me'
'I'm in danger of freezing to death while you take a holiday in the Bahamas'
4 Suggested answers
'It's you who should pay for it ...'
'While you take a holiday in the Bahamas ...'
'If you don't do this before winter sets in, I'll be obliged ...'

The heating problem is, in fact, aggravated by the third and, happily, last small problem that I am confident you will wish to resolve. Three of the windows do not close properly: two at the front of the house, and one at the back. This, combined with a number of broken and cracked window panes, contributes to an enormous heat loss, not to mention the deterioration of the flat caused by the cold and the rainwater entering through the cracks and broken windows. Obviously the windows, like the cooker and the heating, are a matter that requires immediate attention. Perhaps double glazing (the solution adopted by the proprietors of most of the other houses in the street) would be a worthwhile investment: it would certainly protect the value of the property.

1.5 page 94

a

Isokaari 38B
00200 Helsinki
Finland

The Manager   26 June 1996
Windermere Wildside Adventure Holidays
Ambleside
Cumbria

Dear Sir or Madam

I am writing to express my dissatisfaction with the adventure holiday I have just had with your organisation, from the 12th to the 25th of this month. The holiday, for which I paid £380, failed significantly to live up to the promises made in your advertisement.

First, although the holiday was advertised as being based at Wildside Hall, I found myself instead at a youth hostel seven miles away. This meant that, with no car or buses available, I had no access to the Hall's facilities (pool, sauna, etc); at the hostel, the only leisure facilities were a table tennis table and a pack of cards.

Furthermore, at the hostel there were neither 'comfortable double rooms' nor 'talented' kitchen staff: there were four people in a room, and the food was very ordinary indeed.

Finally, the choice of activities was not as advertised. Whereas you claimed that every day we would be able to choose from 'a wide range' of activities, in reality there was only ever a choice of two. I had planned to spend the whole fortnight sailing and windsurfing, but for eight days of the holiday neither of these was on offer.

In view of the many ways in which the holiday failed to live up to your advertisement, which can only be described as extremely misleading, I feel that a refund of at least £190 would be appropriate. Should this refund not be forthcoming, I shall be obliged to refer the matter to the British Tourist Board.

Yours faithfully,

Samanta Brunoni

b

Chris –

I'm glad you asked me about adventure holidays because I can tell you, DON'T GO WITH WINDERMERE WILDSIDE! They were the ones I went with last summer (£380 per person per fortnight), and it was a nightmare. So if you do go, choose Outward Bound. I've heard they're good, but I can't tell you about their prices.

All the best,

6B Applying for jobs, courses and scholarships

1.0 page 95

Paragraph 1: Reason for writing the letter
Paragraph 2: Relevant information from her CV
Paragraph 3: Why she is applying for the job

1.1 page 96

A 1 At least 21.
2 a.s.a.p.; p.a.; min
3 2 jobs for English speakers
4 The au pair jobs since an au pair is part of the family more than an employee.

6C Other formal letters

1.0 page 98

A 1 1D 2A 3D 4B 5C 6D 7A 8A
9B 10D 11D 12C 13A 14B 15B
2 To complain about insurance companies; tell the story of the writer's daughter; to ask for advice on how to deal with insurance companies.

B 1 half-hour   2 murders, including   3 ✓
4 fights   5 falling into   6 ✓   7 'bastard'
8 out. This   9 Captain   10 son).
11 offensive than   12 neck?

1.1   page 100

B
1 1B   2C   3B   4A   5A   6C   7A   8A

2

The Happy Planet Association
63 Crimscott St
London SE1

The Conference Manager
Mrs Lumley
The Royal Hotel
Severn St
Cardiff   February 7th 1996

Dear Mrs Lumley

Further to our telephone conversation yesterday morning, I would like to confirm our
booking for a conference at your hotel from Saturday September 3rd to Monday September
5th of this year, leaving on the morning of the 6th.

The details (subject to amendment) are as follows:

ACCOMMODATION
Sat 3rd, Sun 4th, Mon 5th :   26 single rooms
                                 8 double rooms

Please note that one of the delegates is disabled and requires accommodation with good
wheelchair access.

CONFERENCE FACILITIES
ONE CONFERENCE ROOM on Sat 3rd and Mon 5th (not on Sunday), 4.30 – 7.00p.m.,
equipped with VCR and monitor, to accommodate up to 40 people in space and comfort.

4 SEMINAR ROOMS on Sun 4th and Mon 5th: 10a.m. – 1.00p.m. and 2.30 – 4.00p.m.,
equipped with whiteboards, to accommodate up to 12 people each.

CATERING
Provisionally, our requirements (for up to 42 guests) are as follows:
Sat 3rd   dinner only
Sun 4th   breakfast; lunch (1p.m.); tea (4p.m.)
Mon 5th   breakfast; tea (4p.m.); dinner (8p.m.)
Tues 6th   breakfast

Approximately one third of the delegates will prefer a vegetarian menu.

One last request: we understand that there is an international rugby match at Cardiff Arms
Park on the Saturday afternoon, and would be grateful if you could obtain 6 tickets for us.
Should this be inconvenient for you, please advise how we might obtain them.

I look forward to hearing from you with confirmation of our booking.

Yours sincerely,

Christine Upton

Christine Upton
Association Secretary

7 INFORMAL LETTERS

7A Technical matters

1.0   page 102

1 To thank Arantxa for letting her stay in her
  flat.
  Her stay in the flat; the death of two goldfish

and their replacement; a plane strike at
Heathrow airport.
2 Thank-you; apologies for goldfish and
  explanation; reminder about party.
3 This question is answered by the rest of the
  unit.

1.1   page 104

1 In Arantxa's flat, possibly on the kitchen table.
2 She is in a hurry.
3 By including nothing else. She leaves out all
  unnecessary information. In terms of
  grammar she uses abbreviations, contractions
  and ellipsis.

2.0   page 105

B (letter) Thanks very much; I'll tell you all
about it; Now; It's bad news; the thing is;
That's life; … is no joke; Anyway

(note) Just a quick note; Very sorry; I'm off
now

The use of parentheses; no pronoun (Very
sorry; see you soon); PS; contractions (I'm)

2.0 page 106

C Suggested answers
1 make it / get   2 Anyway   3 got   4 now
5 having / getting   6 so   7 afraid   8 enough
9 problem   10 give   11 job   12 Anyway / Still
13 Love / Best wishes

2.1   page 107

B 1 I'm fed up with this stupid job – my new
       boss is even worse than the last one.
    2 I'm fed up with this stupid job – I want to
       live!!!
    3 I was amazed to see John at the party – I
       thought he was in prison!
    4 I was amazed to see John at the party –
       he's normally very unsociable.
    5 The wild pig didn't attack Emily – it was
       Emily who attacked the wild pig!
    6 The wild pig didn't attack Emily – it was
       just trying to escape.

C Suggested answer

Dear Mum,

Guess what! You'll never believe this, but I'm
going to be famous at last! My new life starts
tomorrow, in Poland! On tour with U2!

It all happened so suddenly. We were just
doing a gig in a small town in the north(,)
when Bono walked in. You should have seen
the look on Kemal's face! Anyway, to cut a
long story short, Bono loved our music and it
just happened that he needed a support band
for U2's East European tour. So we're all off
to Poland next week. By the way, how's your
Polish? Can you still speak the language? If
so, why don't you come with us? I'm sure
you'd really enjoy it - it's not all sex, drugs and
rock 'n' roll, you know!

Must dash. We've got a rehearsal in half an
hour, and my bagpipes are out of tune.

Your loving son,

Edmund.

2.2 page 108

D Sept, thanks, Nov, Aug, 48h; I'll, you've, I'm, I'd, (etc.); had to, see you.

E

> Mike –
>
> Here's my account of what happened at the demo. I've described everything I saw from when we set off from Oxford St to the moment we arrived in Trafalgar Sq. I know you won't agree with me about everything, especially the order of events – I'm pretty sure I saw people throwing stones *before* the first baton charge – but the important thing is to clear Jenny of the charges against her, and I think my evidence here will help a lot.
>
> Hope to see you again at next month's meeting of Fight Racism!
>
> Penelope

7B Diplomacy and tact

1.1 page 109

1 Would make Agatha think that the animal was very easy to look after.
2 Would persuade Agatha not to take the animal.
3 Would make Agatha aware that there were potential problems but looking after it isn't all bad.
4 Would make Agatha feel that she may not have any problems with the animal as it will be in a different home and with different people.

1, 3 & 4 may all persuade her to take the animal, but 1 is completely dishonest.

1.2 page 110

D 1 He enjoyed playing in the garden.
 2 He can be a little excitable.
 3 He's very vigilant at nights, so you won't need to worry about burglars.
 4 He was very companionable at nights.
 5 He was always full of energy and high spirits.
 6 He kept me very fit.
 7 He always tells you when he needs to go out.

1.4 page 111

B is best

A Terrible. This student has not understood that this is a 'real-life' task – a bit like a role-play. Also, it is never a good idea to copy phrases from the question at the best of times; here, it is most inappropriate.
B Fine (though this student will have to use all his/her charm in order to 'explain away' the two disasters mentioned).
C Rather inappropriate. Agnes *didn't* ask for advice about how to look after Attila.
D Too formal.

8 REPORTS

8A Information reports: people

1.0 page 112

A Suggested answers
 1 joining; 2 number; 3 allowed / permitted; 4 her colleagues / the staff; 5 private; 6 her lack; 7 however; 8 punctuality; 9 willing

B 1 All the things mentioned below, but especially his tendency to exaggerate by using superlatives and absolutes in a casual and inexact manner.
 2 a No mention of the epidemic, the strike or Kit's music, all of which are irrelevant in a report that is an appraisal of Kit's work.
  b The exaggerations have been replaced by more measured, moderate language; more formal vocabulary throughout.
  c Annette's report, unlike Gary's speech, is strictly organized. The 5 paragraphs fulfil the following functions:
   1 An overall assessment;
   2 Comment on Kit's social integration at work (note the discreet negative comment);
   3 Comment on Kit's work;
   4 Punctuality, attendance, etc;
   5 Conclusion (not strictly necessary in a report, especially where the conclusion appears in the opening paragraph).
  d Shorter, more economical.
  e (i) an anonymous manager
   (ii) all of the above, but especially the impersonal tone and the impression of 'balance' as opposed to exaggeration.

1.1 page 114

B Suggested answers
 1 . . . his attention to detail sometimes verges on the excessive . . .
 2 . . . she allows her work to occupy a disproportionate amount of her time . . .
 3 . . . her ambition is such that sometimes it is almost as if she is determined to succeed at any price . . .
 4 . . . a natural leader who has yet to learn the value of teamwork . . .
 5 . . . a very confident person who has been known to underestimate his colleagues . . .
 6 . . . finds it difficult to control his eagerness for immediate results . . .
 7 . . . she shows a certain reluctance to work more than the minimum of hours . . .
 8 . . . a free spirit whose provocative contributions do not always promote harmony . . .

1.1A page 115

 2 works well in a team / integrates well
 3 self-confident / self-assured
 4 has a good sense of humour
 5 has a strong character
 6 sociable / integrates well
 7 industrious / diligent / assiduous
 8 meticulous / thorough
 9 discreet / diplomatic / tactful
10 articulate / eloquent
11 well-spoken
12 logical / rational
13 imaginative / has a capacity for original ideas
14 intelligent

1.2 page 116

a See top of next page
b

> Huntingdon House
> 20 North St
> Brighton BN1 1EB
>
> Oct. 9th
>
> Dear John,
>
> I've just written the reference for you, though I'm sure you don't deserve it. I expect you only asked me because you don't know anybody else stupid enough to think you're worth it, but intelligent enough to be able to write a reference in English. Was I really the first person you thought of? And what's this about losing my phone number? You never were a very convincing liar.
>
> Anyway, good luck with the course. And don't forget, I've told them what a good student you're going to be. SO DON'T MAKE *ME* INTO A LIAR!!!
>
> Love,
>
> Dominique

8B Recommendation reports

1.0 page 117

1 drive 2 too 3 both 4 pounds 5 always 6 ✓ 7 to 8 ✓ 9 but 10 all 11 in 12 have

1.1 page 118

Paragraph b is the most appropriate.

Huntingdon House
20 North St
Brighton BN1 1EB

Dr L. Flode
Exeter University
Exeter   9 October 1994

Dear Dr Flode,

I write in reply to your request for a reference for John Kino.

I have known John for eight years, having been in the same class as him throughout High School and having remained in touch with him during the three immensely profitable years I spent at Exeter University.

You mention the problem of students who find it hard to adapt to a new environment and to make new friends. In John's case, there is absolutely no cause for concern. John's recent voluntary work in Rwanda is evidence of his ability to adapt, and as for making friends, there are few people as sociable as John. He has a bright, positive nature which, together with his many social skills, would quickly win him a large number of friends in any new environment.

I also believe that John has the intelligence to handle the workload on the course. And if at times he seems to be less than industrious, I am convinced that, given his competitive spirit and high self-esteem, he will manage to excel in the examinations.

The only question mark, in my mind, would be over John's level of English, which was never his strongest point. However, his natural eloquence and communicative nature would soon remedy this if he were living in England. Perhaps, indeed, this weakness no longer exists: his recent letter to me was written in faultless English.

Yours sincerely,

Dominique Schwarzenbach

PARA 1   k – who you are and why you're writing this.
PARA 2   i – your eye-witness statement, objective and factual. *Don't* include opinions or emotive language.
         j – your description of the stranger, as detailed as possible.
PARA 3   b – your *interpretation* of the events. Include, for example, how you think the 'cigarette package' came to contain drugs.
         h – a sentence of 'character reference' to justify and support your supposition of your friend's innocence.

FINISH with: the DATE, your SIGNATURE and your NAME AND ADDRESS.

B seeming   seemingly
       presumable   presumably
       supposed   supposedly
       alleged   alledly
       certain   certainly

C Suggested answer

8C Eye-witness and narrative reports

1.0   page 119

A Paragraph 1 – the boy with the gun 'becomes real' because of the concrete details: 15, good-looking, blue woollen hat; similarly, descriptive details of the two cars and the gun are given (yellow; Cadillac; rental; shiny; new-looking)
Paragraph 2 – the direct quotation from the car radio
Paragraph 3 – short sentences comprising nothing but facts and concrete details
Paragraph 5 – four action verbs in past simple - *pressed, rammed, turned* and *jerked* - making for fast, dramatic narrative.

B The boy looked about 15 years old and was wearing a blue woollen hat. He told me to open the car door. I refused, and he smashed the window. Fearing that my companions and I would be beaten or shot, I accelerated away from the scene of the incident, colliding with two other cars in my escape.

1.1   page 120

A HEADINGS   e – Start with the heading, TO WHOM IT MAY CONCERN - this means that your statement is not addressed to one person but written for the benefit of any interested party (lawyers, police, Customs, etc). then a subheading describing the contents of the report, e.g. A STATEMENT DESCRIBING EVENTS WITNESSED BY MYSELF, (*NAME*), AT (*NAME OF AIRPORT*) ON (*DATE*) AT (*TIME*).

TO WHOM IT MAY CONCERN

The following is a statement describing events witnessed by myself, Kornelia Ties, on 7 October 1993, at 5.00p.m. at Franz-Josef Strauss Airport, Munich, Germany. I am writing this statement to confirm the innocence of my friend Miss Doris Pescosta of Bolzano, Italy, who I understand is being held in London on suspicion of involvement in drug smuggling.

While Miss Pescosta and myself were waiting in the departure lounge of the airport in Munich, a boy struck up a conversation with her. I presumed he was American because of his accent. He was about 24 years old, 1m 90 tall and well-built. He had short, dark, curly hair and dark eyes. He was wearing Wrangler jeans, brand-new Nike trainers, a white T-shirt with 'Endless Caverns, Virginia' printed on it, and an old denim jacket with green paint marks on the right elbow. I heard the boy ask Doris if she was going to buy any duty-free goods before take-off. She told him she wasn't interested as she already had enough to carry. Then he started talking about the cost of cigarettes in Britain. He claimed that he was only a student, that he was planning to spend four weeks in Britain, and that he wouldn't be able to afford the cigarettes. He said that to save money he had bought 400 duty-free cigarettes, but he was worried he would get caught at Customs, where the allowance is only 200. Doris, believing she was saving money for a poor student, offered to take 200 of the cigarettes through Customs for him, and he gave her a carton of Marlboro in a carrier bag that seemed to come from the duty-free shop. I did not see the other 200 cigarettes he had supposedly bought.

I now believe that everything the boy said was a trick to persuade Doris to carry this packet, which presumably he had prepared in advance and filled with drugs. I am absolutely certain, however, that Doris would never have accepted the packet if she had thought it might contain drugs. I have known Doris Pescosta since we were both children, and she has never in her life had anything to do with drugs or any other criminal activity; her university tutor will confirm that she is a model student of impeccable character.

(signature)

Kornelia Ties, Hamnavoe, Shetlands, 9 October 1993

(name and home address here)

9 ARTICLES AND REVIEWS

9A Openings and closings

1.0   page 122

Opening – B
Closing – C

2.0   page 124

A 1, 6 and 7 – because the other good ones either refer to openings *or* closings and the article is about both.

C 1 a–6   b–3   c–8   d–7   e–2   f–5
       g–1   h–4   i–3
   2 Something to do with changes in the family
   3 9–i   10–h, e   11–e   12–a   13–b
   4 2, 7, 8.   No, they would not be as good otherwise.
   5 2, 4, 10, 11, 13.

2.1   page 126

B A–1   B–4, 6   C–5   D–2   E–3   F–1, 6
   G–4, 6

9B Reviews

1.0   page 128

1 This is a film for every age bracket(,) and is highly recommended for all those who enjoyed Julie Andrews' earlier film, 'The Sound of Music'.
2 If you like your thrillers moody, atmospheric, pessimistic and spine-chillingly bloodthirsty, then this is the film for you.
3 'The Piano' is essential viewing, as diverse and tuneful as the instrument of its title.
4 You'll laugh, you'll cry, you'll love every second of 'Sleepless in Seattle'. Sentimental? Who cares?
5 This is the most tedious of road movies and when the fugitive lovers finally come to the end of the road, shot dead by cynical detective Eddie Mars (Clint Eastwood), the few people in the cinema still awake applauded. Recommended for insomniacs only.
6 Overall, however, the film's faults do not spoil an exciting and stylish piece of film-making, well served by an intense script and fine performances from its cast.

1.1   page 129

1 which   2 a   3 ✓   4 ✓   5 explain   6 to
7 ✓   8 hand   9 with   10 have   11 get
12 ✓   13 of   14 and   15 at   16 to

1.2   page 130

1 than   2 one   3 for   4 was   5 and   6 at
7 who   8 the   9 down   10 each   11 those
12 with   13 when   14 as   15 whose

1.3   page 131

A 1 A   2 G   3 H   4 F   5 I   6 D

B 1 'Stir Crazy' is a pun on 'Stir Fry'.
   2 Opening: a quotation. Closing: an image / picture.
   3 Impersonal constructions: The stir retains its flavour... The starters are mediocre... The vanilla ice-cream is...

10 PUBLIC INFORMATION

10A Leaflets, brochures and information sheets

1.0   page 132

A 1 H   2 G   3 F   4 L   5 C   6 K   7 D
   8 I

B To provide information for people interested in homeopathy. Distributed by homeopathic clinics.

1.1   page 134

B HUMAN RIGHTS BEGIN WITH BREAKFAST

At a time when the world community is considering how to promote universal human rights, War on Want is launching a new campaign called 'A Human Right to Development'.

War on Want believes that it is time that equal attention should be given to social, cultural and economic rights alongside civil and political rights.

Universal human rights will never exist while
• One in three of the world's children are malnourished.
• One in four people worldwide are without adequate homes.
• Lack of decent healthcare means every year 40 million children worldwide never see their first birthday.
• 80% of all sickness and disease is due to unsafe water and sanitation.
• Globally £1.5 million is spent every minute of every day on arms and armies.

For more information on War on Want's work please contact us at :

10B Tourism

1.0   page 135

A The second text.
   a The first text is purely factual.
   b No
   c To make Oxford sound more interesting and mysterious and worth visiting.

1.1   page 137

A 1 ✓   2 rhythm   3 connoisseurs
   4 guaranteed   5 little known / little-known
   6 generosity   7 spaces available   8 ✓
   9 alongside   10 designed   11 paths invite
   12 turning. The   13 ✓   14 force   15 of

B A tourist organisation produced the leaflet for potential visitors to the Landes. The purpose is to encourage tourists to go there. It differs from the homeopathy leaflet in that it uses short sentences, lots of adjectives, and is very positive in the choice of vocabulary.

1.2   page 138

Suggested answers
1 The setting is a private park situated between Scarborough and Filey, only one and a half miles from a sandy beach at Atherton Bay.
2 There is excellent sea fishing as well as the possibility of trout fishing on the River Sharpe.
3 The Cleveland Way, considered by many to be one of the most interesting walks in Britain, is close by.
4 Scarborough, just ten miles away, is the home of (the) playwright Alan Ayckbourn, whose plays are premiered there at the 'Theatre in the Round'.
5 While you are in Scarborough you can enjoy the many restaurants and inns there, as well as a good choice of evening entertainment.
6 There are also opportunities for a large range of activities including steam railway trips, hang-gliding, bowling and horse-racing.
7 The Hall is centrally heated, making it ideal for holidays at any time of (the) year.
8 The pool, open all year round from 8a.m. to 8p.m., is heated to 84 degrees.